OBJECTS
IN MIRROR

DUNCAN CUMBERBATCH

OBJECTS
IN MIRROR

ARCHWAY
PUBLISHING

Archway Publishing books may be ordered through booksellers or by contacting:

Archway Publishing
1663 Liberty Drive
Bloomington, IN 47403
www.archwaypublishing.com
1 (888) 242-5904

ISBN: 978-1-4808-7870-9 (sc)
ISBN: 978-1-4808-7871-6 (hc)
ISBN: 978-1-4808-7869-3 (e)

Library of Congress Control Number: 2019909240

Print information available on the last page.

Archway Publishing rev. date: 07/26/2019

To all those who encouraged me in this endeavor and those who reviewed some pages and gave me the benefit of their comments.

To all those older brothers, many of whom are gone now and who migrated from the South to the East and West Coasts and everywhere in between in search of better lives and whose generation gets very little credit for their courage, strength, hard work, dedication, and love for their people. We stand on their shoulders.

To my ancestors, who contributed their DNA and spirit to me.

To Mom, Dad, my sister, my grandmothers and grandfathers, and all those cousins and aunts and uncles who were and are an important part of my life experiences.

To Omar, Phil, SaRon, Mike, and all the others I had the privilege of calling friends.

To all the women who loved and cared for me, particularly Patricia—may she rest in peace.

To all the nameless brothers and sisters, African American and otherwise, who, over the years, allowed this imperfect creature to share some of their time, joy, energy, essence, and life experiences; to learn from them; to bask in their radiance; and to feel their support, love, and good wishes.

To those who didn't wish me well or tried to harm me—I've learned from you also.

ACKNOWLEDGMENTS

"If a tree falls in the forest and no one is around to hear it, does it make a sound?" is a familiar and often-heard quote. It is generally attributed to George Berkeley. This saying haunted me until I began this work. To not salute the many persons—ancestors, family, friends, neighbors, colleagues, comrades, and some strangers—who have impacted my life in so many ways would be a shame, possibly even criminal. Years ago, I began this labor of love. It is my humble and imperfect attempt to both praise and thank them, living and dead. In my journey, I have been privileged to walk among prophets, angels, devils, scholars, poets, and warriors. I often think of those who have passed on and who don't seem to get any recognition, praise, or credit for their contributions here on this third planet from the sun. This work is dedicated to them.

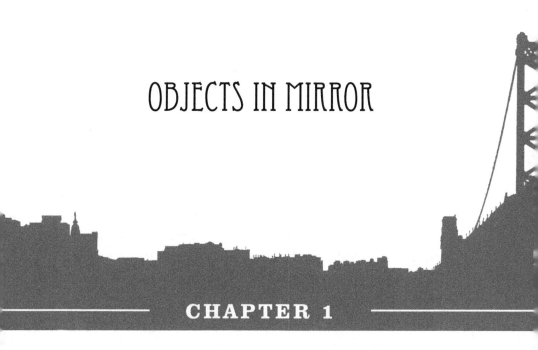

OBJECTS IN MIRROR

CHAPTER 1

He tugged on his sports jacket to get comfortable in his seat as the jet was taking off. He liked the pleated black wool pants he had bought " for a song" at Golden Harry's in Philly. His black loafers were smart looking. He topped off the outfit with a turtleneck sweater. He wore his world time watch on his left wrist. Amir always wore his watches on his left wrist. He could rotate the bezel and tell the time in major cities around the world. The fact that it indicated world time made him feel more sophisticated, more worldly. His Benson and Hedges menthols were in the lower jacket pocket, his Afro comb in the inner left-breast pocket. He had put on some Canoe cologne. His beard was neatly trimmed and groomed. Did he pack rubbers? Yes, he thought. He hoped he would have a chance to use them! He laughed to himself as he recalled how, as an eleven- or twelve-year-old boy, he and almost all his male acquaintances in the old neighborhood would pull out their wallets and show their respective rubbers or let them be casually observed, intentionally, to seem as if they were sexually active. He hadn't been then. He figured most of his buddies hadn't been either. He learned early on that guys could be big liars and how competitive some males were in this area and others. Did he pack a can of Afro Sheen hairspray? Yes, he thought he did. It almost seemed surreal; he was flying to London and Paris in a TWA jet! He had read about and seen—in movies, of course—the cities of London and Paris for years. He wasn't traveling to them because he was in the military and being stationed there or because some employer was sending him there to work or as a participant in some kind of college study-abroad program. No, he was going there simply because he wanted to, in search of adventure, in search of excitement, in search of identity.

He had hoped that one or two of his boys would make the trip also, but it was not to be. He was going anyway! Big Ben, the Tower, and Buckingham Palace were among the sights to see in London. In Paris, the Right Bank, the Left Bank, and the Notre Dame Cathedral headed the list of must-sees. While gazing out the window, staring at the cotton ball–like clouds, almost daydreaming, he reflected on his life, his past, his dreams, his hopes, and his disappointments and wondered what fate, destiny, Allah/God had in store for him. He had left from JFK Airport in New York on his TWA Getaway Tour. He hadn't wanted Mom to worry unnecessarily, so he told her at the last minute. He felt a little guilty about that. Lawrence had been his slave name; his original name was now Amir or Amr Ibn Abdel Aziz. Almost all his contemporaries and comrades called him that. Mom and Dad continued to call him Sonny. He didn't see the need to make an issue out of it. They were from another generation and background, and he respected them.

Bill, his father, had been to London and Paris during World War II, compliments of the US Army. His MOS, military occupational specialty, had been truck driver light, and he had qualified on the MM .30-caliber carbine. He had been to Germany as well. He had liked England, he'd said. He almost decided to stay there after the war and send for Mom, he had shared with Amir. Was that why Amir was a bit of an Anglophile? He also spoke fondly of Paris. "If you had some nylons and candy bars, you could own Paris!" Bet there were some stories there! Of course, Bill couldn't share detailed stories of all his *adventures* with his son, especially female-wise. Dad had personality. He was an Aquarian with a good sense of humor, and he was generally in a good mood.

In fact, Dad had walked around the house speaking some French when Amir was a young boy—"Bonjour," "Parle vous français?" "Oui," "Merci," "Si vous plais." Dad had told him that he was, in fact, French, a French soldier who had met his mother, a poor country girl from rural Georgia, and married her right after World War II. When his mother got around to discussing this with him and explained sometime after that it was a fiction, he was so disappointed, crestfallen, that both his parents were actually from the same area in small-town Georgia!

Back to the present, Amir somehow felt that he was beating the odds, a twenty-something-year-old African American male from North Central Philadelphia flying to Europe under his own steam. He would determine his future, his path, his fate, not some system or accident of birth! Few of his fellow passengers were black. He had anticipated that. Oh, there were two sisters[1] from California, but they weren't foxes![2] He noticed a couple of cute white girls, however. As soon as the plane landed at Heathrow Airport in England, he felt somehow different. Not being in America was like a burden lifted from his shoulders. Sure, he was an American and proud of it, but being abroad made him realize that nationality, at least his, was an accident of birth. As he encountered people in Europe who asked him where he was from and where his people were from, the point was brought home. Born in Philly, he could've just as easily

---

[1] Black girls.
[2] Good-looking girls.

been born in Africa, the Caribbean, or Central or South America. People of color were worldwide, he was learning, and although American, he was also a world citizen. Amir thought that African Americans were not simply what America had taught them they were. His first encounters with people of color with British accents was mind-blowing. The beautiful clerk at the chemist (drugstore) was interesting. This young lady could've been in his family or certainly someone he might have known in America except for the fact that she was British and living in England. No one had prepared Amir for all the people of color he would encounter in both London and Paris. They weren't shown on TV in those times by and large. Walking down the streets of London and Paris, one encountered people of all colors from around the world, speaking English, French, Arabic, Hindi, Dutch, German, Swahili, Amharic, and various other languages.

Sure, he knew that the English had done some horrible things to people of color and others historically. But here they were, people of Caribbean, African, Asian, and other ancestry, former colonial people in many cases who had migrated to the mother country— sort of a "chickens coming home to roost" situation. Some were a bit surprised to meet a black American. Americans to them were white people. Stereotypes! "Do you drive a Cadillac?" "Have money?" More stereotypes about Americans.

The Ponderosa, a.k.a. the Crib

Back in the day, on Sunday evenings, everyone Amir knew watched the TV western series *Bonanza*. It was about the Cartwrights, a wealthy Western ranch family, comprising a father, "Pa," and his three sons. The sprawling ranch the Cartwrights lived on was called the "Ponderosa." Hence one's home was his or her Ponderosa. The other Sunday-night must-see was *The Ed Sullivan Show*. There were only three TV channels to watch in those days—channels 3, 6, and 10, ABC, NBC, and CBS respectively.

On *The Ed Sullivan Show,* you might see James Brown, the Temptations, the Supremes, Jackie Wilson, Moms Mabley, the Four Tops, the Beatles, Elvis, and many other then popular performers.

The only home Amir remembered was the one in North Central Philadelphia, the two-story brick-faced row house in its heart. Only a few blocks over was Broad Street, running in a straight path north to south and vice versa. Broad Street was a kind of demarcation line in Philly. Addresses were whatever number North or South Broad Street often. To the north, it emptied into Cheltenham Avenue. To the south, it went way down into South Philly, to Veteran's Stadium and beyond. Parts were African American populated, and parts were Italian American populated, basically, in the old days. Everyone knew that some of the *good people*[3] lived in South Philly at that time.

The smell of whiskey from a nearby whiskey factory/distillery sometimes wafted through the air on Amir's block. The roar of the crowd from long since demolished Connie Mack Baseball Stadium, formerly Shibe Park, sometimes could be heard on game days and nights in his neighborhood as well. When baseball games were scheduled, his North Philly neighborhood would be invaded by white fans who had parked some blocks away from the stadium either to save money or, for lack of space, be closer to the stadium. Amir was told that at some point the family had lived in another neighborhood somewhere else in Philly when he was younger, but he had no memory of that place or address, wherever it was. Too young at the time, he figured.

As an adult, the house seemed small to him. It didn't when he was growing up there—brick facade, two floors, and a basement with four bedrooms and one bathroom. There were closets and

---

[3] Italian mob members.

a shed kitchen, as well as the regular kitchen. He remembered there had been a coal bin in the basement for a time and a small coal-burning stove there when he was a young boy. There had been coal deliveries where a chute had been run into one of two basement windows, which faced and opened out onto Huntingdon Street, to deliver the coal. Melinda, his sister, a beautiful little girl who would grow up to be a stone fox had developed a penchant for eating or sucking on pieces of coal and was found down in the basement sometimes in the coal bin with coal in her mouth!

He had so many memories there in that house: he and Melinda waking up early on Christmas mornings having given Santa Claus enough time to deliver their presents, of course, and opening them by the Christmas tree after waking Mom and Dad up; putting teeth under a pillow so that the tooth fairy could come by and leave a dollar under that pillow; Amir doing target practice with his archery set in the basement or assembling and sometimes painting balsa-wood airplanes, plastic model cars, ships, and airplanes in his room and displaying them on the mantel; Amir playing with his many toy guns; getting up early in the morning and going fishing with Dad and periodically going to work with him; and getting dressed and ready to set off for Sunday school at church almost every Sunday.

Amir remembered that their first color TV was actually more furniture than TV and the excitement when they got their first Silvertone stereo from Sears, then known as Sears & Roebuck. They could play the music of that rising phenom Aretha Franklin and Sam Cooke, among others, and it had an AM/FM radio! He dressed in his tux for his senior prom, Melinda looking beautiful in her gown when her turn came. Cousins, aunts, uncles, family friends, and others came by to visit or for dinner. Skip, an adult cousin who visited fairly often, had a loud voice and infectious laugh that Amir found unsettling. He was a good-looking brown-skinned man with a thin moustache and curly hair. He had a lot of personality and would sometimes go fishing with him and Dad. Skip was very enterprising; he always had some business venture, investment, or hustle going. He and Dad would also go deer hunting sometimes but rarely seemed to get a deer.

Hell, Amir even remembered the ice man coming along his street when he was very young, yelling "Ice man! Ice man!" In later years, he would always note how Philly, Baltimore, and Boston looked remarkably alike to him with their many often-smallish brick-faced adjoining row homes. There were neighbors on either side of their North Philly home. Sonny Stern, a Jewish man, had a corner store/deli on one side of them. Amir would develop a taste for good pastrami at his deli. "Get him used to good things, and he'll work to get them" was Sonny Weiss's unsolicited child-rearing advice to Fannie Mae, Amir's mom, one day in his store. A Greek family lived on the other side of them. Almost everyone else in the immediate community was African American. It was an interesting situation—white next-door neighbors in an almost all-black neighborhood in an overwhelmingly black part of town. Philadelphia was traditionally a city of home owners, no matter how small or how little marketplace value the home had. In those days, most people washed/scrubbed their stoops and swept the sidewalks. Folks taking pride in the appearance of their smallish North Philadelphia homes was the rule, not the exception.

From a young testosterone-filled male perspective, neighborhood girls jumping double dutch was a bonus. Sometimes you could see up under their dresses or skirts, see some leg, while they were jumping, sometimes some panty! Like in school sometimes, the boys would gather under the stairwell to look up under the girls' dresses as they were negotiating the staircase. Usually boys played stickball, tossed a football in the streets between the cars, or threw snowballs at passing cars. They also made scooters out of wooden milk crates, planks, and roller skate wheels and zip guns out of wood, rubber bands, and nails to shoot flattened soda-bottle tops. Other memories included people going to work early in the morning, some carrying lunch pails or bags, others not. Some wore the uniforms of domestics, auto mechanics, nurses, postal workers, military members, janitors, truck drivers, policemen, construction workers, warehousemen, teachers, and so on. Most adults he knew had jobs and families. Folks on "the welfare" were whispered about. Even the projects, at least the ones Amir had visited, were mostly neat and well kept, at least on the exterior, at that time. There were rules and policies on upkeep, cleanliness, and so on. Young, unmarried pregnant girls often disappeared for a time; they were supposedly visiting out-of-state relatives or had simply disappeared.

A corner store had "Big Jack," as he was called by most, a brown-skinned massive-sized man, sort of menacing looking, with hands the size of baseball mittens, which he used to collect your money as you paid for your candy—Chunkys, Almond Joys, Mars Bars—sodas, loaves of bread, and Kotex (for your mother or sister, very embarrassing). Big Jack had body odor but was friendly enough if you weren't stealing in his store. There was also a sort of hardware store across the street that was owned and operated by blacks. The dad was also an insurance agent.

In addition, there was a black-owned and operated dry cleaner on the other corner. The dad smoked a pipe and had a neatly trimmed, upturned mustache. Dave's barber shop was a couple of blocks away on the right-hand side. Of course, the barber shop was a cultural meeting place for black men, not just a barber shop. The young and the old would gather there for more than haircuts.

The latest neighborhood gossip, current events, politics, religion, women, sports, and racism would all be up for discussion. Trips to the barber shop were a coming-of-age experience for young black males in Philly and many other places big and small across America. Usually, they had a few barber chairs, some old magazines, and chairs to sit in and wait your turn, maybe an old TV placed up on a shelf or on the wall, and usually, a radio of some kind. Some were fancier and more upscale; others were basic and simple. Photos of celebs sometimes decorated the walls, along with depictions of hairstyles offered. It was a place reserved for African American males to meet, commune, and enjoy brotherhood and fraternity. "Will Ali beat Joe Frazier?" "What about those crackers down south?" "Did you hear Aretha's latest album?" "Who you voting for?" "I don't believe Sammy Davis Jr. hugged Nixon!"

Adult male customers were often saluted as "doctor," "professor," "brother," or "deacon" as they entered. Boys or young men were often called "junior." Very few females, young or old, would enter this male bastion, unless they were looking for someone, who, if there then or showed up later, would be teased about it.

Some decades later, Amir would note that this black cultural trapping was very similar to the coffee shops/houses and other all-male gathering places where men drank tea or coffee and sat around conversing and debating like he would see in the distant future in Rabat, Marrakesh, or Fez. The old neighborhood would eventually be called a "ghetto" by the media and others, a term he found racist, stereotypical, offensive, and inaccurate, at least while he was growing up there. It was the Italian name for a concentration of low-income Jewish folks! To him, it was a community!

Decades later, upon return visits to the old neighborhood, Amir could not help but notice how the small, once-black-owned-and-operated businesses in the community were now owned, operated, or run by others—Hispanics, Asians, Arabs. What had happened?

In North Philly, there were also lots of "biergartens," as Mom and Dad called them, and churches, which he thought was interesting. It was an area of stores, shops, restaurants, and mostly hardworking folk trying to make it. He would learn or absorb many valuable life experiences and life lessons there. Many good people lived, worked, loved, raised families, and died there. Dreams were born there. Of course, there were miscreants, but there were miscreants everywhere. Bad people were and are in the minority.

They do not define all of us, he thought. He grew up in a community. The term *ghetto* was not empowering, not life sustaining or affirming, but dehumanizing, disempowering, marginalizing. Poor or working-class urban areas occupied by whites with high crime statistics—for example, Hell's Kitchen in New York City and South Boston—were not usually referred to as ghettos. He would not use the term!

Jitterbugs

Young men who today would be called thugs, gangbangers, miscreants, gangstas, or simply criminals, were called by Mom and Dad jitterbugs. Amir didn't understand this reference as a boy. Was it a southern immigrant reference? Jitterbugs had swagger and were supposed to be tough guys. They often had their hair processed (a hair-straightening methodology that left the hair straight and shiny, often wavy) back in the day and wore du-rags to preserve their processes.

Some brothers used Murray's or Jaybirds hair treatments in their hair to make waves in it or as part of a hair-straightening process. "It burned!" everyone said. Many cool black men wore a process. Also, many black male entertainers had processes or their hair straightened in some manner back in the day—Nat King Cole, the Temptations, the Four Tops, Jackie Wilson, Smokey Robinson, Jerry Butler, and James Brown among many others. The advent of the black consciousness movement and the natural hairstyle would eventually become the death knell of the process. It was to be followed many years later by the jerry curl (a kind of long, curly, wet, dripping hairstyle). These jitterbugs also walked with a stroll, a kind of slow walk with an exaggerated arm swing. Some were criminals, others would-be criminals, and some simply wannabes. They were the essence of cool for the time. In a sense, these jitterbugs/gangbangers both preyed on and protected the neighborhood! Amir never desired to be a jitterbug but tried to have a cordial rapport with them like with almost everyone else in the neighborhood. "What's up, brother?" "Hey, professor!" "Hello, doctor!" "Hey, cool!" "Hey, Mack Daddy!"

This American black male cultural thing about being a pimp or playa was something Amir became aware of as he matured. One of Amir's fellow college students would explain to him years later that the term *pimp* was actually an acronym for paper in my pocket and that he supposedly had run hoes but was then pursuing higher education. This pimp thing has carried on to this day usually among urban black males and most certainly predated Amir's birth. Of course, the vast majority of them were not and are not actually pimps. But the notion that a man can manipulate women for his purposes and be in control of them must somehow appeal to the male ego. There was, of course, the famous "Iceberg Slim," a supposedly real-life pimp who put his life story to pen and paper. There was even a movie about his exploits made! There appears to be something glamorous, something powerful, something appealing about this cultural icon to some black men, the majority of whom have traditionally been denied the respect and recognition due them by American society. "Nature abhors a vacuum," it is said. Amir concluded after years of living and observing that people who are denied recognition or excluded by the majority will sometimes develop their own morals, values, and ethics independent of that society. Why should they buy in to values or standards imposed if they don't receive the recognition, the benefits, for doing same?

Geronimo, a neighborhood character, had reddish-brown hair and a thin, wiry frame. He seemed deranged and wore a hatchet in his waistband. He appeared drunk or high on something almost all the time but seemed to like Amir's family. Years later, he protected Mom in the quickly deteriorating neighborhood while she was living alone there and young men in the pharmaceutical sales business were doing hostile takeovers and otherwise trying to get a leg up on the competition or were settling disputes. Just as he had rejected the term ghetto, Amir rejected the concept of black-on-black crime as well.

Aren't most crime victims victimized by their own group members, be they black, white, yellow, or brown? Aren't most murder victims killed by a neighbor, friend, relative, lover, or spouse? Sure, the media sensationalizes the cross racial/ethnic group crimes, but they are in the minority, and yet we don't say white-on-white, yellow-on-yellow, or brown-on-brown crime!

La Famiglia

In his immediate family, his mother, father, and sister and he were all high yella, redbones, light brights, or light, bright, and damn near white, he would come to understand. Lighter-skinned blacks were often referred to that way back in the day. Mixed, half-breed, plain, yella, and red were also utilized.

In the neighborhood just a couple of blocks away were his grandparents on his father's side—Biggy, his grandmother and family favorite, and Pop, his grandfather. Both were from northeast Georgia. They had migrated to Philadelphia, along with his mother and father. Biggy was a petite, light-brown-skinned, good-looking woman with beautiful hair. Her face suggested strength and dignity. One of Amir's fondest memories of his early childhood would be how he, as a little boy, often sat on the floor near her and watched as she brushed and combed her beautiful hair nightly, handing her a brush, a comb, and hair pomade as requested. Biggy also dipped snuff. She, of course, would periodically have to spit it out into a can or spittoon. Amir knew no one else who dipped snuff. She called him, as all immediate family members did, "Sonny," his nickname. Biggy was a strong, hardworking, loyal Taurus (the bull). She had very little formal education but a whole lot of good common sense, like many of the adults he knew. Her southern accent was not pronounced. You only picked it up when she said certain words (e.g., the word *stab* became "staab"; if something were to happen soon, it would happen "directly"; "Henry" became "Honry"). She was a proud woman and tried her best to instill a sense of pride and strength in Amir and Melinda. "Have your own." "Don't beg!" "Be proud of what you have." She sometimes worked as a cleaning woman in Center City Philly office buildings. She and Pop, her husband and Amir's and Melinda's grandfather, often babysat Amir and Melinda. It was usually fun. Biggy would encourage them both when eating to "eat till you're full." She would give both an entire box of frozen french fries to be eaten along with their respective lunches! Of course, Pop and Biggy spoiled Melinda and him as grandparents are prone to do. When Mom or Dad said no, they would appeal that decision to Biggy and Pop. Often their appeals were successful, causing some tension between Mom and Biggy and Pop.

Pop was interesting. Born in 1900, Pop didn't look stereotypically black by any means. He had a slender build, a narrow face, thin lips, aquiline features, a very fair complexion/coloring, and straight dark hair, which he wore combed straight back, and a neatly trimmed mustache. Pop was handsome. As a boy, Amir didn't pay much attention to Pop's not necessarily black-looking appearance. He was simply Pop to him. Only in later years would he really think about it. He could've been taken for an Arab, a Hispanic, a Greek, or several other Southern European types. Pop didn't have much of a southern accent either. In fact, he used some terms that at the time were embarrassing to Amir but in later years, upon reflection, became quite interesting (e.g., the trunk of a car he called the "boot" and suitcases were "grips"). This from an African American man who grew up in Georgia! Pop, like many black men of the time, carried a small knife on him; some carried straight razors!

Rumor had it that he stabbed someone once. Amir had never probed around that. He would never forget the times Pop would take him to Columbia Avenue, which has since been renamed Cecil B. Moore Avenue, after Cecil, the "Johnny Cochran" of his era in Philly, with him to buy fresh chicken. The Temple University Law School is located very close to the avenue. The store had live chickens, displayed in cages. When selected, they'd be slaughtered, dressed, and packaged up to take out in a back room. The place smelled terrible to a little boy. Pop would often buy him a toy, usually a toy gun, on these forays. Pop worked as a warehouseman. Eventually, he would get frostbite from working out in the cold in his toes.

Mom's mother was known as Big Mama in true southern fashion. Evidently, they had their own farm, including a couple of employees. Back then, there were no official birth certificates for many of these old-timers. The family Bible was often where births were recorded after one was born at home with the assistance of a midwife.

Years later, Amir would remember how he had placed a toy but realistic-looking scale-sized black forty-five-caliber automatic pistol in his waistband for a prison journey, unbeknownst to his parents, to visit some relation called Hank, because you never knew when trouble might jump off. Like most boys of the era, Amir had a lot of toy guns. Some would say he was obsessed with them. He had pistols, holsters, automatics, revolvers, rifles, and so on. In fact, he was rather proud of his collection, some of which were rather realistic-looking. He and other boys played cops and robbers, cowboys and Indians, soldier, detective, FBI agent, and so on. The corrections officer at the prison when he, Mom, and Dad went to visit Hank was not as impressed with his true-to-scale model forty-five-caliber automatic pistol when they arrived, however. He told Amir he would have to hand it over and pick it up upon leaving.

It was a little embarrassing, but his parents didn't yell or fuss at him. The visitee had been in solitary for some reason but was allowed visitors upon their trip. He was low key and didn't say much but seemed glad to see them.

This incident sort of reminded Amir of another one a few years before when, while dressing for Sunday school, he had put on a shoulder holster and a toy automatic. It fit perfectly under his tailored suit. Mom had discovered this and told him to take it off. He explained, "Mom, you never know when something might jump off!" He did take off the shoulder holster, however.

Uncle Dave was a relative, probably a cousin. He was a middle-aged, slender man of less than average height. He was good-looking with a well-manicured moustache and dark curly hair worn short. He didn't talk a lot but occasionally visited the house. There was a framed picture of Uncle Dave in the house. He looked smart in his neatly pressed army uniform, garrison side cap worn tilted to the side.

Back in the day, brothers often wore hats of some kind. "Brims," "sky pieces," and other slang terms were used to describe them. Certain ones had to be blocked, or shaped, usually by hand and with one's fingers. Of course, pimps, hoodlums, sportsmen,[4] and would-be gangsters often wore hats. But so did regular guys on occasion.

Certainly, they protected one from the elements, and some guys really wore them well. There were driver's caps, newsboy caps, Greek fisherman's caps, English-style bowlers, jeffs, cowboy hats (some hats were called Stetson's after the brand name), and Kangols, which were popular with older brothers. Hats were also sometimes called "headpieces" and in years to come, "kufis." The dominant memory Amir had of Uncle Dave was the Philly police at the front door with Uncle Dave, holding him up. He was drunk!

---

[4] Men who frequented certain bars.

In those days, the police often took people to their homes or the homes of friends or relatives rather than lock them up for minor offenses, such as public drunkenness. Uncle Dave apparently had a drinking problem. Amir never actually saw him acting out in any way, however, just standing there quietly, unsteady in the doorway, looking glassy-eyed, with a cop on either side of him. Of course, he'd be taken in to sleep it off, usually bidding them adieu the next day. This would happen again and again.

Aunt Candy visited often. She was not really an aunt but related somehow. She was friendly to Amir and Melinda and always brought fish cakes with her. Amir and Melinda loved fish cakes and were therefore always happy to see her at the door. She was a bit loud, however. Amir never felt particularly comfortable around folks he adjudged as being too loud, be they relatives, neighbors, strangers, or whomever. He liked a peaceful, calm, and tranquil home atmosphere and would often go around the house turning down the volume on the TV or the stereo if he felt it was too loud. This caused arguments with Melinda sometimes. He also at times almost hid when company was coming over to the house, disturbing his tranquil sanctuary.

When Amir was a little boy, there seemed to be more mutual respect among people. So when the brothers, State Store,[5] and two others were holding down the corner of an intersection that cloudy fall day, drinking out of a brown paper bag, probably cheap wine, which they were passing around, and they saw him and Mom coming, one said to the others, "Shh! There's a lady coming!" As Mom and he walked by State Store, they respectfully nodded and said, "Hello," to Mom. The profanity had stopped. This sort of interaction would change, of course, over time. This respect would dissipate over the years to some degree. "Children should be seen and not heard" was an axiom of the era, so when adults visited their

---

[5] Liquor is sold in Pennsylvania via a chain of "State Stores."

home, after paying their respects, kids were expected to leave the area after hearing the obligatory, "Make sure you get your lessons" admonition from at least one of the visiting adults. They would be left to engage in grown folks' talk.

What You See Is What You get

It took Amir awhile to learn that most people seem to judge and assess one another at least upon first meeting on appearance. Decades later, he would learn the terminology—*halo effect, bias, prejudice, ethnocentricity, xenophobia, stereotype*, and so on. He would read studies that demonstrated that all things being equal, for instance, people judged attractive made more money and had more advancement in their respective careers than those not judged attractive and that male business executives, for instance, tended to be over a certain height. The notion was that height suggested leadership ability or some such thing. He learned that obese people, by and large, are handicapped as well and often stereotyped as lazy, greedy, or lacking in character or discipline. Women, of course, were supposed to be the weaker sex and could never be president. Information that contradicted these truisms was often ignored or rationalized.

Human beings tend to see only what they are prepared to see and tend to believe what they want to believe. There are exceptions; certainly attractive women, foxes, tended to be treated better by men than women not judged attractive. They received more benefits and privileges from society by and large. This tended to be true no matter their race or ethnicity. Most of us would say, "Looks are not everything," but does our actual behavior confirm this belief?

Amir observed how most people fawned over cute infants, for instance, but not so much over those deemed not as attractive. Every ethnic group had standards of beauty. They were not necessarily consistent across groups. *But we all have them*, thought Amir—a long neck, aquiline features, big eyes, blue or brown eyes, blond or black/brown hair, a small waist, small feet, a nicely shaped gluteus maximus, big breasts, and so on. In fact, it is well known that some brothers preferred women with huge behinds! Not so much Amir and Omar, who referred to them as buffalo butts or trogladytes. Desirable hair might be long, short, curly, nappy, wavy, or straight. Olive, brown, or pale skin could be desirable. Ironically, many members of groups who fed into these standards didn't actually meet them themselves!

So when Amir witnessed males, young and old, black and white, being helpful and kind to his sister, Melinda, for instance, going the extra mile to assist or help her, he was not surprised or offended. Melinda was a fox and well dressed. She had an infectious smile. He would also go the extra mile for good-looking women. Of course, class and status factor into this equation as well. America proudly proclaims itself a democracy where anyone can make it with no royalty or rigid class standards. But how accurate is that? Isn't society those we used to read about on the society page in the newspaper? Don't we call those who have recently attained some measure of wealth and status the nouveau riche, a kind of dig? Aren't others considered old money? Do most of us really treat those we perceive as wealthy or powerful and high status the same way we treat a neighbor, a coworker, or a homeless person? Don't we give the former more respect and veneration? In our heart of hearts, don't many of us secretly blame poor people for being poor? I'm not poor and destitute, so why are they? Must be some flaw or fault they have! God does not love them as much, many of us secretly believe. Of course, racism applies this thinking to entire races of people, so that a financially comfortable African American can be "nigger rich." Stereotypes, of course, can be dangerous or even deadly for the stereotyped. The American ones about blacks were often horrible. They were and still are used to discriminate against and brutalize them—black males in particular. Other ethnicities have stereotypes as well, but one can educate or earn oneself out of them. And unlike the black stereotypes, their basic humanity is not put up for derision, nor their color, their very appearance. For blacks, however, even wealthy ones, their status is always tenuous at best in America. No matter how famous, how wealthy, how seemingly influential, your card can be pulled! Amir found it so ironic decades later when he learned that the wealthiest human being who ever lived was probably a West African ruler named Mansa Musa I, of the Kingdom of Mali, who is estimated to have been worth about $400 billion in today's dollars, adjusted for inflation!

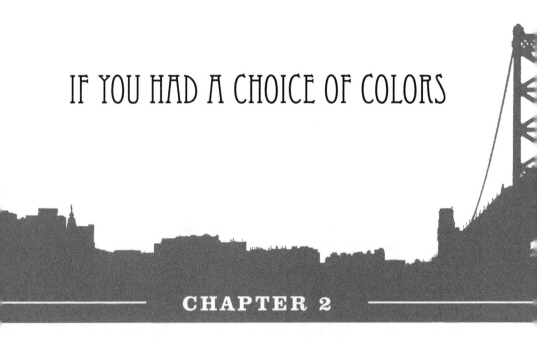

IF YOU HAD A CHOICE OF COLORS

CHAPTER 2

In later years, Amir would sometimes reflect on how, as a very young boy, he was not race conscious. He was not taught to be so by Mom and Dad or others. He didn't hear many derogatory or denigrating comments about whites or other races. There were allusions to the behavior of whites, usually within the context of some racial incident or discriminatory act. In fact, he grew to believe that he, and lots of other young African American kids of the era, did not even know they were black until at a certain age, when typically being called the n word or some other blatantly racist or traumatic racial experience rocked their world.

It might sound a bit silly or incredulous to subsequent generations, but in the late 1950s and early 1960s, when almost all the heroes and superheroes, real or imaginary, when almost all the icons, authority figures, all the folks who were celebrated, who were held up for admiration were white Americans, kids, black and white, secretly or openly identified with those heroes and authority figures. Many young black American kids thought they were white, certainly not black! If not, why were so many genuinely insulted or hurt at being called or referred to as black at the beginning of the black consciousness movement? "Yo mama's black!" was said with anger or hostility as the response of many when called or referred to as black.

Black parents of the era, perhaps to spare their progeny some of the trauma and pain of racism that they had and were experiencing, avoided the topics of race and prejudice at home all too often in Amir's opinion. African Americans always had some pride, Amir felt. But it wasn't always black pride. Many fought against racism, Jim and Jane Crow, segregation, police brutality, and so on. Yet there's a subtle but important distinction between opposing oppression and wanting a better life and being truly proud of who and what you are racially or ethnically. Xenophobia and ethnocentrism among blacks, who had a well-deserved reputation for being accepting and tolerant of almost everyone despite the hell they dealt with daily, essentially did not exist. Amir was often the lightest-skinned person in a class at his elementary school at Sixteenth in North Philadelphia. He was never truly uncomfortable with his coloring and general appearance, however, thank God/Allah, but he often suspected that his sister, Melinda, a beauty by any standard, was a bit uncomfortable with her lovely slightly darker than his skin tone. What a shame, he felt, as he sometimes came across Melinda's sun tan lotions and other skin-darkening-type creams. He determined he wouldn't be picked on by darker-skinned blacks because of his coloring. So one day at his elementary school, when a fellow student, trying to be smart asked him, "What *are* you?" His response was, "First, figure out what *you* are, and after that, know that whatever that is, I'm not that!"

Some other blacks were "nadinolaing it" up (darker-skinned blacks using skin creams and lighteners to hopefully become lighter). Before the black consciousness era began, being black but light-skinned in Philadelphia and elsewhere paid dividends. Some girls preferred the light-skinned guys, with "good" hair. Some employers only hired the lighter-skinned people if they hired blacks at all! Some whites and others seemed more comfortable around the high yella folk than around their darker-skinned brethren. A look at the homecoming queens at many of the HBCUs of the era supported this colorism.

There was an obvious preference for the yella gals—"light, bright, and damned near white"—for many years. Earlier photos of students at historically black colleges/institutions sometimes showed entire classes composed of lighter-skinned blacks. Philly was the town where the well-known organization for well-heeled blacks was founded in 1938 and was and is aspirational for blacks; education, family, and hard work were emphasized. There were cotillions and coming-out-type events. It was also a bastion of color and economic caste when Amir was a young boy. This was the case across America, particularly in big urban areas.

The term *Germantown girl*, for instance, had a definite meaning when he was a young teen. It meant a light-skinned African American girl with wavy, curly, or straight hair, often with aquiline facial features, living in the then middle/upper-middle-class areas of Germantown, Mount Airy, West Oak Lane, or Chestnut Hill in Philadelphia or its environs.

"Light bright" parties were sometimes held, and there were sometimes brown paper bag tests. "If you're black, get back; if you're brown, stick around; if you're red, you're already dead; if you're yellow, you're mellow; and if you're white, you're all right" summarized this caste system. "Hey, cutie, not you, black beauty!" "Ain't yo mama on the pancake box?" Some folks spoke of "brightening up" the race. Of course, there were also the "yo mama's so black" jokes and the "yo mama's so ugly" jokes—"she turned Ice Blue Secret into a rumor," "she has to sneak up on a glass of water," "she'd make an onion cry," and so on. Almost everyone claimed to have a Portuguese or Native American or white distant or not-so-distant ancestor. Referring to or calling someone "black" was an insult. Phrases like "I'll slap the black off you!" were common.

Clearly, whites and lighter-skinned blacks, along with some others, received advantages and privileges over darker-skinned blacks. It wasn't right. It bothered him. It was reactionary. Its roots lay in chattel slavery, American Jim and Jane Crow, and segregation. Blacks had been taught self-hate. He would struggle against it, but it was a reality. And truth be told, some of those redbones were fine! Thank goodness he didn't hear those references at home. No color or racial biases were taught by Mom and Dad.

Amir would never forget the time when, as a young boy, he had innocently asked Mom why Johnny, his darker-skinned neighborhood friend, one of his best friends in the neighborhood, always had dirty hands. In her own inimitable way, she had explained that "that's not dirt; that's the way God made him" and added, "I don't ever want to hear your yellow butt talking like that again!" Lesson taught and learned.

When retail stores and other businesses in Philly that, in the past, would not hire blacks began to do so—slowly and grudgingly or not—they very often hired blacks who were so fair-skinned they were barely noticeable from the otherwise white staff! Many black men had a decided preference for the redbones.[6]

This caste system helped explain some of the hostility the redbones sometimes experienced from their darker-skinned sisters. It was sad. Back in the day, the only colored people/Negroes on TV were on *Ramar of the Jungle* or *Tarzan* or an occasional chauffeur, maid, or butler.

They were usually servile, bug-eyed, and not particularly bright or good-looking and often afraid of their own shadows! Most public schools taught little or nothing about black or African history pre-Columbus. The symbolism was horrible. Black symbolized

---

[6] Light-skinned girls.

evil—the black sheep of the family. The devil's food cake was the dark cake, the good guys wore white hats, a dark cloud was a negative inference, and white symbolized purity and goodness. No wonder not many people wanted to be called black or African!

The black women on TV were not usually the fine ones, whom he knew existed from his own life's experience, but strong, fiercely loyal, sort of asexual creatures attending to whites and their children (Mammy characters). He often wondered if those African natives on television, always dark in color with broad features, speaking some made-up gibberish, not Ki-Swahili, Arabic, Amharic, Akan, Mande, Yoruba, or some other real African language, were out of work or moonlighting African American jazz musicians! Most were certainly not Africans from Africa! They usually had chiefs (an attempt to avoid calling them princes, kings, emirs, or sultans), and they most often carried spears and wore loincloths. They always lived in small villages made up of huts. The real-life Africans, whom he would later learn about, often wore long robes of one type or another, sometimes lived in cities, and were rarely shown on TV. No, these brothers had to be almost naked, sometimes butt naked. Cities, stone structures, or mud-brick structures like those found in Great Zimbabwe, Ethiopia, Timbuktu, or Kilwa or pyramids, like those found in present-day Sudan, were never shown. There was no mention of the University of Sankore or any such thing. They were never portrayed as literate or particularly intelligent. They too were almost never portrayed as brave or heroic; that was reserved for white characters and an occasional noble savage. The Cisco Kid was the first TV show he could remember that had minorities as the central/main characters. Supposedly Mexicans, they were named, respectively, Poncho and Cisco. "Hey, Poncho! Hey, Cisco!" and they rode into the sunset, sombreros flapping in the wind. And yet there was Chief Half Town on TV with his children's show. It was one of the longest—if not the longest—running children's TV shows in the history of television. The chief wore Native American garb and at least looked like (and was) a real Native American! The chief was a big, full-blooded Seneca Indian from upstate New York, Amir would learn years later. He famously said, "Don't call me a Native American; call me an Indian."

Eventually, there would be *Room 222*, with the good-looking and sexy Denise Nicholas; *Julia*, with the beautiful and sexy Diahann Carrol; and *I Spy*, with Philly's own Bill Cosby, but that would be years later. Eventually, some more fine sisters would come along to screens big and small: Pam Grier, Jayne Kennedy, Vonetta McGee, Stacy Reed, Brenda Sykes, and others.

With these images, no wonder so many blacks were ashamed to be black or called black and wanted to be white—or anything other than black! Whites had King Arthur, Camelot, castles, knights in shining armor, Sir Lancelot, Prince Valiant, Robin Hood, Hopalong Cassidy, Roy Rogers, and the Lone Ranger (a character probably based, ironically, on a real-life black federal marshal named Sam Bass). Blacks of the time had Tarzan and Ramar of the Jungle—natives carrying spears and living in the jungle. No one was educating blacks or whites about the West African kingdoms of Ghana, Mali, and Songhay; Kanem-Bornu; ancient Kush or Ethiopia; Nubia; Great Zimbabwe; Timbuktu; or the University of Sankore or about Shaka Zulu, Mansa Musa I, Tarik Bin Ziad, Abu Bakr II, Menelik II, and other African heroes. How ironic, he would grow to learn, that the very people who, according to some scholars, blacks, gave the arts and civilization to the world and the people from a continent where there was no cradle of civilization to be found (Europe) were transposed!

All that aside, Mom and Dad were good-looking, however, irrespective of race, skin color, or caste system. Of course, he was biased, but he felt that his opinion was objectively true. It was often confirmed by others. Bill, his dad, a man of about five feet nine inches tall with a slender to medium build until he got older and gained weight, as middle-aged men are prone to do in the battle of the bulge, was good-looking. Women, young and old, often so stated. He had a neatly trimmed mustache, dark curly hair, a cleft in his chin, and a fetching smile. He parted his hair on the side. He was an Aquarian and very outgoing; he had lots of friends and acquaintances, male and female. He quick with a smile or a laugh, and he did enjoy teasing. Neither Mom nor Dad was a party person. They didn't hang out in bars or clubs, and neither drank a lot as far as Amir could tell—especially Mom, the home-centered Virgo. There would be an occasional visit to Peg Leg Bates's place for a night out. Who was this Peg Leg Bates anyway? Years later, while researching on his own, Amir would find out. This legendary one-legged tap dancer had been quite famous in his day, appearing on *The Ed Sullivan Show* numerous times and having his own resort and entertainment center.

Another of Amir's young adolescent memories was around how he and a buddy from the neighborhood named Thomas had walked several blocks over to the YMCA near Germantown Avenue in order to sign up for swimming lessons. It was a beautiful afternoon as they walked along Lehigh Avenue headed to the Y. They each had big money—possibly two dollars each! As they entered the lobby of the YMCA, Amir had noticed an older teen sort of hanging out near the cashier's window. He looked tough and was wearing a sky piece (hat). As his friend and he were completing the necessary form to take swimming lessons and gathering the fifty cents each it would cost, the guy approached Amir and Thomas and said, "Just like you paid the Y fifty cents to swim, you gotta give me fifty cents too each time you come here." Of course, they were scared but tried not to show it. He was bigger and older than they. He also appeared to be a jitterbug. What to do? They both wanted to learn how to swim but didn't want to get beat up! They decided they would go to the Huntingdon Street gang and seek their help, as they both lived on Huntingdon Street and knew some of the gang members. Peanut Head told them, "Don't worry; I'll send one of my boys with you next time you go to the Y!" He did. He was an older teen also, tall and wearing a sky piece. He had a small scar on his right cheek. In fact, it was Peanut Head himself!

As they traveled to the Y, they passed neighborhood celebrity Cornbread strolling on Broad Street in a bright-red suit with red socks, red shoes, and a red fedora. You couldn't tell him he wasn't cool. At the Y, Peanut Head walked right up to the would-be extortionist, who was still hanging out near the cashier's window and got in his face. He said, "They're coming to the Y, and they're not paying you, dude! If I hear anything else, I'll be back, and you don't want that!" He then patted Amir and Thomas on their respective shoulders and said, "It'll be all right now, fellas." He then turned and walked away with his jitterbug stroll after cocking his hat to the side.

Amir concluded, lessons learned: gangs are not all bad, everyone is territorial to some extent, sometimes force or threats of force must be met with same, even thugs and hoodlums have a code and rules of conduct, the good guy and the bad guy were actually very similar, and his neighborhood was more of a community than some were willing to acknowledge.

Another incident that left an indelible imprint on his young mind happened one day on Seventeenth Street while he was hanging out with Clarence, a neighborhood friend of the same age as he. For some reason Amir couldn't quite remember, they got into a fistfight. This was unusual. Amir didn't like street fights. He would only have a few in his life. Fighting on the streets of Philly for young men was sometimes required but always dangerous. Would it be a fair fight? Or would the other guy's friends take his side and jump you? Or even if you won the fight, would your defeated opponent seek revenge, maybe sneak up on you one day? If challenged, however, it was difficult not to fight. It was a male ego, status thing. You didn't want to be thought of as a punk or a faggot, inviting others to take advantage of or pick on you. Clarence was about

Amir's size. Maybe because Philly was a boxing town, most young Philly guys thought they could hold their hands (box). As Clarence and Amir were fighting or boxing that beautiful spring afternoon near Clarence's house around the corner and down the street from Amir's, they probably were fighting to a draw, when, somehow, Amir got his hands around Clarence's throat. He was really trying to choke him! At some point, he caught himself and stopped.

What later scared Amir was that the act of choking Clarence actually had started feeling good to him! Amir was discovering that like Mom, he had a temper, and when lost, it could become dangerous. For the rest of his life, he would try to control his temper, usually successfully, but on occasion ...

Interestingly, Puerto Rican Philadelphians sometimes approached Amir's dad, Bill, speaking Spanish. He would usually become offended by such "damned Puerto Ricans!" as he was prone to say. Before he and Mom had moved to Philly from Georgia, they had probably not met any Puerto Ricans or Hispanics/Latinos at all! Bill had worked at Perloff Brothers Wholesale Grocers in South Philly for years, hardly, if ever, being late or calling out sick or absent. He would ultimately retire from there. He was also a proud Teamster, a member of Local #107, eventually serving as a shop steward. Dad took him deep-sea fishing with him, usually to South Jersey—Brigantine, Egg Harbor, Cape May, Brielle, and Atlantic City, among other destinations. Bill had some real pain around his southern racial experiences, however. Stories told later partially explained why.

Amir's family had a good quality of life, however. Dad had a good job, with good pay and benefits. He was one of the few African American Teamsters at that time. Jimmy Hoffa was the head of the Teamsters then. Dad loved him! Many black households of the time had pictures with MLK Jr., or John F. and Robert Kennedy mounted on a wall or placed on a mantel in their homes—but not in their house! Robert Kennedy was a "punk" who "had never worked a day in his life." Hoffa was for the "working man," according to Dad. Mom worked on and off at a cigar factory. She was often home when he and Melinda got home from school with soup, hugs, and kisses for their injuries or when they were ill. He and Melinda didn't like taking castor oil or Father John's, however; they tasted nasty.

Sometimes they had to lean over the stove over a pot of steaming Vick's Vapo Rub with a towel over their heads. Biggy would sometimes recommend a hot toddy, some kind of mixture for colds or the flu that had liquor in it, a hot toddy for your body. If they were even slightly ill, Mom kept them home from school.

He would always remember as an elementary school student when one semester, he was placed in a "slow" class. At first, Amir felt devastated and embarrassed. He wasn't *slow*. After a few days of assessing the situation, however, he decided that maybe it wasn't so bad after all. He would almost always know the answers to the questions the teacher asked. He could become a superstar in this group! A veritable genius! It was better to be a big fish in a little pond, he thought. But Mom found out. She came down to the school, spoke with the principal, and demanded he be placed with the regular students, adding that he learned best under young, attractive white women!

Since he had allergies, Mom took him to a clinic weekly. Amir would get a needle for every single thing he might be allergic to. The next week, the doctor would examine his reactions to the specific allergens. As a practical matter, this meant he got six to seven needles upon each visit. His arms were sore from so many needles. Finally, he said to Mom, "Let's make a deal; I can save you from all these trips to the clinic, and I can just take over-the-counter allergy medicine."

Mom agreed; they had a deal. One of the good things about Fannie Mae was that you could often reason with this Virgo woman.

Amir and Melinda were spoiled, he would deduce years later. They received lots of attention, love, affection, hugs, kisses, and great gifts and presents. They had a nicely decorated home to live in, vacations, trips, nice clothes to wear, and so on. He and his sister even received allowances.

Amir would never forget the time, for X-mas, he and Melinda were cowboyed and cowgirled down. Pop had taken them both to a real western clothing store. They were outfitted from head to toe—western hats, shirts, pants, boots, belts, the works! He would cherish a picture of him and Melinda in their western outfits for years. He even had a big mechanical gray horse that he occasionally rode up and down Huntingdon Street to the envy of some other kids.

He and Dad, never with Mom or Melinda, would go fishing, out on party boats, as they were called, deep-sea fishing to catch porgies, sea bass, flounder, mackerel, bluefish, fluke, and others. They usually traveled to South Jersey to do this. These party boats were often former World War II PT boats outfitted with sonar, radar, fish finders, and so on. There was usually a captain and one or more mates on board. They'd be busy steering the boat and cutting up clams, squid, or some other kind of bait to be used for chum. They typically anchored over wrecks to fish. His group, Dad and two, three, or four other elders were often the only African Americans on board the boat. The captains and mates were usually white, of course. Their faces lined like road maps from so much time spent on the sea and in the sun. There would be a pool for whoever caught the biggest fish by weight. You could rent rods and reels if you didn't have your own. They usually had their own. Clams and squid, sliced by a mate, would be used for bait (chum). Sometimes they would throw out this chum to attract fish to the vicinity of the boat.

Usually, they went out far enough that you couldn't see land, only sea and sky. If you got seasick you went below and lay down. The boat wasn't going back because you were sick.

Amir only got seasick a couple of times. Usually, he was okay and had his sea legs. It was fun and exciting—a kind of rite of passage, a man thing. To wake up early in the morning and ride to South Jersey with the men (he was always the only youngster in the group) was a coming-of-age experience for him. By listening, he would learn a lot from these older brothers about life, women, politics, work, and religion. He thought to himself, *These are good men, not angels, not saints, but good and decent people.* Hardworking, family-oriented, most had come to Philly to succeed, had fled the oppression of the American South, and they had a kind of immigrant mentality.

The journey to go fishing was usually long enough that there'd be a lot of conversation in the car as they motored along in the early light, and what a group! Michael T., Whip, Skip, and Uncle Verly were among the usual cast of characters.

"I fucked a white gal over there, in the bushes once," one of them had stated, pointing at some bushes as they drove along the highway.

"What kind of watch are you wearing?" Skip had asked Whip.

"Benrus," Whip had replied.

"That's right; it's been rusted" was the retort.

These guys were funny and very witty. Most were not even high-school graduates. From the rural South, many had to quit school in the fifth or sixth grade to help on the farm. That was an oft-heard explanation. "There was school for the white kids but not us" was also heard. Many were World War II vets who had been to the European or Pacific theaters. Once back home, they would not be denied! "Get your education, boy; the white man can't take that away from you!" was what he heard at the barbershop, on the street, at church, in the park, at the bar, on the playground, almost everywhere. In later years, Amir would figure out they were expressing love, hope for the future, and pride in the past. He liked and respected these men. Amir would always remember the time when his cousin, Michael T., married and with daughters, probably in his forties at the time, was driving him around North Philly/

Nicetown in his car, trying to find a timing belt/chain for his yellow Mustang II, which wouldn't start because it needed one.

Dad was out of town in Vegas for several days. As they drove past certain locations, Michael T. would casually point and say, "I have a gal that works there." Michael said this three or four times!

Probably because of the expression on Amir's face, he offered the following explanation in his Georgia accent: "You see, when you have been married as long as I have, your wife becomes a kind of buddy; when you want to have some real fun, you gotta find someone else."

They eventually located a timing belt, and Michael T. and Whip installed it for him as he watched attentively. All he could do was hand them tools and hold things. It was still part of his education about the vagaries of the internal combustion engine and how to do certain repairs.

Amir would later learn that Dad had been an only child. Biggy had had other children, but Dad was the only one who had survived. Dad seemed to be liked by most, particularly some of the females, as he was handsome and charming. For a time, he had smoked cigarettes, then cigars, then a pipe, and then nothing. He seemed not to be a heavy drinker or frequent card player or gambler generally, as far as he could tell. He rarely even heard him cuss—"Cocks——r!" being the usual utterance issued when he became very frustrated or exasperated while trying to accomplish some manual or physical task.

When Amir discovered some pictures of Dad from World War II, he was very impressed. Dad had swagger in his Ike jacket, his campaign hat tilted to the side. He cut a striking figure.

Dad was not a big disciplinarian. There were no time-outs in those days, however. He and his sister, Melinda, got beatings, or whuppings, usually with a belt and usually by Mom. However, one of the few times that Dad had beat him was when at about age nine or ten he had shoplifted a ten-cent tube of glue from a five-and-dime store on Germantown Avenue. Dad and Pop both took off their belts and beat him that evening, sequentially! He never shoplifted anything else in his life! He had gone at the invitation of some other boys in the neighborhood when one had suggested, "Let's go steal!" He had never stolen anything before! The glue was to build plastic or balsa wood model airplanes, boats, cars, and other things. As soon as he reached out to pocket the glue, the saleslady grabbed his small hand.

Mom, although very loving and affectionate, had a temper. Sometimes, instead of the usual beating with a belt, she threw things at him or them—a plate, something plastic or wooden like a big spoon, and so on. Truth be told, he didn't think he had any lasting scars, physical or emotional, from these beatings. He had always done something, broken some rule, defied some order, been defiant, to cause the beating. To entertain himself, Amir would sit in his room by himself and build his models and then display them. They would usually be displayed in his room on the mantle. He often read books. Amir had learned to enjoy reading. He had learned how to occupy himself. There were only Melinda, his sister, and his mom and dad, so he had to learn to entertain himself. Melinda was a girl and nineteen months younger. "Take your sister with you" were words he dreaded to hear when going outside.

He began reading the Sherlock Holmes stories. Books about Hitler particularly, for some reason, resonated with him. He read Shakespeare later and some poetry. He liked Edgar Allan Poe, Elizabeth Barrett Browning, some Longfellow, and Langston Hughes among others. The poem "Invictus" always resonated with him. He also read some history books and books about sex, as an older teen and young adult. They included the Kama Sutra and *The Perfumed Garden*. He also started reading the Holy Bible and the Holy Koran, not so much for spiritual reasons or guidance but for the stories, the poetry, the drama, and the ethos contained in them. In high school, Amir had developed his taste for Shakespeare, largely because of a very good English teacher, a Ms. Smith, who had made reading Shakespeare fun and interesting. He also read the Ian Fleming James Bond novels as an older teen and young adult, car magazines, and, of course, *Playboy*. He would hide the *Playboy* magazines in his room as a preteen and young teen, under the bed or under the mattress.

Why was he looking in the master bedroom, his parents' room? He was home alone. Was he looking for something specific? He had come upon some interesting things of Dad's. There was a stack of magazines called *Sunshine and Health*. They were full of photos of nude women. They all happened to be white. Dad had a stash of porno! Wow! Sure, by current standards, they were conservative, but it was a stash nonetheless. The pictures were all of healthy white women posing in one-piece bathing suits. Slender or thin was not in vogue yet. These women had curves and serves. He also found Dad's army helmet liner, obviously a souvenir from the war dad had brought home. The most exciting thing he found, however, was a German Luger. He knew it was real, so he'd be careful with it. A real German luger, was it loaded? Another war souvenir? Exciting finds! He carefully put everything back exactly where had found it. A few minutes later, he heard the front door opening. Good thing he had put everything back!

Omar, a fellow high school student, a year or two behind him, would eventually become the brother he never had or his brother from another mother.

Short to average in height, he was light-brown-skinned in color. He had dark-brown to reddish hair, which he usually wore in a kind of wavy style. He was good-looking with an impish smile and a twinkle in his eye. They first met in high school, where Amir was a year or two ahead of him.

One fateful day, while Amir was hall monitoring, sitting out in the hallway, on guard, he had observed Omar sneaking up the stairwell on his way to the roof with a girl and a blanket! He was on a mission. Amir's and his eyes met, and Amir smiled. Omar nodded in thanks and continued on his mission.

Mom, or Fannie Mae, was a good-looking woman. About five feet six or seven, she had a round face, almond-shaped eyes, one dimple on her left cheek, high cheekbones, and dark hair. Her coloring was like the desert sand. She was a curvaceous woman and buxom. Her overall appearance, he would realize years later, suggested her part Native American heritage (Lower Creek). That's where the high cheekbones, almond-shaped eyes, and dark hair probably came from, he decided. A loyal and hardworking Virgo, if Mom had your back, you had nothing to worry about! While friendly, witty, giving, affectionate, and loving to laugh, if you crossed the line with her or one of hers, you had a fight on your hands, both figuratively and sometimes literally! She had a short fuse and a capacity for violence when she deemed it necessary.

Be Prepared

Maybe he had a thing for uniforms, adventure, travel, camaraderie. Maybe it was because Dad had been in the military. He enjoyed being a Cub Scout.

The pack was attached to the family church. They had a den mother, of course, who lived on Seventeenth Street, just a block and a half away. Meetings were held at her house. A motherly, attractive, light-skinned woman, she was warm and friendly. She had one or two (he couldn't quite remember) cute daughters older than he and the other cub scouts though. It was fun earning merit badges, reading the handbook, wearing the uniform, going on trips, sleeping in tents, being around the campfire, singing songs, cooking hot dogs and s'mores, and hiking. It was all good. The Boy Scout Troop was also attached to the family Baptist church. Only now the troop leaders or scout masters were men. "You have to be twice as good to get half as far!" Competence, hard work, and tenacity were stressed. "You have to be better than the other boys!" The camaraderie, the adventure, the getting away from home, jamborees, and being outdoors (when not too hot or cold) were enjoyable to him.

This all eventually led to Amir becoming, as an older teen, a Civil Air Patrol cadet and believing, at least for a time, that he wanted to be an officer and a gentleman, by an act of Congress, probably in the US Air Force. Years before he had ordered and received brochures and catalogs from the Valley Forge Military Academy in Valley Forge, Pennsylvania. He thought the cadets looked so smart in their winter uniforms. The campus was impressive also. Amir finally had to admit to himself that even if he could get in, his parents probably couldn't afford the tuition.

Cherchez la Femme, Part 1

Amir was now in his early twenties and had pretty much overcome his basic shyness and bashfulness for the most part. He was working full-time and living in his small bachelor pad. So many women and so little time! His boy Omar used to say, "They come at you in human waves."

Je t'aime, te amo, ti amo—he had learned to say "I love you" in multiple languages. Seduction was an art after all. He would not use these phrases loosely or too often though, just to score, just to get some. Telling someone you loved him or her was serious stuff! You might love what you were doing, but that didn't mean you loved the person you were doing it with!

"What part of Ethiopia are you from?" he had asked the beautiful young Ethiopian-looking woman sitting alone at a table in the lobby of the YWCA, located conveniently just down the street from his Center City Philadelphia apartment. When she smiled back at him, flashing her beautiful white teeth, he knew it was showtime, and he had his foot in the door. She was café au lait colored with fine features, beautiful skin, high cheekbones, and big beautiful dark eyes. He had just recently done a little research on Ethiopia, its people, culture, history, and so on with photos.

Her lips were thin yet sexy. She had one dimple in her left cheek and a beautiful smile. Although she was slender, she looked lithe, supple, and sinewy. Her hair was black and thick. He thought, she was a fox! "Every poor boy's dream and every rich man's prayer"— that line from the song popped into his head.

Nadia carried herself with grace. She was soft-spoken, yet strong. She had class. It was almost like interracial dating, he came to believe after a time. She was different from most African American girls he had known. She was a college student; she had lived and gone to school in London for a while, and her family was back in Ethiopia. Her accent wasn't strong, but it was sexy. Her eyes sparkled. They would become significant in each other's lives for years to come.

Amir had grown up around and with good-looking, powerful, and strong females—his mother, Fannie Mae; his sister, Melinda; his grandmother Biggy; and numerous aunts, cousins, neighbors, and fellow students, among others. Biggy, his grandmother, had cautioned him to not bring anything home "with flies on it!" "Look so good, smell so sweet, makes things stand that have no feet" was a popular saying of the era. Although he didn't really have a type, they had to be attractive to him. Looks might not be everything, but they did matter! They could be short, medium, or tall and have curly, straight, kinky, wooly, or wavy hair. Generally, he preferred dark hair over other colors, but one must always be willing to make exceptions, a redhead here and there. He even dated a naturally blond sister for a while. Skin coloring could be from pale to very dark. He also felt he was attracted to the unique, the different, the unusual, the exotic. He was attracted to women with accents, particularly the English accents. French, of course, could also be romantic and sexy as well.

As far as white girls were concerned, he was usually attracted to the Southern European or Mediterranean type more so than the blond or Nordic European look. There were notable exceptions. Marilyn Monroe was incredibly sexy, after all, as was Brigitte Bardot. Sophia Loren oozed sexuality. They all had that ho quality that he and the brothers sometimes spoke about—that almost indescribable combination of a certain look, a way of carrying herself, the voice, the eyes, a certain spicy quality, a certain attitude. They, white girls, were not better than black girls but a different flavor.

Over the years, there would be many women, younger, older, his same age, very bright, not so bright, nice, sensitive, insensitive, half crazy, selfish, nurturing, troubled, unmarried, married, one-night stands, relationships, friends with benefits, brief sexual encounters, and so on. There would be black women, Latinas, an occasional white woman, mixed race, and Turkish but never an Asian for some reason. They were usually seen with white guys if dating outside their respective groups at all.

Disco Lady, Part 1

He was at the funky, dark, Center City go-go bar he sometimes frequented that warm summer's night. It was located under a railroad trestle. Usually, all the patrons and go-go girls were black. There would be an occasional white or Asian dancer, but sisters ruled. Typically, each dancer selected three songs to be played while she danced seductively and got tips, which would usually be handed to her or inserted in the elastic of the pasties or G-strings they wore. Dollar bills were the most frequent tip, but some brothers even tipped twenty-dollar bills, occasionally more! Amir grew to believe guys did this to impress the other guys really, more than the dancers! That male ego again. The psychology of the go-go girl or exotic dancer was interesting, he thought with a roomful of men, a platform where the dancers danced, elevating them up above the patrons, and the dancers, usually with good figures, sometimes with fantastic figures. The good ones were, of course, good dancers, skilled at flirting with you or interested in or curious about you! Of course, these ladies were working, and most were clear about their real goals: tips and money.

Amir would learn after years of patronizing such places that some of the women were in fact lesbians, not interested in men at all. Perhaps this was what enabled some of them to dance and gyrate around almost naked or naked in a roomful of men, usually strangers! Of course, Amir would learn in years to come that sexual orientation and identity were more fluid than he had realized.

Sometimes he went alone, sometimes with his boys, often with one other friend or associate. Rain, snow, sleet, or hail, they drove all over Philly and beyond to these establishments—Center City, West Philly, North Philly, South Philly, Germantown, Overbrook, West Oak Lane, Jersey, and so on. One of Amir's early favorites was Beverly T., a tall and statuesque dancer with a great body and long, auburn hair, which she always wore down or in a ponytail. She danced at a go-go bar on Sansom Street, in Center City.

He would walk there from his Center City apartment. He would often be the only black patron in the bar. He liked her. She always played as one of her three dance selections, the Supremes' "Love Is Here, and Now You're Gone." *USDA Choice, all beef, no filler,* he thought as he watched her dance. Bet there's a back story there! Shame he couldn't get close enough to put his application in. In those days, the dancers were kept segregated from the patrons. That would drastically change over time. He would eventually see a piece about Beverly T. on local TV news. She was attending medical school while go-go dancing!

School Daze or the Gang's All Here

The then recently opened community college was situated in Center City, Philadelphia. The tall building housing it had been the home of a department store. A large ground floor central lobby, a set of escalators, and elevators were still there and operational in addition to the classrooms. African Americans were attending college in record numbers. There was something in the air! For inner-city young people who didn't have a lot of money to spend or who couldn't gain admission to a four-year university initially, it seemed ideal. Some poor and working-class whites also found it attractive. Go there for two years and then transfer to a four-year school and get your bachelor's was the usual formula. Amir planned to take lots of arts and sciences courses, mostly political science, anthropology, and western civilization courses.

There was a sizeable black demographic at the college, followed by whites and a few Hispanics and Asians. Amir would have some of the best times in his young life there at the school. Friendships would be made, some enduring, some not. Some of the most interesting and intelligent people—black, white, and others—he would ever meet he met there. For a community college, he was pleased to learn that some of its instructors and professors were also teaching at other more prestigious colleges and universities in the Philadelphia vicinity. One, Dr. Weldman, he really enjoyed. A slender, bald-headed, clean-shaven man of average height, he had two PhDs, two suits, and two pairs of Hush Puppy shoes, which he wore alternately. He taught history courses, such as Western civilization. Weldman had a student following. Students who had not signed up for his courses, often turned up to audit them. Weldman challenged students. You could give any answer or response to a question he asked that you pleased as long as you could logically and rationally back up and explain your response. He was sarcastic at times. "General Motors would be proud of you!" Weldman had said to one student, a young Catholic school woman whose response to a question he found ill considered. During his classes, an occasional student was brought to tears by some of his pointed comments.

"I wouldn't give a crippled crab a crutch if I owned a lumber yard!" Harry had said in the lobby of the school that winter day. A little older than the rest of the students, he was a vet. He had been to Nam. He had a cute wife named Marsha. "Friendship is like chicken shit. Sweep it away, and some more will appear." Harry was on that day. He was quietly holding court in the lobby. But talking shit, rhyming, rapping, spouting poetry and rhymes, and engaging in witticisms, repartee, plays on words, and puns were all quite the theme of the time. If a brother couldn't, then he had a weak rap or a Saran wrap. The girls tended to like guys who could rap, guys who had some conversation and who were quick-witted, articulate, and had game. The school's cast of characters also included Louise, who was a platonic college friend. She was tall and attractive and "big-boned". She was fun to be around and witty, with a ready smile. Louise had jokes and big stockings. She could hang with the fellows. Cool Breeze or Breeze was another. She had personality plus. This cute brown-skinned sister with the engaging smile talked a lot of shit. She could hold her own with the crew as well. She was a platonic friend and fun to have around. Ben was a likable fellow student. He was dubbed "the other man" because he was always quoting some famous person in his conversations.

J. Vinson was dubbed "Vinson and Hedges" after the then popular Benson and Hedges cigarette brand, because of his hedge-like hairstyle. He was a nice, nerdy kind of guy, very bright, wearing horn-rimmed glasses and ill-fitting clothes.

SaRon was from Manayunk and a few years older than the rest. He would eventually become "Cheap Ron" because he "never met a check he liked to pay," according to the Dude.

Coffy was not really in the crew but an associate. He was a tall, dark-skinned slender brother from Nice Town, who was explaining that they called him Coffy not because he had a dark skin tone but because he could grind so fine! He would proclaim that he was a gangster of love.

Amir was dubbed British Peter by SaRon, a nod to his being a bit of an anglophile, including his habit of wearing English-style clothes and knowing a bit about English culture.

One member, Forty-Four, a.k.a. the Forty-Four-Caliber Dude, was so named because he allegedly had forty-four lovemaking positions to offer the honeys, a detailed description of which he carried around with him on a sheet of paper to display when desired! His declarative sentences often started with the word "shiit."

Candy was a few years older than most college students and truly attractive. She was of above average height with reddish-brown hair worn in a short, sexy, becoming hairstyle. Candy had naturally blue eyes. This was unusual in Amir's experience for an African American girl. She also had an hourglass figure, big legs, and a nice booty. She dressed like other coeds but in a way that always showed off her assets. "Hey, fellas," she had said the other day, in the cafeteria at their table. "I made the easiest fifty dollars I've ever made last night! He just wanted a golden shower!" (A golden shower refers to being urinated on.)

"You go, girl!" Omar responded.

The crew enjoyed her bubbly personality and her revelations about life as a sex worker. It was part of their education. When she was cleaned up, most would not guess her part-time profession. She looked like a well-dressed young female office professional. At least she was getting her education!

Tarik was dubbed the Militant from Nob Hill. While he presented as so militant or radical, his middle-class roots were obvious to a discerning eye. He was a professional student, attending universities across the country, some expensive. He also traveled a lot. Some thought he was an agent, a nod to the understandable paranoia of the time. Light-skinned and short, he was a good-looking brother with a prominent kind of hooked nose and dark hair. Sometimes, he wore a Hitler-like mustache. He was a good person who never said a bad word about anybody. His rap was weak though.

Fat Frank was a brown-skinned, eyeglasses-wearing, tall, and rotund brother. He had an outgoing personality, an infectious laugh, and a way with the ladies. He sort of reminded Amir of Bill Cosby's fictional character Fat Albert. His particular bag was to give massages to females. Massages, of course, often led to *other* activities. At least he had some game.

Cool Ron was just that—cool. He was tall, about six feet four, thin, dark-skinned, handsome, and always elegantly dressed. He was suave with a baritone voice, and when wearing sunglasses, he looked like he could be one of the Temptations!

Omar was then called Dude or the Dude. He was a short, good-looking, light-brown-skinned guy who was obviously very intelligent and very articulate, but because of his age (he was younger) and assumed lack of experience, he was dubbed Dude.

Of course, Amir had met the Dude at high school, the school they both attended as an on-duty hall monitor who winked at the Dude as he was sneaking up the fire tower during class with a honey and a blanket. They would grow to become friends for life! They would share many adventures and experiences. The group amusingly spoke of the 4-F Club (as opposed to the 4-H Club). It was an acronym for "Find 'em, feel 'em, fuck 'em, and forget 'em."

"I wouldn't fuck her with your dick!" "He'd fuck a snake if you held its fangs!" They were young, single, bright, cocky, arrogant, chauvinistic, and full of testosterone and bluster, along with hopes and dreams for the future. Amir always felt they were not necessarily a typical group of young inner-city black men.

Phil was a little older than the rest. He was from West Philly. Of average height, he had an olive-colored complexion and a stocky build. Phil had a slight stutter, which didn't mask his high intelligence. He had obviously traveled a bit and was quite sophisticated. He could recite Al-Fatiha from the Holy Quran one minute and start singing "Deutschland, Deutschland, Uber Allies," the next!

Many of the guys and girls had original names as well as slave names. Back in the day, if you were a scientific brother or sister, you usually had an original name. Islamic converts almost always did. Folks joining the Nation (the Nation of Islam) would have to write a letter to Chicago to be given an original name. Others, like Amir, Tarik, Omar, Khalil, Ahmed, and Peter Brown-Bey often named themselves by selecting a name they thought was aspirational or descriptive of themselves. Some female friends had names like Sharifa, Naima, Nadia, Jamila, Yasmine, Rodina, and so on. This was occurring across America. They typically greeted each other with "As salaamu alaikum," or simply "salaam," the greeting of "peace and paradise" according to the Nation. Why this attraction by blacks to Islam and things Islamic? Amir would learn years later and after much study that the first Muslims to come to America were not, in fact, Arabs, but some of the African captives brought to America to be slaves. Some of their respective names are even known. Islam had reached West Africa before the trans-Atlantic slave trade had begun. Many of the African captives we now know were from West Africa.

Never, or Peter, had attended high school with Amir. They were friends. He was called "Never" as a takeoff on the Fellini movie *Never on Sunday*. He claimed to have sexual activity almost every day of the week except Sunday, his day of rest, hence Never! He was also said to possess a most prodigious sexual member. Amir would always remember the day at the college when two girls he did not know came into the cafeteria looking for Never on the strength of his reputation alone or that time at the house party in West Philly when in the midst of the dark, calm, and grinding, a young lady ran down the stairs from the second-floor bedroom/coatroom where she obviously had been with Never yelling, "He's not going to put that in me!" He was also a man ahead of his time, during an era when many black men did not participate in cunnilingus, for the most part. Never had become a cunning linguist! While many brothers said things like, "That's nasty," and "I don't have to do that!" Never had walked around high school with a napkin conspicuously dangling from his rear pants pocket and a fork! There was no shame in his game. He would sometimes practice his tongue moves as if they were martial arts forms. His oral-genital skills made him quite popular with the girls, of course.

Flash, a.k.a. Ron, a.k.a. Super Negro/Nigger, was a friend of the Dude's from his church and neighborhood. Tall, dark-skinned, good-looking, articulate, intelligent, and quick-witted, Flash had a sense of humor and was a good conversationalist but couldn't be trusted around the ladies. Even their own! At one point, he tried to come on or talk to SaRon's, Dude's, and Amir's girls! "I am more man than him," he allegedly told all of them in turn. SaRon got angry, and Dude and Amir laughed about it. Flash would bring his kit with him when he went courting. It consisted of albums, books, condoms, and other assorted items.

Back in the day, neither Amir nor his friends knew what a Sikh was. They had never heard of the Punjab Region of India. But the Indian student at CCP rocking the turban was cool. He was always sharply dressed and flirting with the honeys. They liked him. So, when he came around, he was dubbed "Gunga Din" from the Rudyard Kipling poem. He seemed to like the moniker. "You're a better man than I, Gunga Din" was how they typically saluted him. Decades later, while doing research for a course he would be teaching, Amir would read about an African American musician who, because of racism and discrimination, created a persona for himself where he was not presenting as African American but as Korla Pandit, a turban-wearing South Asian who then enjoyed some success as a musician, including several albums and a TV show!

Many folks, male and female, young and old, wore Afros or natural hairstyles in those days. Even Amir's dad would a couple of years after the craze began! Many guys kept an Afro comb or pick casually displayed in a rear pants pocket. Some had huge, perfectly coiffed Afros and others more moderate ones, with and without parts. Even blacks who had hair that was wavy, straight, or curly and not easily styled into an Afro tried to wear them. Some whites and members of other groups—Jews, Arabs, Hispanics, and so on—wore Afros! Amir tended to wear a medium-sized 'Fro. A musician friend, a drummer, Omawalde, had a huge, perfectly manicured 'Fro.

Amir and many of his friends also grew beards, which were usually neatly trimmed and groomed. "You look handsome with your beard," the African American redhead he was dating at the time told Amir. That felt good. Another woman, middle-aged, told him subsequently, "I don't trust men who wear beards; they have something to hide." *Nonsense*, he thought. *Guess you can't please or appeal to everybody!*

Many students and others had sworn off eating pork.

Yogurt, wheat germ, tofu, fruit and vegetable juices, and other health foods were becoming popular with many. The reading of certain books, such as *The Autobiography of Malcolm X*; *The Wretched of the Earth* and *The Pedagogy of the Oppressed*, both by Franz Fanon; *The Miseducation of the Negro*; *Message to the Black Man in America*; *The Invisible Man*; *Mao's Red Book*; *Kaddafy's Green Book*; *The Peculiar Institution*; *The Communist Manifesto*; *Before the Mayflower*; *The Spook Who Sat by the Door*; *Message to the Black Man in America*; and *How to Eat to Live*, among others, were mandatory reading for the conscious or scientific brothers and sisters.

Black women were often referred to as "queens," and almost every black man was a "brother," unless of course he had sold out or was suspected of being an agent or spy of some kind. Some were learning to speak Arabic, Ki-Swahili, Hausa, Mandinka, Ibo, or Yoruba. Some were studying the Holy Quran, the Egyptian Book of the Dead, the Torah, the Talmud, Buddhism, and the Hindu Vedas, as well as the Holy Bible.

They often gathered, many times when they were supposed to be in class, during late evenings, on weekends, or at parties to intellectualize, to philosophize, and to debate. Many discussions were memorable. Points and counterpoints abounded. Books and philosophies were analyzed, dissected, discussed, and debated about. Was America the "whore of Babylon" referred to in scripture? The Statue of Liberty the beast with the seven horns from the book of Revelation? Was the white man the devil? Was religion the opiate of the people? How long would American civilization last? Was the white man's time up, as taught by the Nation? Was an actual violent revolution coming? Were concentration camps secretly being readied for blacks by the US government? Was Marx's dialectical materialism really the explanation for many major historical events? Was W. E. B.'s analysis correct? Booker T.'s? Marcus Garvey's? The Honorable Elijah Muhammad's? MLK's? Noble Drew Ali's? Was Socialism/Communism the way? Capitalism? Were the black man and white woman the two most oppressed groups in American society? Do white Americans suffer from a kind of mass cognitive dissonance and blacks from natal alienation due to American slavery and Jim Crow? Would America ever truly get past its race problem? Would the black man ever truly be free in America?

Amir's first boyhood crush had been on Ellen, in elementary school, walking distance from the crib. He used to get crooks in his neck turning to gaze at her as she sat in the back of the room and he in the front. He sometimes passed notes to her with deep and profound messages like "I like you" and "Do you like me?" among others. He particularly liked her nose. He didn't understand why, but he did. She grew into an attractive, tall, long-legged, caramel-colored young woman. Their families both attended the same church in North Philly. They never really dated, but their lives would intersect from time to time. At Mom's suggestion, Amir took her to his senior prom. He was told in later years that she was a lesbian.

Patricia, a.k.a. the Lone Ranger, was tall and very fair skinned. During the winter, she would become pale. Her face had an Asian or American Indian kind of appearance. She had almond-shaped eyes, a round face, dark hair, a wonderful smile, and was healthy. She was pretty, he thought, a fox, as he gazed at her on the No. 2 bus every morning on his way to work. He was working part-time at the Free Library of Philadelphia as a page. The transportation system was the Philadelphia Transportation Company (PTC) then, later to become the South Eastern Pennsylvania Transportation Authority (SEPTA).

The No. 2 ran back and forth from South Philly traveling through Center City and continuing to North Philly, Nice Town, Tioga, and points further north. It ran south on Seventeenth Street and north on Sixteenth Street. It was a veritable unofficial tour bus of the inner city and central Philly. He often thought of it as the Inner City Express. Much of his young life would be spent riding it. He had noticed the tall, beautiful, long-legged young woman getting on the No. 2 bus every morning after he was seated. She was always alone. How could he not notice this gorgeous young woman?

After getting his nerve up, he approached her early one fall morning as she sat alone on the No. 2.

"Hi, good morning. May I join you?" Rejection would've been very embarrassing, crushing. There were other passengers after all.

He wasn't rejected but offered a warm and beautiful smile in return. Her name was Patricia. *Life is good*, he thought, as he sat down beside her. He had his foot in the door. She seemed nice, she had class, and she was *fine*. He got her digits. They would talk on the phone. Eventually, he would be invited over for dinner. He was in love. He could sense and feel it. Patricia wouldn't be just another girl! He would never forget his first visit to her Diamond Street home, near Temple University, not far from Broad Street. He was a bit anxious, as the leaves blew down Diamond Street on that cold winter night. What about the Diamond Street gang? He lived on different turf. He didn't have a car and would have to ride the No. 2 bus to visit her. Back in the day in Philly, there were lots of gangs—Old Heads, Young Boys, the Zulu Nation, the Valley, the Klang, the Moroccos, Huntingdon Street, and many more. But he was in love. He would not be denied!

Simone was a truly exceptional-looking young woman. Tall and lithe, she was café au lait colored with beautiful big, dark round eyes. Her facial features were sharp and delicate. She carried herself like a dancer, moving deliberately but gracefully with style and class. Her hair, worn long, was reddish brown. Simone was so good-looking she always drew attention. Blacks, whites, and others would often stare at her, consciously or unconsciously. "Romance without finance is a nuisance!" was one of her oft-repeated sayings.

Omar, Amir, and the rest of their crowd made it a point to try to be on at least speaking terms with all the fine girls at the college, and Simone was one of the finest. A smile from her or simply walking a couple of blocks with her in Center City was a thrill. She had aspirations to be a model. That was understandable, Amir thought. Simone would periodically take the train to New York City in that connection. She did ultimately do some work for the famous Ford agency in New York. Amir smiled to himself one afternoon while driving to AC on the AC Expressway, thinking of the time he had put his application in with Simone. It was an unusually quiet day at the college, and he and Simone were two of the few people in the cafeteria. Amir approached her by a vending machine with a smile and asked, "Do you have a moment?" They sat down at one of the round tables dotting the cafeteria. "Simone, I'll be frank," he said,

"I know you must have a man, as fine as you are, but do you have any spare time? Just a little? I could be your part-time man."

She laughed as she let him down easy. "Amir, I like you but not in that way."

Rejection had rarely been so tactful, he thought, and charming. He still liked Simone in a platonic way.

Jocelyn was a fellow CCP student and Amir's then girlfriend. She had a real job at the post office! She would occasionally give Amir presents, often Oleg Cassini shirt and tie sets, quite the rage at the time. It was good to have a working girlfriend. Light-brown-skinned with a cute little nose and a good body, he liked Jocelyn. She looked great in her skintight jeans, which emphasized her nice but not overly big booty. Her mom seemed nice, and her dad was not present.

Like his dad did to his mom, he would gently slap Jocelyn on her booty from time to time. "You're a Puerto Rican," her grandmother had said to him when he rang the front doorbell as he stood on the porch of her West Philly home. "I know what they look like, and you're one!"

He had tried to explain that he was not and that his last name wasn't even Hispanic! It was no use; she didn't like him. Sometimes when he was visiting Jocelyn, sitting on the love seat talking with her, her grandma would start to vacuum—at nine, ten, eleven o'clock at night!

Meanwhile, back at school, he always thought it was interesting that SaRon seemed jealous of Dude's success with the ladies. Dude, later Omar, was good-looking and quite charismatic, and he could see why some women would be curious about or fascinated with him. He was energetic and talked a lot of shit, with a twinkle in his eye.

SaRon and the Dude were particularly skilled at changing the lyrics of popular tunes of the day so that the title of the late Donny Hathaway's (after his untimely death by falling, jumping, or being pushed out of a window of a hotel up in NYC) lovely duet with Roberta Flack, "Where Is the Love," became "Where Is the Ground?" Sam Cooke's haunting "A Change Is Gonna Come" after he was shot and killed in a motel or hotel had its lyrics changed to "I was born by the river in a little tent, and I died in an apartment." The lyrics of Jimmy Ruffin's "What Becomes of the Brokenhearted?" "Those who've loved and now have parted" was changed to "Those who've loved and now have farted." Dionne Warwick's beautiful and melodious "Déjà Vu" became "Deja Boo." The Hugh Masekela hit "Grazing in the Grass" became "Grazing in the Bulrushes." Tom Jones belting out of the James Bond Thunderball movie theme became "Thunder balls!" The popular Luther Ingram hit "If Loving You is Wrong" became,"If loving you is wrong, let's do something wrong." Among the crew, Barry White was the "walrus of love!" The six-million-dollar man of then TV fame was "the one dollar ninety-eight cents dude." These guys were witty and funny! Amir didn't have the musical talent, acumen, or skill of Omar and SaRon but flattered himself by writing a couple of blues songs—"I know her daddy's got some money; I can tell by the way she walk," and "I really like your apples, girl. I think I want to shake your tree."

Pat was a prime example of what he and the guys liked, or said they did, a superstar with pretty hair and a tall, voluptuous, sinewy-looking body with a small waist and big legs. Her tan skin tone was beautiful and radiant and her eyes big and brown. She was a stallion, as they used to say, a stone fox. Pat had a nice personality and butt to go with it, shown off by her spray-painted-on jeans and booty shorts. She was a picture of health. She was USDA inspected, all beef, no filler, as they described such women at the time. "If she wrapped those long legs around you, brother, you'd be in paradise at once," someone had said. SaRon would utter, "That damn Dude! I wanted Pat!"

Amir and the Dude never had a competitive tension between them toward the ladies. As far as Amir was concerned, they both generally felt that there were plenty to go around, even among the fine ones, so why the need for animosity over a particular girl? In fact, their shared code for calling attention to a particular girl for the others' perusal was to say, "That's you, brother," to him softly while pointing her out ever so subtly at a party, on the street, on the subway, at school, in a store, at the library, wherever. Maybe SaRon, full of bravado and machismo, actually had some insecurities. "I'm too much man for one woman!" "They can't keep up with me." "I gotta have sex every day." Sure, SaRon.

Sanaa, who had a genuinely nice personality and artsy presentation, also had a balcony you could do Shakespeare from! They seemed to look at you when she was facing you. She seemed to be attracted to Mike, a really nice, bashful, low-key guy from West Philly. "You better get that, boy," "You should be hitting that, boy," he was often advised. Light-skinned with dark hair, of average height and build, Mike had unusually large keloids on his face that formed a kind of beard around it. "That boy ain't had no pussy since pussy had him!" was once cruelly said in reference to Mike. His facial issues didn't seem to bother the guys. All the crew seemed to like Mike. He was part of the inner circle.

Amir and Omar seemed closet to him, visiting with and hanging out with Mike. Amir would grow to believe over the years, however, that hanging out with him, Dude, SaRon, Fat Frank, Phil, Tarik, Forty-Four, Kahlil, and the rest probably was intimidating to Mike, probably made him even shier or more withdrawn!

These guys all had personality plus, pizzazz. They all were flirtatious, witty, and outgoing. "Girl, you need to try something new. I'm new; try me." "Girl, you need an upgrade—me!" "I'll rock your world!" "You ready for some excitement? Well, you're looking at it!" "I'm not just good; I'm slow good!" "Satisfaction guaranteed, or take your loving back!" "You've heard of the Wonderful World of Disney? How about the Wonderful World of Dizzy?" "I can get references." "It's not the size of the ship; it's the motion of the ocean, girl!" "I'll have you following me around like a puppy." "You'll be speaking in tongues when I'm done, girl." "It's not how long I make it; it's how I make it long." "Do you believe in the hereafter? Then you know what I'm here after!" "All I got to offer is stiff dick and bubble gum, girl, and I'm fresh out of gum!" "No reason to be nervous, girl. You gonna git the best of service."

They seemed to have an endless supply of lines, retorts, quips, and witticisms for almost any and every situation. The really fresh or obscene sayings were not usually said to the girls or around them but in all-male company. Young men have this need apparently to present as fresh and aggressive toward females to each other. Few were better at repartee!

"Your eyes may shine, your teeth may grit, but none of this p— will you get!" Amanda was a Catholic high school grad attending the college. She was truly exceptional with beautiful tan skin, pretty dark eyes, a mole on her cheek, and a few freckles. She was smart, sophisticated, and well dressed. She had star power. That girl was a stallion. She was well and tastefully dressed, often wearing ho heels. Amanda had big legs (curvaceous calves) and a body by Fisher. She knew how to work it. She was fine, smart, and classy! "You gotta have a j-o-b if you wanna be with me."

Margaret had a cute pixie-like face, dark curly hair, a very curvaceous body, big legs, and a friendly, sexy manner with a beautiful smile. Margaret sort of reminded him of Marilyn Monroe with a nice tan. Her dresses were attractive and short enough for you to see some leg. Carol was always pumping (wearing high-heeled pumps well), which made the total effect even more captivating. You could hear music play in your head as she glided across the lobby of CCP in syncopated motion. One evening, she actually appeared unannounced at his Center City apartment while some fellas were visiting. They blew it for him! The expression, "Yum, yum, give me some" came to mind each time she strolled across the lobby of CCP in all her glory.

Tina B. was petite and dark-skinned, with a great body and attractive face. Tina pumped a lot, pulling the calf muscles in her already outstanding legs. She was bright and talked a lot of shit. She was a good student, flirty, but not overly. Every time you looked at her, you just wanted her. "The blacker the berry ..." had to be a reference to Tina! She was hot.

"Damn, did you see that sister Ahmed brought to the set last night?" asked Tarik. "She was ugly!"

"No, brother, she wasn't ugly; that girl was fugly!" proclaimed Phil.

Everyone in the small group laughed. The old double standard again. Men didn't have to be handsome or cute as far as they were concerned. Females, though, to some extent, would always be judged, at least in part, by their looks. Amir was never obsessed with white women, as some brothers were. Hell, he knew guys who preferred dwarfs or Chinese women or women with disabilities! Amir's and Omar's tastes were catholic. Sure, he'd see fine white girls, and he found some of them very attractive, sexy, but no more so than black, Spanish, and Asian women. He thought he'd try a couple at some point to see what all the hubbub was about! Those Asian women had slanted pussy was the street wisdom from the oldheads.

"You're not fully Negro, are you?" the young pretty blonde asked Amir on the stoop in Center City on Walnut Street one balmy summer night.

"I'm not a Negro at all," Amir had calmly replied. "I am a black man, descendant of the Moors and a member of the lost found tribe of Shabazz!"

She looked puzzled. He had expected that. She was probably looking for that black experience, he felt, some soul pole, it was sometimes said—"Once you go black, you can never go back" and all that. "It's all pink inside," "They all look the same in the dark," "My dick can't see," "Eight to eighty, blind, crippled, and crazy,"

"My dick has no conscience!" and so forth and so on. They never got together.

Latifa was from Turkey. She was beautiful with her big, dark eyes and thick, jet-black hair. Talk about exotic. She was petite and had a small waist with a pumpkin butt. She also had big legs. Her accent was sexy, and she was fun. But her student visa was almost expired, and she didn't want to go home. They made sweet love together in his Center City basement apartment even when she had a cast on her leg for a time! As he drove her to the Philly airport, it was sad. He would miss her and their easy friendship. He didn't want to see her leave either, but what could he do? Marry her? For years, he would cherish the beautiful gold pendant and necklace that read "Allah" in Arabic, a gift from Latifa.

Omar, then working at an audio store nearby Amir's apartment on Chestnut Street, would make love tapes for him upon request on eight-track tape. Amir and Omar both loved music. Omar, in addition to having an encyclopedic knowledge of music, could actually sing himself, having sung on a church choir. His deceased dad, he explained, had been a jazz pianist. For a time, Omar had a group that actually went out on the road. Ultimately, however, he decided that he liked the business more than the show in show business.

On these love tapes, there would be selections by Black Moses (Isaac Hayes), Smokey Robinson, Barry White, Jeffrey Osborne, Jerry "the Iceman" Butler, Tom Jones, Bobby Womack, and others. Whether it was made in Muscle Shoals, Alabama; Memphis, Tennessee; Detroit, Michigan; Philly; London; or elsewhere, rhythm and blues, jazz, some rock, folk music, some country (not much), some Broadway show tunes, even a little opera were all enjoyed and appreciated by Omar and Amir. If the tapes, incense, dim lighting, convertible sofa, and his lines didn't work on the honeys … oh well!

Hanging Out

Rittenhouse Square, a.k.a. the Square, was Philly's version of New York's Washington Square Park. Located in a rather ritzy, upscale part of Center City, surrounded by luxury high-rise apartments and condos, hotels, restaurants, and townhouses, it was a neutral zone, where black, white, Spanish, Asian, and every other ethnic group felt free to congregate. Whether sitting around talking philosophy, playing guitars, reading, citing poetry, courting, smoking dope, walking dogs, or simply seeing and being seen, it was a gathering place for the young and not-so-young members of the hip, cool, radical in crowd. Interracial couples abounded, as did hippies, musicians, artists, poets, nationalists, con men, hustlers, and pimps.

Amir and Omar sometimes hung out in the Square, sometimes together, sometimes alone. It was a short walk from their respective Center City apartments. They (he and Omar) had been "hanging out over there with white women," Jane, a fellow college student, had reported back at the school. "Are they talking black and sleeping white?" she questioned. They were allegedly "hanging out with white girls." Omar and he just laughed. Of course, they liked all kinds of women! But they didn't prefer white girls! "It's all pink inside!" "Hips, lips, and fingertips." Black girls had the best butts and white girls the best legs was the common wisdom then. White girls were allegedly more freaky, however, than black girls and would give it up more quickly. A big selling point! Was Jane's possible motivation the fact that she didn't get much play? Jane was a booga, not particularly attractive and lacking in personality as well!

The big pub-like restaurant was another of their Center City haunts located on South Broad Street. It was a big place with lots of tables and booths and a long counter located at a busy Center City intersection. It stayed open until the wee hours of the morning, so it was perfect for an after-discotheque/club/date meeting place with friends at two or three in the morning, usually a Saturday or

Sunday morning. The customers themselves were a show, sleepy-eyed, drunk, or half-drunk patrons who had partied and clubbed all night and were hungry or needed to try to sober up; musicians who had finished their gigs; an occasional actor/actress, all seeking a quick bite; hustlers, con men, pimps, regular people, Of course, there were the honeys, of all types; foxes, oxes, wannabes, has-beens, and never-weres were all in abundance. Flirting and cross-table conversations among strangers abounded. It could be a hook up environment.

One evening while dining with Omar at another one of their favorite Center City eateries, Amir could not help but witness him flirting with the pretty young sandy-colored waitress with the body by Fisher and mind by Mattel, who was serving them. "If you were my woman, you wouldn't be waitressing and you'd be wearing silk suits, carrying Gucci handbags, and wearing blue diamonds." Her broad smile and response showed she was flattered. He and Omar were both skilled flirters. Sometimes it was just good fun or target practice as Omar called it.

"Bullshit the baker, and you might get a bun; bullshit me, and you get nareeee one!" SaRon was waxing poetic at the pancake place on Walnut Street in Center City during the cold early morning hours of that Sunday, after a night of discoing with the fellows. He, Omar, and Amir were seated in a booth; all were tired, sleepy, and hungry. They had been to the Hippo, the Funky Donkey, the Fox Trap, and the Cave. SaRon had fallen asleep with his face in his pancakes and had woken up. He and Constance, his current older woman girlfriend, had allegedly broken up! She was too old for him, according to SaRon but did his hair for free, his jerry curl. Curious justification for a relationship, they all secretly felt.

Switch Hitting

Back in the day, when Amir was growing up, there were faggots, do-do chasers, sissies, punks, fags, and queers for males and for females, lesbos, dykes, bull daggers, and mananimals, among other references for homosexuals. In the neighborhood, there were a couple of young guys who were obviously different. Sometimes they carried themselves in an effeminate way. Some "walked funny." Sometimes they played with dolls or loved to play house. They were picked on and teased or laughed at to some extent in his experience. Clearly, these folks were an integral part of the community, however, including the black church, where they often were choir directors, organists, musical arrangers, and so on. Very interesting, thought Amir. Their behavior was officially condemned by church doctrine and society as a whole, and yet for the most part, they were tolerated by the black church! Amir believed that every family probably had some gay and lesbian members, whether they were acknowledged or not! You saw them, and you interacted with them. In some cases, you liked them as people whether you understood their bag or not! "I'd rather fight than switch!" some said. Black culture, of course, as he knew it, had its macho expression just as Hispanic cultures had their machismo expression. African cultures, to Amir's understanding, tended to be intolerant of homosexual expression. Even psychology used to teach that homosexuality was a mental illness. Personally, Amir felt no hatred or animus toward gay and lesbian folks. He didn't understand their lifestyles emotionally but wished them no harm. He thought the lesbian women who acted extremely butchy were curious though.

Amir's personal awakening would happen years later when he was working for the government and was forced to share a hotel room in Harrisburg, Pennsylvania, with a coworker he was fairly sure was gay. The signs were classic; he never had anything good to say about any female, hated his mother, was obsessively neat, and was into the theater. He had studied for the priesthood, but something had happened. Amir enjoyed his company, however, and had nothing against him. The guy was funny with a sense of humor. They were in Harrisburg for training. They would have to share a room, the government being cheap and all. This coworker made no advances in the slightest toward him. Amir had some apprehensions, some uneasiness, even putting his pajamas on in the bathroom after his coworker was already in bed. Later, he felt somewhat embarrassed within himself for having so many anxieties. In his adult life, Amir certainly would feel true friendship, affection, and caring for some males, fellow students, coworkers, friends, and so on but never felt sexual desire for one. His personal analysis was heterosexual relationships were difficult and complicated enough. Adding another layer of complication, homosexuality, particularly for someone black in America, was piling on the challenges.

The fluidity of sexual orientation was also interesting to Amir. There was the case of a female coworker who was a lesbian activist, appearing on TV and other media, who one summer returned skipping through the office from vacation declaring, "I'm in love!"

When Amir, who liked his coworker and neighbor, inquired, "What's her name?" he was somewhat surprised when she answered, "It's not a she, but a he!"

Amir had met other supposed lesbians and gays who were sleeping with the opposite sex. *This sexuality thing gets complicated*, decided Amir.

BEHIND THE COTTON CURTAIN

CHAPTER 3

Elberton, Georgia, located in northeastern Georgia, a couple of hours by car from Atlanta, was/is the "Granite Capital of the World," according to the big sign on display as one drove into Elberton on the main drag. It purportedly produced more granite monuments than any other city in the world. It is located not far from "America's Stonehenge," the mysterious Georgia Guide Stones located in Elbert County, Georgia. When Dad and Mom took Amir and Melinda down South, usually to Elberton, for a week or so in the summer—some summers, not every one—it was interesting. Cars were big and heavy in those days. Mom and Dad were in the front seat, he and Melinda in the backseat fighting over the sharing of deviled eggs and chicken wings! The ride was a long one. Dad always drove. Amir, as he grew older, noticed how Dad's fingers sometimes gently played in Mom's cleavage as he drove with his left hand on the steering wheel and his right placed so that he could reach her cleavage. Mom never learned how to drive and didn't seem to want to.

In later years, he would come to understand why Mom packed so much food to eat along the way, and why after arriving at a certain point in the South, when they stopped at the filling station, they could purchase gas but not utilize the restroom facilities! Mom and Melinda, if they couldn't hold it, had to go in the woods while he and Dad stood guard.

He would also remember the "White Only" signs he often saw out the car window on some of the restaurants and hotel doors and windows they passed as they drove through the South. His dad seemed to have real pain and anger around his southern experiences—segregation, Jim and Jane Crow, and southern etiquette. Once in Elberton, however, it was fun for a few days' stay. They would usually stay in one of Mom's sister's houses. They would then venture out and visit other relatives. He and Melinda were like celebrities to the southern kids around their age. "Y'all from Philly?" they would ask. Some wanted to be shown the latest dances in Philly.

Others admired the clothes they were wearing, the latest styles. Some of the southern girls were good-looking, and there was a certain southern charm that some of them had. Melinda and he would go country (take their shoes off and walk around barefoot like most of their young cousins did). They would pick blueberries, help shuck some corn, churn ice cream, and go to church, and Amir would shoot BB rifles with his cousins. He enjoyed that! Being little boys, they were mischievous, however, shooting birds out of trees with the BB rifles. They also shot some chickens in the butt with their BB guns. They thought of it as fun.

Upon first arrival, Melinda and he usually got stomachaches. They were told it was because of the fresh food they were consuming and not used to. The eggs, milk, and much of the meat were not from the supermarket like in Philly—no, this was fresh. Butter floated on the top of the milk. They helped make homemade ice cream, turning the device around and around. The ice cream was delicious. They saw chickens being slaughtered, usually by women, who often held them by the head as they spun them around until the head came off. Interestingly, even with their heads off, the chickens ran around for a few minutes like chickens with their heads off! until they keeled over.

He saw a hog being slaughtered and hung up in a smokehouse, where there were other sides of meat as well being cured. They saw people storing things in Mason jars, like peaches, apples, and other things.

The guy behind the counter in the small country store laughed when Amir asked for a bottle of soda. He called out to another guy from the back of the store and said, "This fella wants a soda!"

They both laughed.

"Do you mean a bottle of pop?" the man asked.

Amir said, "Yeah, that's what I want," as the man pulled a Coke out of the ice box. A soda in Philly was a "pop" in Georgia. He learned something that day.

Two features of their southern adventures Amir and Melinda did not like. One, the heat could be oppressive, stifling and brutal. Philly summers could be hot enough as far as Amir was concerned. Georgia heat in July or August could be intense! Two, using an outhouse was an experience they could've done without also! Some relatives lived in town and had indoor plumbing. Others lived out in the country and didn't have indoor plumbing. Getting up in the middle of the night and walking out of the house one was sleeping in to an outhouse in the dark, which was often smelly, to sit on a wooden plank with a hole in it and do one's business was not their idea of a good time!

The red clay of Georgia was kicking up as they traversed the county roads. They were headed to the family church. It was a fairly long ride from their aunt's house, which was in town. It was August and hot. In those days, many of the roads were unpaved. They passed houses along the way, some small, some bigger and nicer, and also a few shacks. The shacks were depressing, with metal roofs, newspaper for wallpaper, and falling-down porches; they reminded you of a "third-world" country. The small wooden church had a chapel but was not impressive looking. It also didn't have air-conditioning! In the pews were the obligatory fans from funeral directors. By Philly standards, the experience was underwhelming.

He did feel a sense of tradition on some level attending the family church and sharing a meal with the local community, however. On the whole, Amir thought he sensed or knew why his parents and so many others had left the South, though they did enjoy the trips down S outh, the kinship, the traditions, the shared love, the sense of community, and feeling a part of something. Amir would never forget the time, however, when in Elberton, on another Summer trip while very young, he and Melinda had walked into town. Town was a joke by Philly or New York standards. It had a few traffic lights, a few stores, one movie theatre, and so on. They had spotted a mechanical horse in front of a store. Having a little pocket change, they went to ride it. While taking turns riding the horsey, a man who happened to be white exited the store behind the horsey and faced them. Just like in the moves, in a perfect southern drawl, he asked, "You all aren't from around here, are you?"

Simultaneously, Mom had rounded the corner and having heard the comment, replied in a very emphatic tone, "No, they're not, but I am, and they're riding the horsey!" Mom was no joke. The man, sensing her fervor, turned and went back into the store. Amir reflected years later how brave this was of Mom and also how this could've ended very badly.

He would have put his money on Mom had it become physical, but then they would've had to get out of Dodge quick, fast, and in a hurry.

Years later, another southern experience would roll around inside Amir's head. He and a male cousin as little boys had walked into town, and Amir, spotting the only movie theater in town, had suggested, "Let's go to the movies!" He then headed for the box office where other kids were in the queue. His cousin then cautioned, "We don't go in that way."

Amir, confused, didn't understand as he was led around to the back of the theater, where he saw other kids in a separate queue. Upon entry, they went to sit in the balcony. In and of itself, the balcony seating didn't disturb him. Back in Philly, he sometimes sat in the balcony in the Uptown Theatre on Broad Street and joined other balcony sitters in throwing spitballs down on the folks on the first floor. But this somehow felt different. Years later, Amir would deduce he had been to a segregated movie theater! The kids in the queue at the front box office were all white. The kids in the queue around back as well as all balcony sitters were black. Dad had randomly and abruptly once told him, "White people are no damn good; they don't want you to have anything." His dad, an almost always friendly, amiable man, had shocked him with this comment. In years to come, he would develop some understanding of his dad's comment and the painful reasons for it.

Just prior to one of their family's southern sojourns, Tarver, an older brother from the neighborhood who owned a house just down the street, had cautioned Amir, "Be careful. Those crackers down South are no good!" Tarver was a short, very dark-skinned, powerfully built brother. He had had a career working for the railroad. He was collecting a pension. Tarver, a regular churchgoer, referred to black people as mules. Whites were crackers. He had been born and reared in the South, South Carolina, Amir believed, around 1921 or so. Amir could only imagine some of the trauma, the indignities Tarver had probably undergone in the South of that era.

He was wiping down his black deuce and a quarter that summer day when Amir encountered him. During the war (World War II), he was explaining, the trip to Europe by ship via the North Atlantic had been rough. A lot of GIs got sea sick, barfing all over the place. He had fought in the European theater. He, like so many other older brothers, had had to drop out of school to help on the farm at an early age, he had explained to Amir. "Get your lessons. The white man can't take that from you!" he would say very earnestly. Tarver's current problem was that a "haint" had appeared in his bedroom, he told Amir. Amir didn't really know what a haint was. Listening to Tarver, he deduced it was some kind of spirit, or succubus, he concluded. Tarver seemed truly concerned and apprehensive about this haint. Tarver kept his cash money in an envelope in the trunk of his car. Curious, Amir thought, but none of his business. Amir also noticed a Redd Foxx comedy album in the trunk on this particular day. Too racy for young folks, his comedy was for grown folk. Tarver would get really sharp on Sundays for church, typically wearing a sharp suit and a kind of Hamburg hat. He also carried a small pocket knife. Many brothers of that generation did. An earlier generation of black men had been known to carry straight razors, a formidable weapon when wielded by a skilled user. These brothers believed in self-defense!

On any given day, Tarver could be seen sweeping the sidewalk in front of his smallish row house and beyond of candy wrappers, cigarette butts, bags, and other litter discarded by the trifling mules who had tossed them carelessly onto the sidewalk. Amir liked Tarver.

On the Town

"Damn, boy, you put your foot in that," Omar said to SaRon.

He and Amir had enjoyed the tofu burgers and fixin's SaRon had prepared for them. Omar and Amir had driven to SaRon's place that summer afternoon. They didn't like his neighborhood. It was a typical lower-middle-class Philly neighborhood. The street was so narrow you could barely drive a car down it. There was nothing exciting or different about the area—restaurants, nightclubs, stores, and so on—to draw anyone there. *The residents probably shouldn't be blamed*, Amir thought to himself. They were probably victims of housing discrimination, red lining, high unemployment rates, high crime rates, poor public school education, and the exodus of the best and the brightest from the area. SaRon, who constantly complained about his hood, wouldn't move! He had grown up in this house and had occupied it by default, family members one by one either moving away or dying. Amir and Omar were of the "I'm gonna fight my way out of here" school, just like the lyric to the song "Dead End Street." SaRon didn't seem to be doing that. Sure, he talked a lot about moving, but never moved. Why couldn't this somewhat sophisticated and urbane guy pull the trigger? Omar and Amir did. He couldn't bring sophisticated honeys to this spot, they both agreed. He had his bachelor's and was working on his master's. Did he fear success? Was he lacking in confidence?

Around the crib were very graphic pictures posted that he had cut out of *Penthouse, Hustler, Playboy*, and other girlie magazines. He was intending to bring company home with these on the wall? They were starting to be concerned about him. Sure, they enjoyed looking at beautiful and sexy nude females too, but they didn't plaster these pictures on their apartment walls. "I have a young freak who licks my ass," SaRon was explaining, but all females now seemed to be freaks to SaRon.

They were becoming uneasy. "Got to go, brother," said Amir after thanking him for his hospitality. "Be good, and if you can't be good, be careful, and if you can't be careful, name the first one after me."

"Later, brother."

As they drove away, he and Omar shook their heads. What was wrong with this brother?

"Let's go to Jim's on South Street for cheesesteaks," Omar suggested, as Amir accelerated out of the neighborhood.

Wedding Bell Blues

Melinda and Donald had had a small wedding. Amir knew, of course, they had been high school sweethearts. The three of them had all attended Olney. Donald was the same grade level as he, and Melinda one grade behind them. He would occasionally bump into them walking near the school, holding hands and making goo-goo eyes at each other. He was somewhat neutral about Donald; he didn't particularly care or not care for him. Amir was only nineteen months older than Melinda, so he thought she was a bit young to get married, only twenty-one! He knew he wasn't even thinking about marriage. He was enjoying being single.

Of course, Amir would attend the wedding and wish them the best, but he had his doubts about their compatibility and the possible longevity of their match.

Melinda was bright, exceptionally good-looking, high energy, well dressed, and ambitious—Donald, not so much so, in Amir's estimation. She was doing eighty and he fifty-five, thought Amir. Time would tell. For the time being, Melinda was expecting. Wow, Amir was excited about this and excited generally. He would arrive at Hahnemann Hospital on North Broad Street before Donald or anyone else had arrived the day his niece was born, a beautiful, light-skinned, dark-haired baby. Melinda seemed to be doing fine. Wow, a new addition to the family! He was now an uncle!

The marriage of Donald and Melinda would eventually become annulled. When she was murdered, leaving his young niece behind, Dad, Mom, and Amir all agreed she would want for nothing. Amir would become a kind of surrogate father over time to his niece, along with his dad. Mom, of course, was a surrogate parent as well, taking her into the family home and raising her. Amir took his niece to museums, movies, fairs, concerts, and the library; fishing, out to eat, on road trips, and so on. Amir enjoyed it. She was kind of the daughter he hadn't had yet.

Blind Justice or Just Us?

Melinda was probably the first or certainly among the first homicide victims in Philly of 1976. Her body was found in the apartment of her former boyfriend; she had been shot in the head.

Amir had never liked him from the first meeting, which was unusual for him. When Aunt Lucy had phoned the house that evening, he happened to be there. Somehow, he sensed, felt, that it was about Melinda and that it was something tragic. Dad was out on the road at the time and was not told exactly what had happened but was ordered back in by his employer. Amir thought he knew who had done it right away.

All the immediate family did. Melinda and this guy had had a stormy relationship, a toxic one, of some duration, involving physical abuse, much of which she had hidden from the family, at the time of the occurrence, like the time Amir had visited Melinda at Hahnemann Hospital on North Broad Street. He had thought it was because she'd had dental surgery, only to find out much later that she suffered from a broken jaw! Dad had spoken to the man and told him that he didn't want him beating on his daughter. He had listened respectfully. This abuse had gone on for quite some time evidently. Melinda would not stay away from him permanently. Initially, the man was hiding out after killing her. They didn't know where he was. People, some relatives, were looking for him. Amir had actually gone to a bar he and Melinda were known to frequent himself, unarmed. He wasn't there, of course. Stupid, Amir would later think to himself, to go unarmed looking for him! When he surrendered to the police, he had a lawyer, one of Philly's best, Cecil B. Moore, and pleaded not guilty to the charges. Cecil was a well-known part of Philadelphia, a celebrity, Philly's own Johnny Cochran of that time. He was an attorney and civil rights leader (head of the North Philadelphia Action Branch of the NAACP until he and the NAACP parted ways). Cecil was considered one of the best defense attorneys in Philly. He had a café au lait color and a neatly manicured mustache and wore a part in his wavy styled dark hair. A dapper dresser, often wearing silk suits, Cecil was tough and smart. He could cuss like a sailor and did. Amir had witnessed Cecil's mastery of a courtroom, sitting in the back along with a few law school students in the recent past.

The former Columbia Avenue in North Philly was renamed Cecil B. Moore Boulevard in his honor on Temple University's campus near its law school. Almost all African Americans in Philly who needed a lawyer wanted Cecil. He had been in the marines in World War II. Cecil once famously said, "After nine years in the Marine Corps, I don't intend to take another order from any son of a bitch that walks." Another of Attorney Moore's famous quotes was "I don't want no more than the white man, but I won't take no less!" Amir had read somewhere that Cecil had attended Temple Law School at night after his discharge. Cecil smoked cigars and drank daily. He was an interesting mixture of toughness, legal acumen, street smarts, and down-hominess. At one point, Cecil was so busy he was given his own courtroom and judge! Amir knew Cecil and had seen him do a few trials. Cecil thought he knew him as well. When they saw each other on the street, usually in Center City, Cecil would call him Lorenzo, probably thinking he had represented him at some time. He didn't mind, being in the company of this charismatic local celebrity even briefly was always interesting and exciting. In his hoarse, gravelly voice as he and Cecil sat at the counter, he had heard Cecil ask the shapely brown-skinned waitress at the hamburger joint, "You like old money, honey? How about old jewelry? Now, how about an old man willing to give them both to you?" This was during an accidental encounter in Center City, near city hall on a hot summer's day. They were eating at Philly's then version of Jersey's White Castle. There were several in Center City.

"I'm tired of Jews in my business!" he had heard Cecil say in anger in open court one day as a young Jewish assistant district attorney had continued to object as Cecil was cross-examining a witness on the stand in a case where he was representing the defendant. When the judge cautioned and then threatened Cecil with a fine or a weekend in jail if he didn't behave in her courtroom, Cecil replied by pulling a big wad of money out of his pants pocket and stating that he had been locked up before! Cecil sort of reminded him of a slightly darker-skinned Adam Clayton Powell Jr. He was smart, street-savvy, arrogant, talented, skillful, committed to the cause, and prideful. He would go on to win the longest-running battle in Pennsylvania Supreme Court history, the breaking of the will of Stephen Girard, which then allowed orphaned black boys to attend Girard College, with its beautifully manicured campus located in the heart of mostly black North Central Philly but to which admittance had been restricted heretofore to "poor white male orphans" as per the will of the late Stephen Girard, a wealthy businessman. He was rumored to have stolen part or all of his fortune from Toussaint Le Overture of Haiti!

Cecil, along with another activist lawyer in Philly named C. B. was also responsible for stopping the Mummers, that famous and traditional Philly New Year's Day event (string bands) from having their traditional blackface contingent as part of the Mummer's Day Parade.

Cecil had stared at him across the courtroom, possibly because he recognized him as well.

Dad one day during a court recess reminded Cecil that Melinda, his daughter and the murder victim of the man he was defending, had walked around the Girard College walls with him during the demonstrations. Amir would be in court from the pretrial motions, through jury selection, through the trial and sentencing, through the posttrial motions. He didn't trust the system. The Philly police, he thought, didn't care as much about black victims of black perpetrators, or black life generally. If Melinda had been white, it might be a different story! Amir found it interesting that in the

courtroom, the people who knew least about the law—the jury—
were the people charged with finding innocence or guilt!

Also, since X had rights, the jury was not allowed to hear about
how this guy had shot a woman before! Of course, he understood
the reasoning; he was being tried for this crime, no others. But
knowing something about a person's past behavior could be quite
telling and even necessary, he felt, to judge current acts. Of course,
X had been cleaned up for court. He was freshly shaven, goatee removed, and wearing a suit, and he'd had a recent haircut. He carried
an attaché case with him. Amir discovered one day as X opened it
that there was nothing in it! Image, image, image. Of course, it was
explained to the jury that his failure to take the witness stand was
not to be held against him because of his Fifth Amendment right
against self-incrimination. It was a circumstantial evidence case,
no known witnesses, no murder weapon, no confession. But what
circumstances! Her body was found in his apartment. The box a
revolver had come in was found, empty, in his place as well. They,
Melinda and he, had been together New Year's Eve at a popular
Philly night spot, according to the bartender working that night.
He had a history of physically abusing her. Threats made by him
had been heard.

There was a witness who testified that she had heard him
threaten to kill Melinda. This witness had been difficult to find,
and Philly detectives had to go and ferret out this reluctant witness from another state. She was handcuffed when brought to the
courtroom to testify. She was probably afraid of X. He was a scary
guy, known to carry a gun daily. Amir was not called to testify. He
had not really witnessed anything. Fannie Mae did testify, however.

Amir thought that Cecil might be in for a surprise when he
cross-examined her, and he was. Holding a picture of Melinda
modeling some beds but standing erect in front of them and fully
clothed, Cecil tried to infer that she was a porn star or prostitute
because of the beds.

Fannie Mae, not to be intimidated by anyone, replied very clearly and strongly after grabbing the picture from Cecil's hand and bringing it close to her face, "Can't you see the price tags hanging from these beds? The child was obviously modeling the beds; that's all!"

Cecil quickly said, "No further questions."

The trial went on for a couple of months. Amir was there every day, Mom and Dad most days. Because Dad was a Teamster, before the trial actually started, he had made some phone calls. Dad and Amir would go to Palumbo's restaurant/hall in South Philly for a Mayor Frank L. Rizzo event. There, they were determined to meet the mayor and ask for an appointment. Upon arrival at Palumbo's that evening, it was obvious that Amir and Dad were among the few blacks there. But this was important. It was necessary. The system didn't really care about his murdered African American sister! They had to do something extra! Something more. Melinda and her memory deserved it! Rizzo, sharply dressed as usual and accompanied by his big black police detective bodyguards, was working the room.

When he got to the table where Dad and Amir were seated, he smiled broadly and extended a big hand for a handshake. After pleasantries and telling the mayor they had to see him on a personal matter, he said while passing out his card, "Call my secretary and make an appointment to see me next week." Mission accomplished; they would.

Arriving at Philly's city hall that cloudy afternoon, Amir was a little nervous. They were going to talk to the controversial mayor of America's then fourth-largest city, who was thought to be a racist and a fascist by many Philadelphians, particularly many black Philadelphians, about Melinda and the upcoming trial of the guy they were sure had murdered her. After they were politely ushered into the mayor's inner office and seated, the discussion began. After a brief description of what had happened, the mayor said, "Because there's a jury, I can't promise you the outcome, but I can assure you that an experienced and competent Assistant DA will be put on the case, and the police will leave no stone unturned," further adding, "Call me if you need to."

They rose and all shook hands. He and Dad thanked the mayor for his time and assistance. The mayor, labeled a racist, a law-and-order Democrat, a Fascist, seemed sincere, in his assurance of aid. You live, and you learn.

Daily, X was only sitting a few yards from Amir and Dad or Mom at the defense table. He sometimes thought how easy it would be to grab and choke him or shoot or stab him, right there. Amir was angry and wanted revenge. No, that was not the way. What would happen if he missed or the shots didn't kill him? Would a mistrial be declared? If so, would he be retried? If successful, would one of X's relatives take revenge against Mom or Dad or his niece? Would Amir be shot and killed in the attempt to get to X? Ultimately, he was found guilty of second degree murder and weapons charges. It should've been first degree, but the jury probably didn't clearly understand the difference. They had asked the judge to clarify this difference at least two times. He got twelve to twenty something years. Years later, he would often hear on television the family and friends of murder victims speak of closure. *There is no such thing*, thought Amir. This person has been taken from you; if you cared for them, it leaves a hole in your heart. You go on, but your family is never quite the same.

BLUE SERGE OR "YOU HAD A GOOD HOME BUT YOU LEFT, RIGHT, LEFT ..."

CHAPTER 4

I don't know, but I've been told, Eskimo pussy is mighty cold, sound off, one, two, sound off, three, four." "Jack and Jill went up the hill to have a little fun; stupid Jill forgot her pill, and now they got a son! Sound off, one, two, sound off, three, four, sound off, one, two, three, four." "My father was a jockey; he taught me how to ride. He said, 'Son, you got to hit it from side to side.' Sound off, one, two ..." These were repeated along with other rhymes as they drilled. Squadron #1016 met every Friday night at the Ben Franklin Institute at 1900 hours. They made formation just beneath the beautiful, gigantic marble statue of Benjamin Franklin in the main lobby. The Civil Air Patrol (CAP) is a US Air Force Auxiliary, and Amir had thought he wanted a military career at that point in his life. It seemed like a natural evolution to where he thought he wanted to end up—Cub Scout, Boy Scout, CAP, and then US military. An officer and a gentleman was what he thought he wanted to be. Besides, a lot of girls liked men in uniform at that time. CAP cadets wore US Air Force uniforms. If you passed all the required steps, you earned your Certificate of Proficiency, meaning that if you joined the US Air Force, you entered as an airman third class (one stripe). The CAP's most famous cadet was probably Lee Harvey Oswald. Amir actually would begin the process of applying to the US Air Force Academy in Colorado Springs, Colorado, a couple of years later. He would meet with Congressman N. C. Nix, one of the first twentieth-century black US congresspersons, as a congressional recommendation was required to gain entry into the academy.

His first time flying in an airplane was with the CAP in a small Piper Cub with a pilot who wore Coke-bottle glasses thicker than his! When they began to hit air pockets, he did get a bit scared but couldn't show it, of course. The only difference between the uniforms CAP cadets wore and regular US Air Force uniforms were a few distinguishing patches. People didn't seem to usually read them and often thought they were airmen. He liked that.

"James Bond has a license to kill, gurl, but I have a license to thrill! I'll be going back to Nam in a week. Give me something to remember you by." It was a great line for the honeys, Amir thought. They'd often meet young women in Center City after the squadron meetings as they would walk around proudly in their smartly pressed uniforms and spit-shined shoes. Usually they'd end up at a pizza shop or some other inexpensive restaurant. Most of the cadets were African-American and most of the noncoms and officers were white. It didn't take Amir long to figure out that the higher the rank, the better; then you could tell at least some people what to do as opposed to being ordered around by everybody else yourself.

"Drop your cocks, and grab your socks! Drop your nuts and move your butts!" Sometimes, there were redcaps (real emergencies), usually downed private airplanes that they would be called upon to help search for, usually in rural Pennsylvania. They would put on their fatigues and combat boots, pile into a van, and tear off to parts unknown, at least to him. Secretly, he always hoped they'd never find any dead or mangled bodies in treetops or on the ground on these redcaps. Amir would never forget how one winter evening as he and some other cadets were riding in the back of a panel truck in fatigues and combat boots during a redcap on their way to upstate Pennsylvania, some jocularity was occurring, and one of the noncoms who happened to be white joked to the mostly African American group of cadets how maybe he would pick up some watermelon for them. Amir shot back, "And maybe some bagels and lox for yourself!" He eventually became a staff sergeant and had earned a few ribbons. He liked that, calling his squad to fall in and make formation. He even went away to Officer's Candidate School (OCS) for a week, somewhere in rural Pennsylvania. That was interesting. He was one of only 2 or 3 other blacks at the whole place as far as he could tell. They were plebes, maggots, faggots, and ladies and had to run everywhere on campus.

They were called other names as well—lowlifes, girls, worms, queers, pond scum, and turds, among others. An upperclassman might approach you and say, "Give me fifty" (push-ups), which after doing, you'd say, "Thank you, sir!" You could be asked to recite some paragraphs you had been required to commit to memory, which made no sense, without any mistakes. Of course, there was always the drilling, the marching, the PT, sometimes in the rain, and the fancy drills with their intricate steps. Reveille didn't bother him too much, as he could always get up early in the morning.

They had to eat at attention in the mess hall. Their uniforms had to be worn crisply and perfectly. They got demerits if upperclassmen felt it was warranted. He'd never forget the dance that was held where a white female cadet had asked him while socializing if he was from an island. Should he slow drag with her, try to get a grind? Better play it safe and not!

He remembered the obstacle course, particularly the part where you climbed a tall pole and just jumped off it with your gear on! He had heard that one cadet had broken his leg attempting to do so. They often did PT in the rain. The CAP was trying to make this experience as realistic as possible, he thought. He did everything asked of him; however, out of a sense of pride, he had to represent. Although he successfully completed OCS, he never was made a second lieutenant back at the squadron. He was told that they were not allotted to have another.

Dem Bones, Dem Bones, Dem Dry Bones

"They dropped bums on Germany!" *How cruel*, he thought at first, until he finally realized that these brothers, most of whom were from the rural South and had dropped out of elementary or grade school in the fifth or sixth grade, often because they were needed to help out on the farm, meant bombs, not bums! In later years, he would find it interesting that when immigrants from foreign lands spoke broken English, it was often seen as charming or quaint, but this did not apply to southern immigrant blacks, however. They were simply adjudged uneducated, ignorant, and so on by American society.

These brothers were often country. They had accents. They sometimes talked funny, and they weren't always sharp dressers. Many drank. Many cheated on their wives. Most were male chauvinists by today's standards, but in the main, they were some of the finest people he would meet in his life from anywhere. On the whole, they were strong, decent, and hardworking.

Some southern blacks were "geechees." Amir didn't know for years what that meant. Finally, he learned the term had to do with the Gullah people and the low country of South Carolina and Georgia and those from those regions. His future stepmother would be a geechee. These black immigrants were usually very family oriented, with a love for and a pride in their race and their culture, which slavery, Jim and Jane Crow, segregation, brutalization, discrimination, and police harassment and brutality had not obliterated. They actually sought a kind of political asylum from the harsh womb-to-tomb caste system, segregation, and brutishness of their lives in the American South and elsewhere. "Get your education, boy. The white man can't take that from you!" These words were said to him and other young blacks by these brothers so often, he grew tired of hearing them.

At the barbershop, on the street, in church, at the baseball stadium, in people's homes, at the bar, in the pool hall, it became their mantra. Years later, he would realize these were words of hope, love, and motivation, of dreams and fulfillment, of the future. It was amazing, Amir would come to believe in later years, when one considered the gristmill they had gone through, which was American society for African Americans, particularly of their generation!

Whip looked like an Arab sheik to him. He was very fair-skinned, and he combed his jet-black hair straight back. He had a thick, dark, well-trimmed mustache and a little tuft of hair below his lower lip. He also had a prominent nose. His wife, Sue, was good-looking, he thought, a little plump now, but good-looking. When she was young, she probably was a fox, he thought.

Whip was related somehow, a cousin perhaps from Georgia on Dad's side. He was a chainsmoker, but that didn't bother him. Whip always seemed to be working on cars, fixing their air-conditioning systems or something else while chainsmoking. Whip had helped him several times with various car troubles—poor air-conditioning operation, broken timing belt, and so on. You could count on him. He was part of Amir's network.

He and another cousin, Michael T., also from Georgia, could both be counted on in a pinch. Two FBI agents had come to the ponderosa looking for Michael T. when Amir was a little boy. He had thought the two suited white guys were insurance agents. Usually, white guys in his neighborhood with suits on were insurance agents collecting premiums! Of course, Mom was not going to give him up.

"No, I haven't seen him," she had said.

Wow, real FBI agents at his house! Just like on the TV show with Efrem Zimbalist Jr.! Cousin Michael T. had just recently visited.

Savile Row

When Amir was growing up, there was a lot of emphasis on dressing well or stylishly in Philly's black communities. You wanted to be in style, sharp as a tack, and clean as Dick's hat band. A well-dressed guy was a yok. Stab-me collars (big, long, pointed collars) on shirts were out. Chest protectors (big, wide ties), like their dads often wore, were out as well. A suit could be a vine. "The brother is clean" was a compliment, as was "he's clean as the Board of Health." Amir even had a couple of tailor-made suits as an adolescent. For the rest of his life, he decided, he would be clean, no matter what. When visiting London years later, he would make a pilgrimage to the famous Savile Row area just to see it, to pay homage.

Philly's local DJs, many ministers, some politicians, the Temptations, the Four Tops, Jackie Wilson, and Smokey Robinson, among others, were always clean. As was James Bond, Shaft, Our Man Flint, the Trouble Man (Robert Hooks), Peter Gunn, Bat Masterson, Cary Grant, Clark Gable, Sidney Poitier, actor Calvin Lockhart, and JFK. "That's a bad suit, brother!" was often said, or that's a boss vine. Guys who didn't dress well were farmers. Stacey Adams was one of the popular brands among the clean guys in Philly, in terms of shoes and hats especially. In Philly, the best-dressed guys were usually the black, Jewish, and Italian guys overall. Dad could get sharp when required. On isolated occasions, he and Mom even went out to cut a rug (dance). Amir and Omar particularly liked the European styles popular in the late 1960s and 1970s—Pierre Cardin, Yves St. Laurent, and Oleg Cassini, among other designers. On South Street, down in South Philly, there was a large discount men's store. They sold shirts, ties, suits, sports jackets, overcoats, and so on. They sold the kind of clothes young hipsters liked. Many African Americans shopped there. M. Gross, the owner, who happened to be Jewish, was a bit of a celebrity, tooling around town in a Bentley convertible. A sharp, dapper man, he dressed somewhat like a pimp, Amir thought. He and Omar sometimes went there for overcoats, sports jackets, and the like. The well-known large men's store on Market Street had stylish clothes but was getting too expensive. The GGG brand was one of the most stylish but was an expensive choice in suits and sports jackets back in the day. Moshe's on Chestnut Street in Center City had a stylish selection of men's clothes. Amir would never forget the day he was browsing in Moshe's and Cecil came in. He went directly to the rack that contained his suit size, grabbed two armfuls of suits, looked at the salesman, said, "Put these on my account," turned, and walked directly out of the store!

The crew had a relationship with Sam at Golden Larry's near Spring Garden Street, where many quality designer men's suits, sports coats, pants, overcoats, and so on by Yves St. Laurent, Pierre Cardin, and others were to be had, often at half the normal retail price.

During this era, some of the Cardin pieces actually read "Made in France" on the label. Sam, a salesman there who happened to be Jewish, would actually call Amir at work as new shipments arrived. "We just got some Yves St. Laurent overcoats, some leather blazers, some Pierre Cardin sports coats …"

"Thanks, Sam. Set aside a 46L for me please, in the fawn color. I'll be by after work!"

Amir and his close friends all loved a bargain, and paying retail was seen as a defeat. Bragging about how much one paid for something was not cool in his crowd. Amir, Omar, and SaRon, with their shaped, European-cut jackets and suits, with the high arm holes and tapered waists, were smart looking. Amir particularly liked the English look with the jackets having shape, double side vents, and a ticket pocket, often tweedy. He particularly liked the glen plaid patterns in sports jackets and suits. There was the time, for instance, they both purchased English twill double-breasted overcoats with peaked lapels for a New Year's Eve party from Krass Brothers.

"Those brothers are clean!" they heard as they arrived at the New Year's Eve party in Germantown. "Check out the brother's vine!"

Omar, Amir, and their close circle were some of the most stylishly dressed young men in Philly at that time.

The crew (Amir and his close friends) were somewhat popular in their way. They had foresworn fraternities as nationalists. The thinking was that frats were Eurocentric. Why all the Greek references? Why not Arabic or Ki-Swahili references? Instead of alpha and omega, why not alif and ya? The Greeks were not older than the ancient Egyptians. Ancient Egypt was seminal!

"They're here!" they sometimes heard when they (the crew) made their entrance at social functions (usually fashionably late). They were energetic, good-looking, charismatic, and witty. Oh to be young, gifted, and black!

Little Light in the Basement or "Parti 2-Nite, Y'all"

From about age fifteen on, there were those house parties. It was hot, dark, and crowded in the basement of the smallish Philadelphia row house. "Niggers draw heat," he had heard someone utter on more than one occasion. He didn't like or use the "n-word" himself, but many used it. It was almost always hot and crowded at these parties. Someone's parents had often gone away for the weekend or at least allowed their son or daughter to invite a few friends over for a party. Typically, you had to say someone's name to gain admittance. "I know Jamal" or Ronald or Curtis and so on. There would be chairs arrayed along the basement walls for seating, some kind of punch or Kool-Aid to drink, and often just pretzels or potato chips to eat. Music would typically be provided by a record player playing 45 rpm records. They had a hole in the middle into which a plastic disc was inserted. Dancing would typically occur in the middle of the floor. Occasionally, a couple would be grinding up against a wall.

If it was local, you might know some of the kids there. He always hoped the girls would be plentiful. Maybe some foxes would be there, and he would get a grind or two or three. "A kiss and a grind would do me fine. I missed the kiss, but I got the grind" was a Philly axiom among young folk. To get the grind, you had to have the nerve to ask some girl to dance.

This meant it helped to know the intro to songs that were good to grind to. Smokey's "Oh, Baby, Baby," the Dells' "Stay in My Corner," and "Oh What a Night," "The Love We Had Stays on My Mind," "Give Your Baby a Standing Ovation," "You Got to Pay Some Agony If You Want the Ecstasy," or "Would I Love You," also by Smokey, were all great grinding records. You had to be quick to ask for a dance or only the skanks[7] would be left to dance with! He liked girls well enough, but during his preteen and early teenage years, he was very shy and bashful. He watched as the more aggressive guys got dances with the foxes! He would determine that he had to get over his shyness or he'd always be left at the starting gate. He worked on that diligently and by his late teens had, for the most part, overcome it. "One yes makes up for a lot of nos" became his mantra. "Nothing ventured, nothing gained."

When he did get a grind, his eyeglasses typically became greasy because of the hairstyles the girls were wearing then and the fact that he was usually taller than his dance partner. So after the dance, he'd return to his seat and wipe off his eyeglasses! For years, grinding was the closest thing he and many others had to real sex. A kind

---

7

of simulated sex was occurring as their young, hard bodies, ever so close, slowly rotated and gyrated and rubbed up against each other around their respective pelvic areas. Typically, a young man would pop a hardy (get an erection) while grinding. Some actually came.

"Hey, man, what's that on your pants?"

"That's syrup" would often be the answer.

"Damn, you must eat pancakes every morning!" was the retort.

When you couldn't get a slow drag, you were left with having to watch others who did. The expressions on people's faces and the ability of some to move every part of their bodies except their feet while sweating profusely was often amusing! It was primal and exciting, as some writhed in ecstasy. Facial expressions were lustful. During a certain period of time, he was considered quite the catch by some girls, he was light-skinned and had good hair, according to some. This good hair thing really bothered him, however. People were good or bad, not their hair! Hair was straight or curly or nappy or wavy or wooly, whatever. Blacks, however, or too many of them, seemed stuck on this good hair thing. It was obviously a remnant of white superiority and poor Black self-esteem and self-hatred. Amir determined that he would never use the phrase and didn't. Philly was steeped in the black colorism and caste system of the era. This would change, for the most part, in a few years as the black consciousness era evolved.

When the James Brown records were playing, such as "Papa Don't Take No Mess" or "The Big Pay Back," with their irresistible and primal beats, sometimes everyone was on the floor dancing in syncopated motion, in the dark, in the heat, and it seemed almost spiritual, almost tribal! Among dances then were the jerk, the fly, the dog, the Philly dog, the twist, the mashed potato, the James Brown, the twist, the monkey, the twine, the cha cha, the rock, the watusi, the funky chicken, the two-step, and the stroll. Some Philly kids could really dance. It was a bit intimidating for Amir, who was only a mediocre dancer at best. Of course, Philly was a musical town. *American Bandstand* was broadcast from Philadelphia for years, from a studio in West Philly under the L tracks.

Many singing groups and individual artists came out of Philly, among them boy preacher Solomon Burke, one of the founders of soul music; the Stylistics; the Delfonics; Harold Melvin and the Blue Notes; Chubby Checker; the Intruders; Teddy Pendergrass; Sister Sledge; Brenda Holloway; Barbara Mason; Tammy Terrell; Frankie Avalon; Bobby Rydell; Fabian; Billy Paul; Pearl Bailey; and others. Even the great opera singer Mario Lanza was from Philly! Kenny Gamble and Leon Huff had Philly International Records, and they were churning out hits for artists like the late Lou Rawls, Dionne Warwick, the Spinners, and on and on. Jazz legend Grover Washington Jr. was also Philadelphia based. Guys could be seen and heard walking up and down the city streets harmonizing, day and night, sometimes singing under bridges and trestles for the acoustic effect. During winter, they might gather around an oil drum with a fire in it. Some professional groups got their start this way. His sister, Melinda, learned to dance by holding a pillow while watching *Bandstand* on television and dancing with it right in their living room. Years later, Amir, never a particularly good dancer, used to think to himself, *Maybe I should've done the pillow thing too!* As Amir got older, he and a buddy or two would venture all over Philly to attend parties—Germantown, West Philly, West Oak Lane, Powelton Village, South Philly.

WDAS AM and FM were the radio stations most black Philadelphians listened to in those days. There was also Jerry Blavat, "the geator with the heater." He was a half-Italian, half-Jewish guy who talked a lot of shit and was popular with blacks and whites. The Geator would go on to have a TV show and eventually promote dances in South Jersey and Philadelphia. He referred to his mostly teenaged TV audience as foxes and coyotes. Popular local DJs were celebrities; they included Jimmy Bishop; Jocko Henderson; Georgie Woods, "the Man with the Goods"; John Bandy, a.k.a. Lord

Fauntleroy; and "Butterball" Tamburo, a.k.a. Butter, a.k.a. Fast Butter in the City.

Disco Lady, Part 2

Whether it was in Center City, West Philly, Germantown, South Philly, Overbrook, West Oak Lane, North Philly, Camden (New Jersey), New York City, or elsewhere, it was the era of the go-go girl, later to be called an exotic dancer. The clubs included Pony Tail, Coupe De Villes, the Bird Cage, the Place, the Living Room, the Trestle Inn, the Half Moon, and so on. The crew or Amir alone would travel all over Philly and beyond to partake in this social phenomena. In most bars or clubs, the dancers were all white or all black. He and the guys went to both!

"We don't serve black people here," the smart-ass white bartender had said with a smile on his face at the Center City bar.

"I didn't want to order black people," Amir had responded. "Just three Buds!"

The bartender laughed and complied. He wasn't worried; he had his boys with him, including Luther! Some of the dancers were beautiful, with great or exaggerated body proportions, some not so much. Of course, one had to have money for tips, usually several one-dollar bills if one wanted their attention. Amir made sure he had change before going, as did most guys. "A dollar will get you closer," the female DJ would say at the club on Locust Street in Center City on Men's Night (no female customers would be admitted). The dancers would actually come and jump in your lap there and gyrate and twist in a sort of lap dance after initially coming out in a kind of burlesque review, costumes and all—a bride, a cowgirl, a policewoman, a nurse, a businesswoman, a French maid, and so on. Eventually, they would strip down to pasties and G-strings. It was quite a show. The female DJ was a trip!

On one occasion, as Amir and SaRon were enjoying the show, two sinewy, muscled, sweet-smelling, oiled, brown-skinned lovely twins were gyrating on Amir's legs. Awww, sooky, sooky now! Some guys were so cool they tried to act unmoved by the dancers. Of course, he realized it was really all about the tips, but how often did a fella get to have two good-looking, sexy, curvaceous young women gyrating in his lap—twins yet? "A shout out to all you gappers, finger snappers, toe tappers, and love lappers" was another of the DJ's quips.

The oils and lotions, scents, and sparkles the dancers wore would get on and in your clothes and facial hair if you had any. They witnessed the evolution of the go-go girls from pasties and G-strings and segregation from the patrons to topless and sometimes completely nude to engaging in lap dances, oral sex right out in the open, or sex acts committed behind a curtain or in a room—for a price, of course. "Put your clothes back on!" could be heard at one nude dancer joint if the woman didn't look pleasing completely naked.

At one spot in West Philly, the dancers danced on a long horseshoe-shaped bar above the customers, as they worked the room. This sometimes led to cunnilingus being performed right there in front of everyone! "Here's Mikey!" (This was from the then popular TV commercial about a little boy who would eat almost anything). "Mikey will eat anything," he heard in the dimly lit West Philly go-go bar. "Mikey," seated at the bar, then proceeded to turn his baseball cap around backward and perform cunnilingus on the dancer above and astride him right on the spot! Amir had concluded years before that one didn't go to the go-go bars looking for love or sex or romance and didn't drop one's entire paycheck there or seriously try to take one of the dancers home. Of course, there was the incident at that Center City bar between Amir and the dancer he had dubbed "S&M" because she wore black leather, spikes, and other sadomasochistic-looking gear. But that was another story …

This was almost always business to the dancers, so no matter how skilled they were at flirting with you, making you think they had really noticed you, liked you, wanted to go home with you, and so on, it was usually all part of the job! They were after tips! Occasionally, something odd or unusual did occur, like the time when in a smoky Center City predominantly white go-go bar, a dancer, passing him standing at the bar, had slipped a note into his pocket as she passed by reading, "I like you!" He didn't follow up. She looked high.

There was another notable occasion when at a Center City bar on his way to the men's room, he noticed a line. It was curious for a men's room. As he continued to walk, he realized what was going on. Men were in a line, single file, facing a seated woman who, in turn, was giving head to those in the queue, for a price, of course! He continued on to the men's room. Amir did briefly date a dancer once, or twice, but it didn't last, just a few dates. Then there was the beautiful summer's day when, while out at lunch from work, walking on Broad Street, he looked to his right and up a small intersecting street for some reason. What he saw was a first for him. A line of cars in single file were driving up to a takeout type window, where each paused, but instead of food being dispensed, a woman from inside the building lowered her upper body into the car through the driver's side window and committed fellatio on the customer. Truly a unique takeout service!

SaRon was once conflicted about dating a very attractive and shapely dancer who was a part-time student at the college. He threw the question out to the crew one day at their favorite cafeteria.

"The girl is fine and sexy, and she's a college student."

"She seems like a lot of fun" was among the responses made to him.

Someone questioned, however, would he be able to pick her up from work if required or requested to at two or three in the morning and wait for her, having to watch her flirt (part of her job) with men to get tips? Or observe men hit on her without getting angry? These were the real issues, was the consensus, not her vocation as such.

"Being a dancer doesn't make her a ho," someone stated, "but can you handle it?"

"She was a dancer when you met her. Are you going to ask her to stop?"

Omar would later remark, "That brother is cuntfused!"

Amir would never forget the day the lady in question came skipping into the lobby at school, radiant and beaming, opening her blouse to show him her new breast implants! She was charming, bubbly, and likable enough, but did she have to actually lift her blouse up like that in public to show them off?

Later that afternoon, as the guys gathered, Omar asked Kahlil, "Hey, brother, have you heard about the Idaho resolution?"

"Idaho resolution?" Kahlil repeated with a quizzical look on his face.

"Yeah, akhi, if they're big enough, they're old enough!"

Everyone laughed. SaRon retorted, "You crazy, boy."

To Protect and Serve?

The Philly police, a.k.a. the Rizzopo, during the late 1960s and 1970s, earned a well-deserved reputation for being one of the most hostile and brutal police forces in America, at least to black and Latino communities. Houston, Texas, and LA shared that distinction with Philly. Police brutality and harassment ran rampant in the City of Brotherly Love. Far too many black and Latino males were killed unjustifiably by the cops, and many others were beaten unmercifully without legitimate cause. False arrests abounded.

Those who sued the force for police brutality, false arrest, or wrongful death usually did not prevail. The jury of their peers, most often white and suburban, would not take the word of a black citizen over that of a usually white police officer. Witness testimony and medical documentation also didn't usually sway them either.

The Rizzopo was named after former police commissioner and two-term Philadelphia mayor Frank L. Rizzo, a South Philly High School dropout who had a meteoric rise in the Philadelphia Police Department to become its commissioner, a.k.a. the Big Bambino and the Cisco Kid. He was a law-and-order Democrat during the Nixon era. His tactics and brutality in the black community won fans among many whites who were racists or who feared change and progress, and possibly miscegenation. Some blacks liked Rizzo as well. He did provide jobs with the city for some. An Italian American, Rizzo was a big man of Sicilian descent with olive skin and dark, slicked-back hair. Well dressed with a quick smile, he was hot tempered and had a reputation for brutality. One example occurred while the crew was walking back from the college one afternoon. Near Logan Circle, Amir, Omar, and SaRon actually witnessed the Rizzopo attack demonstrators protesting outside the Philly Board of Education administration building, mostly students interspersed with a few administrators. They saw pregnant women attacked and girls pulled down the street by their hair. Some of the officers were mounted on horseback for intimidation. Amir would never forget the scene.

Amir's first remembered personal experience with Philly cops was when a busload of junior high school students, including himself, from his junior high were driven directly to Seventeenth and Montgomery, the local police precinct! He had been sitting in the back of the No. 2 bus, not a school bus, but a public bus, with the bad kids, whom he enjoyed, as they cursed, shared anecdotes, and sometimes smoked cigarettes. Amir, wearing thick glasses, a part in his hair, and carrying a briefcase, while rocking a sports jacket must have looked the perfect nerd!

Sort of like an extremely young college professor. Someone, not on the bus, had thrown something and broken a window on the bus. Hence the express ride to the precinct for everyone on the bus by the bus driver! You had to call your parents to get picked up. Amir's dad often worked late, so he'd be among the last to get picked up! As he talked on the phone, trying desperately to explain why he was at the precinct, he could hear in the background Dad initially saying, "Jail? Leave him there!"

Biggy could be heard also, however, in the background saying, "Go get my grandson! If you need my bankbook, here it is!"

It felt good to know that Biggy was on his side, that she had his back. She would aid/rescue him several more times before her untimely and premature death. While he was waiting at the police station for his parents to pick him up, some of the detectives had shown him some pictures of alleged gang members. He recognized Peanut Head and Ice Man and Nasty Man along with some others, but he couldn't snitch. "Snitches get stitches!"

When told "we could keep you" by one of the detectives, Amir replied, "Any lawyer worth his salt would get a writ of habeas corpus, and I'd be out in no time!"

This caused raucous laughter and guffaws among Philly's finest.

"What do you know about a writ of habeas corpus?"

"I know because I read about it in the *World Book Encyclopedia!*" Amir replied.

The family had recently acquired a burgundy-colored set. All of his adolescence and adulthood in Philly would include having to carefully deal with Philly cops. Being followed for no good reason while driving, being questioned on the street for no valid reason, being taken to a police station, and being held a few hours in a cell with real criminals for no legitimate reason, false arrest—this harassment was common in Philly at that time.

Of course, there was also the occasional cop who gave him a break or who was actually courteous, respectful, and professional to him when he approached (e.g., driving the wrong way on a one-way street only got him a warning to "be more careful in the future"). Of course, it could've been worse. He was never beaten or killed by them!

"Where you going?" he was asked by the cop as he exited his patrol car when Amir was exiting the phone booth that Friday night in Center City. He had a hot date and had just gotten off work.

"I'm going on a date," he had replied, whereupon the officer explained after looking him over and checking his driver's license and owner's card that a "black man driving a VW Beetle had just robbed a bank!" He assured the officer he knew nothing about that! The cop allowed him to carry on. He thought if he had been driving a pink Rolls Royce, he would've used the same pretext. Bad police shootings were common.

Handcuffed black men were shot numerous times, and prisoners in jail for minor traffic violations hung themselves for no apparent reason. Allegedly escaping prisoners were shot numerous times while supposedly running in handcuffs! Philly was rough in those days. Amir and his friends refused, however, to cower in their homes out of fear of gangs or the police! They wanted to do what young men do—explore, travel, flirt, meet all kinds of women, see and be seen, be in the mix, the ebb and flow of humanity. So, they traveled not only around Philly but to NYC, Camden, Atlantic City, Washington, DC, and Baltimore. Locally, the Funky Donkey, the Cave, the Hippo, the Living Room, the Library, the Fox Trap, the 4-6 Club, the Electric Factory, the Latin Casino, Casablanca, discos in hotels, dances at veterans clubs, college/university mixers, and parties were all regular stops for R&R for the crew. This meant they would encounter law enforcement periodically. They had to develop coping skills!

One freezing winter night, as he and his boys were walking

to the trolley stop after a party in Germantown, the strong winds whipping around them, he noticed the paddywagon slowly pulling up parallel to them. The policeman pointed at him and Phil and said, "Get in"—the moment of truth, again. Do you simply get in and hope you don't get abused, or do you resist, get beat up, possibly shot, and charged with resisting arrest and assault on a police officer? They chose to simply get in. Paddywagons have a bumpy, hard ride he was to learn that night—or did the cops intentionally give them a rough ride? At the precinct, they emptied their pockets before the desk sergeant. The tall redneck-looking officer standing behind them was trying to be intimidating, beating his gloves against his palms in turn, first the right and then the left.

"What do you guys do?" they were asked.

"We're law students at Penn," they both responded simultaneously with no preplanning or prior agreement.

When Phil was asked what the condoms were that he had taken out of his trouser pocket, he responded, "Ask your mother; she would know!"

Amir was bracing for the punch, kick, or baton strike he thought would surely follow. It didn't, but he and Phil were led to their respective cells. As the seemingly normal-looking officer was escorting Amir to his cell, he couldn't resist the temptation of asking the officer, "With all due respect, Officer, why are you doing this? We both know I haven't broken any laws!"

The cop calmly replied, with a wry smile, "It's cold tonight; by bringing you guys in, I get a chance to keep warm in the precinct for a couple of hours!"

Typically, you'd be placed in a cell with two to four real criminals. One disgustingly filthy toilet and no toilet paper rounded out the scene. After four, five, or six hours, you'd be let go—no phone call, no apology. This happened to him on several occasions. Many other young blacks and Latinos and some whites experienced the same!

Ye of Little Faith

The atmosphere was austere at Temple of Islam, Muhammad's Mosque No. 6 or 7 or 12. It was simply and sparsely furnished, but on the wall, there would always be a small framed photo of the Lamb, the Honorable Elijah Muhammad, the little soft-spoken man from Georgia, wearing his kufi with stars and crescents on it, always a cross with the words "Slavery, Suffering, and Death" around it. There was also a star and crescent with the words "Freedom, Justice, and Equality."

The message was clear! He admired the discipline and organizational skills of these clean-shaven, bow-tie-wearing, sharp-dressing men. Shouts and affirmations of "Make it plain!" "Teach!" "Expose that beast!" and "Take your time, brother minister" would be heard as the minister spoke. Christian ministers were "that lying preacher" and "that chicken-bone-eating preacher." "You believe that the white man lied to you about everything but God?" Of course, men and women would be separated. He already knew that Muslims and Jews, among others, did that at their respective houses of worship. Everyone would be searched for weapons before entry. The brothers in the Nation had to sell copies of *Muhammad Speaks* and bean pies. He liked both! The Fruit of Islam (FOI) was impressive. Those brothers seemed sharp and disciplined. They were the paramilitary wing of the Nation. They, among other things, provided security for the NOI.

The articles in *Muhammad Speaks* (*Speaks*) were often well written, he felt, and timely. The cartoons were often very critical and unflattering toward African Americans and their lifestyles. Gambling, drinking, too much partying, fratricide, and not working were all soundly criticized. "The black man is the original man." "The white man is the devil, grafted/developed by an evil black scientist, Dr. Yakub!" "The Lamb was taught by God/Allah, who came in the person of Master Farrad Muhammad." "The Bible is the poison book." "The white man's time is up!" Their message of pride and independence and self-reliance struck a chord in him. (He didn't believe the white man was the devil, however.) Other groups had origin stories and creation myths. Some seemed quite fantastical—Romulus and Remus, for instance, and the origins of ancient Egyptian gods. Why shouldn't African Americans? The red-fez-wearing Moorish Americans had a different take on things. National identity. "You should not be known as colored, black, Negro, or Ethiopian," they taught. "You are a descendant of the ancient Moors. You are a Moorish American. You must claim your national identity to get your national rights." Everyone's last name was El or Bey. Men wore red fezes, women red scarves. They weren't as popular or as well known as the Nation. They taught that the Lamb, years before, had been a member.

"Hey, Professor!"

"Wassup, Doctor?"

"What's going on?"

"Ain't nothing going on but the rent!"

"Nothing shaking but the leaves on the trees, and they wouldn't be shaking if it weren't for the breeze!"

"Just trying to keep my dick hard in the wicked world of the white man, brother!"

"Going to the mixer tonight at the college?"

"I may check it out."

"Bringing your queen?"

"I don't bring sand to the beach, brother, or oil to the gas station!"

"See you around eight or nine then?"

With those words, Amir and Tarik agreed to meet later at the mixer. Amir and some of his friends tried to turn the college into a real campus even though it was clearly a commuter school. They often stayed around the campus long after the last class, into the evening. They often hid at the college until the mixers started rather than go home and come back. There might be some foxes there, and they didn't have to pay to get in if they stayed around and just mixed in with the crowd. Another frequent activity for the guys was going to hear various famous or well-known militants speak. Amir and Omar had heard Dr. Ron Maulana Karenga, from California, of the US organization speak at the Church of the Advocate in North Philly. Dr. Karenga of course was the creator of Kwanzaa. On stage, he had two bodyguards positioned on either side of him, armed with crossbows! Amir had missed Huey's (Huey P. Newton of the Black Panther Party) lecture for some reason. Walt Palmer, a local nationalist and scholar, lectured frequently, as did Playthel Benjamin. Of course, Cecil was leading marches around Girard College as part of his attempt to break the will of Stephen Girard so that black male orphans could be admitted. Amir's sister, Melinda, sometimes joined the marchers.

The Cafeteria, or What's Your Bag?

A visit to the cafeteria at CCP, housed in what was formerly Snellenberg's Department Store (the escalator was still there in the lobby and in use, as were the elevators), was educational. A series of large round tables and vending machines constituted the cafeteria. Students generally sat at the table that reflected what bag they were in, so that there were light-bright tables, militant/nationalist tables, white tables, party people tables, and a few diverse ones.

Amir and his group comprised a diverse table. Usually, he and his friends weren't so easily classified. They were black, white, South Asian, male, and female. Phil, a bit older than most and quite intelligent, was part militant movement and part con man, ripping off the system when desired. He was an interesting guy. Sometimes, he would go to John Wanamaker's Department Store to liberate some goods with White Mary, assuming, usually correctly, that store security would watch him as White Mary liberated items! They would then return to the college and divide up and sell their booty. Upon the change of seasons, Phil would usually travel to a good restaurant, enter the coatroom, and liberate someone's nice overcoat! He was an excellent shoplifter and thief, bold and quick.

Brother Tarik looked more Middle Eastern than stereotypically black, with his prominent hook nose, and had been dubbed "the militant from Nob Hill" because of his obvious middle-class background and attendance at expensive universities across the country. He was always carrying and reading a book and was supposedly supermilitant. Tarik had a really weak rap, however, his basic line being, "Miss, miss, can I go with you?"

Amir and Omar would admit with a smile that they were each a combination of elitist, nationalist, pseudointellectual, and ladies' man. Ron, a.k.a. Super Nigger or Flash, after Flash Gordon, was always educating young ladies with his album collection and some books. He was a real man! All you had to do was ask him, and he'd tell you so! Mike, from a nice middle-class West Philly family, was cool and not very political. He was painfully shy, but he had a reason. SaRon also thought he was a ladies' man and a raconteur and bon vivant. White Mary was cool. She wasn't particularly attractive but fun and was Phil's liberation partner. They worked well together. Jimmy Vinson was a very nice, nerdy guy, quite intelligent, who wore baggy, ill-fitting clothes.

It was Summer and time for Omega by the Sea, the annual ball or gala given by Omega Psi Phi Fraternity in Atlantic City (AC), New Jersey, every year. Amir and some high school buddies had been going, on and off, every year since becoming high school juniors. None of them had pledged Omega. That was not the point. There would be lots of young African Americans, particularly chicks, there! There would be the parties, often held in hotel/motel rooms. They wanted to go. Whoever could borrow their dad's or mom's ride would do so. Not having much cash, they would all pile into a single hotel or motel room, once fooling the hotel clerk by pretending that just one or two persons would occupy the room. Some would have to sleep on the floor.

"Is Muhammad ibn Abdullah your real name?" the nervous middle-aged white female desk clerk had asked.

"Of course!" would be the typical response. They would state they were from the Sudan or Morocco or Mauretania, depending on the mood. Hanging out on the boardwalk was fun, seeing and being seen, lots of honeys walking around, some dressed for the beach. "That girl has a great future behind her!" "That must be jelly 'cause jam don't shake like that" was said about the shapely young lady in the pink terrycloth hot pants as she passed the fellows strutting her stuff.

This was precasino AC, and folks actually used the beaches there. Of course, blacks typically went to Chicken Bone Beach, the portion of the beach where the soul people hung out. Whether that had started by choice or as a result of de jure segregation, he was never quite sure. In those days, Kentucky Avenue was electric, a several-block area near the AC Boardwalk, where Club Harlem, restaurants, bars, and discotheques abounded. That was where the soul people partied! Only an occasional white person would be seen. He was always reminded of the night, alone, while hanging out on Kentucky Avenue he heard girls screaming at one particular club and saying the name "Squirrel" over and over. The Chi-Lites were appearing, and Squirrel evidently was their favorite group member!

It was interesting, he thought, segregation was both good and bad! Rather than be overlooked, ignored, marginalized, or mistreated by whites, blacks had developed their own counter/alternative cultures where one could fully participate. There were black-owned and operated banks, insurance companies, news-papers, magazines, funeral homes, catering outfits, construction companies, and so on. Blacks, at least some, had a sense of pride, a sense of destiny, of agency, of dreams. A golden era was in place, he felt!

While lying on blankets on the beach at AC with Ahmed, Rita, Never, and Omar that beautiful summer day, Amir's eyes had started to slowly open from the nap he was taking. As he looked around, he could not help but notice that Rita and Never were walking together toward the pier, sort of under the boardwalk. Rita's man, Ahmed, was still sleeping. Although he felt guilty for continuously watching them. Amir did. They were passionately kissing under the boardwalk in the shadows. Eventually, they both were submerged in the water. It didn't take a rocket scientist to figure out what they were doing as the bubbles rose to the surface. Damn, Rita was being unfaithful to him as her man slept a few yards away on the beach—just like the popular song sung by the Drifters, "Under the Boardwalk!"

A Way out of No Way

The Dude had an eye for the ladies and several of them found him quite charming, which caused some consternation to SaRon, who often quipped, "that damn dude" when he felt Omar had beat his time with some girl. Omar was an avid reader, consuming several newspapers and periodicals a day. He was conversant on many topics—for example, the stock market, politics, history, religion, and music, among others. And, boy, could he turn a phrase! "white people generally succeed in this country because of the system, blacks in spite of the system." "We, black people, are at war; there are lulls in the fighting, but make no mistake, we are at war!"

They would spend much road time together—Philly, Los Angeles, New York City, Camden, Atlantic City, and Washington, DC, among other locales. They would stay at, among other elite hotels over the years, the Beverly Wilshire Hotel in Beverly Hills and the Pierre Hotel in New York City. They would ride in chauffeured limos together and on subways and buses, be in car accidents together, have good and bad times, experience tragedies, and know each other's lovers and heartbreaks, family members, and strengths and weaknesses. They would share many meals together and many philosophical discussions.

There was the time for instance that Omar called late one evening to advise Amir, asleep in his Center City bachelor pad, that he was in the company of two stallions, who were models, and that he needed a little assistance. Amir went over immediately. Or the time they double-dated to AC and were walking along the boardwalk on a beautiful spring day with two fine women in tow to the envious stares of many they passed. At times, they commiserated about how they both had lost sisters to murder. They talked about what the future portended, what old age would inevitably bring, and many other topics.

Hips, Lips, and Fingertips (Cont'd)

Young and single and loving to mingle, Amir occasionally set goals in the female department: a girl with huge breasts, a girl with naturally long beautiful hair, one with red hair, one with big stockings,[8] one with an accent (he loved foreign accents), one with blue or hazel eyes, a natural blonde, a natural redhead. He kept a big, laminated paper map of the world on his wall in his one-bedroom bachelor pad and put pins in the countries where women were from that he had made love with. He particularly liked those British accents coming from women of color! Sure, he had always liked girls, but he was a bit shy growing up. During puberty, he read books about

---

[8] A girl with nice, shapely legs, not thin/skinny.

sex, bought *Playboy* magazines, and so on. He'd never forget the time Mom had found one under his bed in his room while she was cleaning it. She was cool, however; she didn't embarrass him. She simply smiled and handed it back to him, while saying, "I found this."

He learned that some older women thought he was good-looking. "The girls are going to like you when you grow up," Cousin Whip's attractive wife had told him with a smile. Another cousin's wife used to always come up to his room alone when he was a little boy, when she and her husband visited the house. She was attractive and slender with freckles and a pixie haircut but an adult. She would rub her fingers in his hair and tell him the girls were going to love him! Maybe she would take advantage of him? A win-win, he thought. His adolescent sexuality was raging. She was cute and an adult, so if they were discovered doing something, she would get blamed not he! She never did bust a move, however.

The very first female to awaken his nascent sexuality was Ms. Vance in elementary school, a teacher, the color of café au lait, with mahogany-brown hair, which she often wore pulled back in a ponytail. She wore eyeglasses and appeared quite intelligent. Amir would always remember Ms. Vance typically wore black high-heeled pumps and stockings with seams in the middle. They complemented her pleated skirts. As he watched her walk down the hallway, the pleats moved in syncopated motion as the high heels pulled the muscles in her calves! She was classy and sexy. He knew nothing about sex at that point, but he knew Ms. Vance affected him. How to get her alone, so he could talk to her? He purposely acted up in her class one day, got an after-school detention, and was finally alone with Ms. Vance! He turned from the blackboard where he had been writing "I will not talk in class" one hundred times at the behest of Ms. Vance and stated, "Ms. Vance, let's get married!"

Shocked, her response was "Amir, you're a little boy and shouldn't talk like that."

He then said, "I drink my milk, and I will grow!"

Ms. Vance explained that she was a married woman, to which, he said, "Then get a divorce!" Well, at least he tried! He would never forget the incident or Ms. Vance.

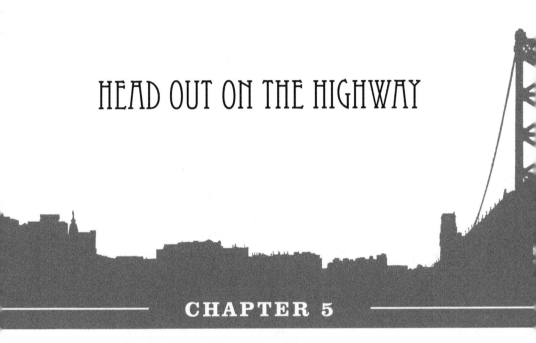

HEAD OUT ON THE HIGHWAY

CHAPTER 5

Amir was just casually walking along Market Street on that pleasant Autumn day, feeling the same old ennui, when he heard the car horn beep. The exhaust rumble of the white Triumph TR6 sounded good to him. He and some of his friends liked sports cars, particularly the British sports cars—Austin Healey, MG, Jaguar, Triumph, Sunbeam, and so on. Most didn't own one yet, but they knew about and could identify them on sight. He had never seen Phil driving before! But there he was, pushing a white Triumph TR6!

"Want to go to New York?" he asked.

"Brother, I only got twenty bucks on me," Amir had replied, with a shrug of his shoulders.

Phil said, "I got ten. Let's go!"

Exactly at that point, Amir noticed that the outside rearview mirror on the passenger's side was broken and loose. "What the hell, let's go!" He was learning that some of life's best times weren't necessarily planned but impromptu. Phil only drove at two speeds, fast and faster!

It was the quickest run from Philly to NYC he had ever experienced. Occasionally, Phil would ask Amir to turn his head and look for traffic as the mirror was of no use. What an adventure! Once in NYC, they hung out in Washington Square Park for a while, with the folk singers, hippies, militants, pimps, hustlers, poets, chess players, and hos. They went to some clubs and bars and ended up at Small's Paradise in Harlem. In those days, it was rumored that someone big in the pharmaceutical trade owned Small's. As he was sitting at the bar sipping his usual ginger ale, on the lookout for some foxes, suddenly Phil came running from the back, shouting, "Let's go! Let's go!"

He ran with Phil to the TR6. He thought he had heard a gunshot or two as they were running to the car.

"What happened, brother?" he asked Phil.

"I'll tell you later. Right now, we have to get the hell out of here!"

Made sense …

Those in the inner circle believed that Phil probably had been a member of the Nation and maybe some other groups as well. Could it have been some old enemies? Some dispute over a girl? Over some money? A real or imagined slight of some kind? They flew out of Harlem. Later that evening, they returned to Philly. Phil, a Gemini, was many things, but boring wasn't one of them!

As he was enjoying a cheeseburger and fries one beautiful spring day in the restaurant on Market Street near Seventeenth, Amir noticed Muhammad Ali, sans his entourage, crossing the street. What's he doing here? he wondered. Then he remembered the Champ was now living in Cherry Hill, New Jersey. When Ali entered the restaurant, he became excited. It really got interesting when he sat down near him! He had to get his attention.

"As Salaamu Alaikum," he said as he smiled at the Champ.

Ali flashed a warm smile back and said, "Wa Alaikum As Salaam, brother."

The first thing he observed was that TV did not do him justice. He appeared much bigger than on TV. He also was "pretty," as Ali had proclaimed many times, meaning that he had this beautiful coloring and skin tone. They conversed for ten to fifteen minutes. No one else in the restaurant seemed to know who Ali was at first, but after ten minutes or so, waitresses and customers started to stare at and recognize him and head toward where they were seated. He then bade farewell to "the Greatest" and let him do his thing.

He would never forget this chance encounter with one of his heroes and at that time, the most well-known, recognized person on earth! He had been told that Ali had, of course, a very nice house in Cherry Hill, New Jersey, and that he was neighbors with a certain Major, a smallish black man who always wore a cowboy hat and was, according to the media, in the pharmaceutical business. Sometime later, a person or persons unknown would enter his Cherry Hill home and execute everyone found therein except for a little boy who managed to escape. Gangsters, pimps, hustlers, con men, athletes, and folks in pharmaceutical sales were not foreign to Amir and his friends. If one spent as much time in the streets, clubs, and at parties as they did, one was bound to rub elbows with them.

The crew was driving all the way to Pittsburgh, Pennsylvania, in Amir's car, of course. Only he and SaRon had rides at the time. SaRon had an Oldsmobile Toronado, one of the first mass-produced full-sized, front-wheel-drive cars on the market in America. He had demurred about driving, of course, probably because he was so cheap! Gas and tolls cost money. Real Philadelphians thought that Philly was the only happening place in Pennsylvania. It was a long ride from Philly to Pittsburgh, about three hundred miles as the crow flies. As they motored along that beautiful winter afternoon, Omar casually mentioned that he had an office in Pittsburgh, meaning he had a girlfriend and lover there. Brother Omar had offices in several locales—NYC; Detroit; Easton, Pennsylvania; Harrisburg, Pennsylvania; and Boston, Massachusetts.

Amir couldn't remember the last time he had been to Pittsburgh—maybe when he was real young, taken by his parents. Mike volunteered he had a cousin who attended Pitt. Tarik was quiet for the most part. He was recovering from a broken heart. He had a penchant for dancers, and this member of the Dance Theatre of Harlem had broken his heart. He had been cuckolded. She had been caught with another man!

"Damn, bro. That's rough," they had all agreed.

Of course, Tarik was seeing someone else also. But they all supported the old double standard.

"You'll find another akhi!" he was assured.

"You're a cunning linguist, I've heard, boy," added Omar with a smile, upon which everyone guffawed.

Should be plenty of honeys at the affair they were headed to, they all thought.

"These bitches is killing me," Mike had interjected with a half smile.

"What happened, akhi?" asked Amir.

"I took dis girl to dinner, and afterward, she wouldn't give it up!"

SaRon stated, "Treat the ladies like hos and the hos like ladies, and they'll love you, boy!"

"Well, brother, did you talk shit, swap spit?" asked Omar.

"No, I just asked her to give it up," replied Mike.

"Damn, brother," responded Tarik. "You have to rap to these honeys if you want the panties to come off."

"Develop some game, akhi."

"Boy, you know you been paying for it," retorted SaRon.

Everyone laughed.

The hotel was in the distance, finally, after all that driving.

"Let's have some fun," Amir urged. "Let's put Brother Omar in the center, form a phalanx around him, and act like bodyguards when we get to the hotel." They did. It was fun. The looks and expressions of surprise, shock, and fear on the faces of the hotel guests and employees were worth it. They would all go to the restroom and have a big laugh. The affair was jumping, lots of women, a live band, good food, zaats boogaloo!

When Amir looked up from the table to the dance floor, Omar was doing the funky Broadway, Tarik was doing the rock, and SaRon was attempting the cha cha with a stutter step. Cries of party over here and party over there could be heard as well as "the roof, the roof, the roof is on fire" throughout the night!

In a sort of anteroom to the main ballroom, there was a big punch bowl filled with cocaine. Many partook, but as far as he could tell, none of the crew did. They weren't into drugs.

It sort of reminded Amir of LA. Once in Beverly Hills at a supermarket early in the day, an acquaintance of Omar's picked up a big-legged white girl and was taking her back to his hotel room.

As the group of them were walking down the street, she asked, "You fellas got any Coke? I got some friends, and they like to party too!"

Of course, Amir, SaRon, and Omar had no drugs. They didn't know about Omar's acquaintance. Amir thought to himself, *Guess I won't be partying then. The only Coke I have is in a bottle! Shame, that girl was fine!*

One of his early life lessons would be that the bad guys weren't always as bad as depicted and the good guys were not always as good. Amir seemed to have the capacity to communicate with a wide range of people from many walks of life, the ability to be in it but not of it. So he and his friends could go to parties where others were doing drugs and not do drugs themselves. They could listen to stories from people who had injured or harmed others and appear nonjudgmental. Their mission was usually focused and singular—adventure, fun, travel, and meeting some foxes and some honeys to get those digits! They wanted to romance the ladies and rub elbows with celebrities, life in the fast lane.

Hotel, Motel, Holiday Inn

The Palm Motel was on Admiral Wilson Boulevard in Camden, New Jersey. For about a three- to four-year period, he took so many girls there to make love, he felt that there should've been a wing there dedicated to him with a plaque with his name on it! After meeting them at discotheques, clubs, and so on, if they were so inclined, he and they would often end up at the Palm.

Sometimes, it was just sex. Other times, there would be actual lovemaking. At times, there would be something in between the two. Often, he wasn't even sure of their names and maybe they of his. This was the era of free love, and he and his buddies felt they should get all they could. He was discriminating, to a degree. He didn't subscribe to the "eight to eighty, blind, crippled, and crazy" mantra often quoted in those days. He didn't have a set type relative to height, size, coloring, hair length, and so on. They had to be appealing to him on some level, however. Lighter-skinned, darker-skinned, long hair, short hair, petite, tall, and thirty-six, twenty-four, thirty-six were not the only measurements that qualified. Some had huge breasts. Some had pretty long hair, their own or store bought. Others had short, sexy hairstyles. Some plump or rubenesque women were very sexy or attractive. Some girls had back, or junk in their trunk. Hourglass figures were nice but not necessary. Amir had learned that a woman's stats didn't really relate to how good a lover she would be. He grew to believe that was more of a mental or attitude thing. He had been with numerous women with great bodies who were not good lovers!

As the sun filtered into the room that Sunday morning, he looked over at the woman in the bed with him. The sheet was just below her perfectly round butt, exposing the curvature of her lower back. A beautiful sight. Her medium-brown skin was glistening in the sunlight. A vision to behold. He couldn't remember her name. He did remember that they had had quite an enjoyable lovemaking session the night before. Amir had learned that it was important to try to please the woman, not just himself, and he usually tried to do so. He would drive her home and then return to his apartment often in the wee hours of the morning as others were getting up.

Bobby Womack's "Daylight Is Gonna Catch Me Up Again" became his theme song for this period in his young life. They were mostly African American. There would occasionally be a white or other type of girl. It wasn't that he didn't respect them, but he was a young man who desired frequent sex. One of his rules was to never say, "I love you," if he didn't mean it just to get them in bed. Once in bed, he really tried to be a good lover, sometimes successfully, sometimes not so much. He had learned that you can't please them all. Of course, he had also learned some women were not good lovers. Some just lay there no matter what you did! Others overresponded; some, you knew they were having a good time! Sometimes he was using them, sometimes they him. Sometimes mutual use.

By the Sweat of Your Brow

As he stood in the adult store talking with Little Johnny about the part-time job he was being hired for, he couldn't help but think that Little Johnny was straight out of central casting. An Italian American, a Sicilian, in fact, he was short in stature but tough looking. He had dark hair, a cleft in his chin, and brown eyes. He owned and ran a series of adult stores in Philly and a few nightclubs. He had a big home in Jersey with a pool and always had two nice late-model cars.

He had an attractive wife and a sexy girlfriend. Obviously street smart and tough, he had a circle of other Italian *friends*. "Hey, if the police raid the joint, call this number, and we'll have you out in a few hours," Little Johnny was explaining to him.

The US Supreme Court had not ruled on what constituted pornography in those days, and such places were sometimes raided. "Okay," he had replied. He liked Johnny, you didn't ask, but you knew what and who he was! If Johnny wasn't in the mob, there was no mob! The job, however, was perfect for a college student. Part-time, they paid in cash, and he would be the cashier, working the register. During daily lulls, he could study. Adult movies, magazines, creams, lotions, gels, black leather products, dildos, ben wa balls, cock rings, butt plugs, vibrators, edible panties, inflatable dolls, handcuffs, masks, vaginas (to be filled with hot water) in different colors, whips, chains, a human-style foreman with a clinched fist for fisting, and more were all for sale. No questions asked. The store never was raided on his watch, but it was a sex education for him. There were products for heterosexuals, gays, lesbians, necrophiliacs, bestiality fans, sadomasochists, pedophiles, and others by section. He would play this mental game as customers (most often men) entered the store, guessing which section they'd head for. He got to be pretty good at it. Almost invariably, the more conservative-looking guys, with suits, attaché cases, and close-cropped hair, were the biggest freaks!

His and Little Johnny's paths would cross again years later when Omar would become the DJ and overall manager of the Hippopotamus, a big, New York–style disco club in Center City, located in Sansom Village on Sansom Street between Twentieth and Twenty-First. He and Omar were both living in Center City in those days in their bachelor pads. Young, single, working, and well dressed, they, for a time, truly were princes of the city. They would go to clubs in Center City and not have to get in the sometimes long queues, waiting for admittance. They also often did not have to pay the cover charges usually asked at discos.

"Just go in, fellas," they were usually told.

Omar, in the music and club business, tended to know the other club managers and owners, especially in Center City.

As a group, he, Omar, Tarik, SaRon, and Mike, therefore, had carte blanche on the benefits of the nightlife scene in Center City. Amir would usually go to the Hippo, hang out at the DJ booth with Omar, and when the Hippo closed, they'd make the rounds of the club circuit in Center City—the Funky Donkey, the Cave, Casablanca, the Electric Factory, the 4-2 Club, Fields, and others.

The honeys often congregated around the DJ booth at the Hippo, a plus for him and Omar. He would meet Lionel Ritchie and the Commodores, Rufus and Chaka Khan, Betty Davis, and Cuba Gooding, of the Main Ingredient, among others, there. A young Chaka Khan was gorgeous and incredibly sexy. Omar typically booked the acts. Little Johnny was smart enough to have many black staff, bouncers, bartenders, waitresses, and, of course, DJ Omar for his disco, whose patrons were mostly black.

When his fellow Italian and other associates would come around for meetings, they would go to Johnny's office in the basement and close the door. He and Omar didn't know what they were discussing, nor did they want to know! Johnny's friends had names like Fat Nick and the Hunchback. Johnny and his Sicilian friends sometimes referred to each other as "sigis." He encouraged Amir and Omar to use the term also. They didn't feel comfortable doing so, however.

He would always remember and be touched by Johnny's comments to him one evening when, as he was sitting at one of the bars in the Hippo, nursing a ginger ale, probably looking depressed, Johnny approached him and said, "I heard about your sister. Let me ask you a question; was the man who killed her black or white?"

Amir replied, "Black."

At that point, Johnny responded, "I'm sorry to hear that. I can't send my people into a black neighborhood looking for a black guy. But you know what I would do if he were white, right?"

Among those he recognized who stopped by the Hippo and engaged Johnny in conversation were a couple of Philadelphia City Council persons, several high-profile Philly attorneys, and some black and white civil rights and labor union leaders.

Miho was beautiful, Japanese and black, Omar had explained to him. Her dad was a black American GI who had been stationed in Japan, her mother Japanese, of course. Omar had spotted her walking past the Hippo and had chased after her. He had pulled her. Omar could be deadly with the ladies. Somehow, he had gotten the digits, and they were a couple now. She dressed very fashionably and had style and class. She was a show stopper, all right. Omar seemed to love having showstoppers on his arm—black, mixed race, white, or otherwise. He had been accused of having a penchant for redbones, which he vehemently denied. Certainly, he would admit that they had to be fine, had to be foxes. Over the years, he would meet and be aware of almost all of Omar's great loves: Miho, Shahida, Trina, and Pat, among others. And Omar would his. Trina, a nursing student who actually lived in a kind of nunnery in Center City, would do him wrong. Amir had seen her, quite by accident, getting into the Dodge Charger of his neighbor from the old neighborhood. To tell or not to tell? That was the question. He had grown up around the corner from Pete, knew his mother and father, remembered when he had set off for Howard University. But Omar was his boy! He would wait for the right time and then tell him. While loyal to Omar, he didn't relish the idea of being the bearer of such bad tidings. When he did, Omar thanked him and never mentioned it again.

Laissez le Bon Temps Rouler

The SOS Band's hit "Just Be Good to Me" was starting to play as Amir walked into the club inside the big hotel on City Line Avenue. Great, he liked the song; it was almost like having your own theme music, like some of the black superheroes in the current crop of so-called black exploitation movies. It was a big club with a couple of bars and tables and a big dance floor. The lighting was dark. It was a mixed club. Amir had caught an attitude while waiting in the queue to get in. He had observed the guy on the door asking some blacks who clearly looked over twenty-one for proof of age IDs. White associates working at various other clubs and discotheques had told him and Omar how sometimes club owners or managers wanted to discourage too many blacks from entering their mixed clubs. They feared this would reduce the numbers of white patrons. So they hassled some at the door. So when Amir walked up in turn, he declared to the guy on the door, "I'm over twenty-one, you know it, and I'm not showing you anything!" He was admitted with no hassle.

He spotted the girl with the classy but tight brown dress on a few minutes later. She was dressed in expensive yet sexy clothes. She was even wearing pearls. About five feet seven, she had a good body, great legs, and a nice booty, not overly large but nicely shaped. Amir didn't like too much behind. "Buffalo butts," "troglodytes," "Bertha Butt" and "the Butt Sisters," he called them. Some brothers loved those giant behinds that some sisters had. Not Omar and Amir. This girl had long, sexy legs; a small waist; and medium-sized but perky-looking breasts. The high-heeled pumps she was wearing were sharp. Her toes were exposed. The color of her toenail polish was coordinated with the rest of her outfit. Her movements were almost catlike. *Maybe she's a dancer*, thought Amir. As he sat at the bar observing her and drinking his usual ginger ale, he noted that she sat at a table with two female friends. They were cute also. He thought she was checking him out also but wasn't sure. He wouldn't watch her for too long. He didn't want to make her nervous or uncomfortable. Yes, he'd make a move.

As she was walking back to her table from the ladies' room, Amir intercepted her. "Hi, my name's Amir. I don't want to hold you, but I must ask you a question, if I may."

She smiled curiously, and after a pause, Amir asked, "Your toenail polish, is it acrylic or enamel?" She giggled. It had worked; he could now start gaming her.

"Do you always go around staring at women's feet?" she asked.

"Only when they're as stare-worthy as yours," he responded. "You have good-looking feet," he added.

She said, "Thank you."

"Join me for a drink," he suggested.

She did. They sat at the bar and conversed for about an hour. She was intelligent and articulate, and their conversation flowed. She also had jokes.

"Do you have a foot fetish?" she asked.

"Proud to say I do," he answered. Amir got the digits before he said, "I must be leaving now," and added, "It was a real pleasure meeting you." He said to himself while walking away, "I think I'll call this girl." He wouldn't get his hopes up too high, however. This had happened before. He'd get the digits, but every time he called, she was not available for a date or she was busy or the number you were given was no good.

The club scene was weird. Folks got dressed up and well groomed, often looking sexy and dressed provocatively to be in a coed environment. Many, however, were not out to or open to meeting someone of the opposite sex. "I came out to talk to my girlfriend," "I am tired," "My feet hurt," and "I only dance slow with my man" were all among the responses a guy might hear when asking a woman to dance. In fairness, it must be acknowledged that guys were often accused of holding up the wall also. Why? The club scene was sometimes described as a meat market.

What contributed to the dynamics? The presence of sometimes many attractive guys and gals? The competiveness of such a situation? The posturing some felt the need to do? The inflated egos of some? The poor self-esteem of others? Simple laws of supply and demand?

If you only went out to dance and you could find people to dance with, many great evenings could be had. But if you were on the prowl and dancing was really only incidental, like with Omar, Amir, SaRon, and most of their associates, who were usually hunting, you would have good and bad nights.

"The pickin's are slim tonight, bro. My hand is starting to look better and better."

"Is this the SPCA? So many dogs here!"

"Catch you later, brothers. I have a pressing engagement."

"Excuse me, gentlemen. I have to make a nighttime deposit in the fuzzy bank."

It seemed, however, for one reason or another, relationships with women they met in clubs rarely developed into real relationships in Amir's experience.

It was interesting, however, one night when Amir and SaRon were hanging out at a popular disco on City Line Avenue, they were both getting frustrated. Each had asked several girls to dance at the predominantly black club.

"My feet hurt," "I came out to talk with my friends," "Maybe later" were among the rejections they both received.

Frustrated, they crossed the street and went to a predominantly white club. They weren't in there for more than fifteen minutes when a young lady who happened to be white approached the two of them and asked, "Would one of you guys like to dance?" Interesting, they got no play at the black spot but got some play at the white spot.

Amir knew from listening to the old heads that Philly was also historically a big jazz town. Some famous jazz artists, like Grover Washington Jr., were Philadelphians or had spent considerable time in Philly. The list was long—Billie Holiday, Art Tatum, Bill Doggett, Jimmy Smith, John Coltrane, and Dizzy Gillespie, among others. So from time to time, Amir would make the rounds of a few jazz clubs he had discovered, located in Center City. They were usually small and dimly lit. The crowd was older, more sophisticated. Some patrons belonged to Philly's black elite. Furs and pearls were often displayed. There would be no dancing, but some of the music really was good. Several times, he stumbled upon jazz singer Arthur Prysock or Arthur and his brother, Red Prysock, who played sax. Arthur's baritone voice and good looks seemed to work magic on the older ladies as he sang "I Worry 'Bout You," "When You Walked in the Room," "When I Fall in Love," and other hits of his. They were of another generation. But their sophistication and hipness was attractive to him. Good-looking women often hung around Arthur Prysock at the clubs. He had even sung a beer commercial, "Let It Be Lowenbrau." Prysock was always in the shadow, he felt, of Billy Eckstein, so he never got really large but was known among jazz aficionados. Amir was usually alone when he visited the jazz spots; it was a change of pace. This jazz scene was cool.

He thought it harkened back to the old days in Philly's black culture, when color, hair grade, education, and income were stratified, with light-skinned folks with good hair being on top. Certain privileges and benefits flowed therefrom, in employment, housing, education, number of choices of available boyfriends or girlfriends, and so on.

The still somewhat existent tension between the brown-skinned and darker black women and the redbones or high yella ones was proof of this. She's light, bright, and damn near white was sometimes heard, as was she's dark, but pretty or good-looking. Many brothers seemed to have a preference for the redbones. Omar was accused of this and was often protesting that it wasn't so and that his history disproved this charge. Amir didn't really have a color preference. They had to be attractive though with good bodies. He was drawn to exotic-looking women whether black, white, Asian, or Hispanic. Hair could be long, short, or somewhere in between. He found accents of almost any kind very sexy. He hadn't dated an Asian girl yet. He wanted to try one! Some were *fine*! They seemed to prefer white guys, however.

Philly's Fairmount park was purportedly the largest city park in America. Parts of it was located in North and West Philly, as well as West Oak Lane, Wissahickon, and other areas. George's Hill was a hill in Fairmount Park, a kind of Lover's Lane. The view from George's Hill was nice. On a clear night, the night sky could be beautiful. Amir, like many young men and women, would occasionally drive to the Hill.

"Girl, are you gonna be a Chesterfield [a once popular brand of cigarette that was advertised as "satisfying"] and satisfy or a Camel [another popular cigarette with a camel as a logo] and walk?" he had said with a broad smile to the young tenderoni in the front seat of his car. They would indulge in heavy petting in the parlance of the time, not actually have sex, but of course some did, as you could tell from the parked cars with engines off swaying or rocking!

Years later, the Plateau, a location also in Fairmount Park and memorialized in song by actor / rap artist Will Smith (a Philadelphian), in one of his songs, "Summertime," became a gathering place initially for young fraternity and sorority members and others who would picnic, drive around, and hang out around the nice spacious outdoor area very self-consciously, seeing and being seen in their casual best. Later, nonfraternity/sorority members started attending as well. At some point, he understood an undesirable element started coming and causing problems.

Nationalists/Revolutionaries

"It's as cold as wolf pussy in here!" Phil had uttered with a half-smile as he entered the house they shared in West Philly one dark autumn evening, rubbing his genital area with his right hand. Another philosophical discussion ensued almost immediately.

"I can't stand those Jews!"

Unlike most African Americans, who seemed to view Jews as just another subgroup of white people, black nationalists, in solidarity with their Palestinian brothers and Muslims generally, as well as other revolutionaries around the globe felt an obligation to express some hostility toward Zionism and Israel particularly. Amir had read about Deir Yassin, the Hagana, Urgun, and Stern gangs, the blowing up of the King David Hotel, the UN Partition Resolution, and so on. Besides, common wisdom of the time declared that Jewish merchants weighed their thumbs on the scales at the neighborhood butcher shop in the ghetto and were often slum lords.

Weren't they a buffer between blacks and real white people in an American context? Hadn't they been heavily involved in the international slave trade? Conversely, weren't they smart? Weren't many of the best lawyers Jewish? "Have your Jew call my Jew" was a common expression, as was "Jewing someone down" on a price or cost.

Many public school teachers at that time were Jewish. In fact, some of Amir's favorite teachers were. Years later, Amir would reflect this hadn't been real hate, maybe prejudice, maybe ignorance, but not hate. Amir, Omar, Phil, Tarik, Ahmed, and others considered themselves more "Nationalists" than "civil rights activists" or "integrationists." So Israel was referred to as "Occupied Palestine" or the "Zionist Settler State of Israel." They sometimes referred to Jews as "Yahoodys" from the Arabic. Malcolm X was much more popular than Martin Luther King Jr., "Black Power" more than "We

Shall Overcome" and nonviolence. W. E. B. DuBois, Noble Drew Ali, and Marcus Garvey preferable to Booker T. Washington, fighting back and self-defense more than nonviolence. They didn't wish to physically harm whites or deprive them of anything but had a kind of mistrust of whites and saw a need for a reexamination and redefining of who their enemies and friends were.

Nationalists and scientific brothers and sisters generally, had to have read and be familiar (or pretend to be) with certain books and writings: *The Autobiography of Malcolm X, Message to the Black Man in America, The Miseducation of the Negro, The Invisible Man, The Wretched of the Earth, Mao's Red Book, The Pedagogy of the Oppressed, Khadaffy's Green Book, The Communist Manifesto, Before the* Mayflower, *The Philadelphia Negro, The Spook Who Sat by the Door, The Souls of Black Folk,* and the *Invisible Man,* among others.

Their heroes and sheroes included Harriet Tubman, Nat Turner, Denmark Vesey, Gabriel Prosser, Jomo Kenyatta, Kwame Nkrumah, Patrice Lumumba, Fredrick Douglas, Shaka Zulu, Nelson Mandela, Hannibal, Yaa Asanteewa, the Mahdi of the Sudan, Dead Wood Dick (Nat Love), John Brown, Gabriel Prosser, Charles Leslonde (German Coast rebellion, 1811), Muhammad Ali, Malcolm X, Marcus Garvey, the Honorable Elijah Muhammad, W. E. B. DuBois, Robert F. Williams, Cecil B. Moore, A. Phillip Randolph, Fannie Lou Hammer, Joanne Robinson, Rosa Parks, Angela Davis, Noble Drew Ali, Ahmed Ben Bella of Algeria, Gamal Abdel Nasser of Egypt, and Adam Clayton Powell Jr., among others.

Among required viewing were the films *The Battle of Algiers; Three the Hard Way* with Jim Brown, Jim Kelly, and Fred Williamson; *The Liberation of L. B. Jones; Shaft* and *Shaft in Africa, Omar Muhktar, The Lion of the Desert, The Spook Who Sat by the Door, Lawrence of Arabia,* and years later, *Sankofa* and the TV series *Roots* and *Shaka Zulu,* among others.

Amir was proud of the fact that he was working for an

organization named FOLK (Freedom, Opportunity, Liberation, and Knowledge), located on Point Breeze Avenue deep in South Philly. Located in a storefront, they had a breakfast program and taught African American history to neighborhood kids, along with health, nutrition, and good citizenship. A fellow CCP student named Bob had gotten some kind of grant or government funding. Amir was doing something he enjoyed, and he was giving back. The kids seemed to be enjoying it too as they talked about Africa, family, and respect. Each got an African name, listened to music, and learned a little of Africa's glorious past.

The Revolution

The poem "The Revolution Will Not Be Televised" by the Last Poets was, of course, very popular among his contemporaries. Some of them were actually preparing for a violent revolution in America by blacks. At parties, there were deep discussions by the scientific brothers and sisters. Sometimes, there was no dancing but hours' long discussions sitting on the floor with soft drinks, pretzels, and potato chips, debating the merits of various strategies.

"I'm storing can goods for the time the tanks are coming down the street!"

"I've been going to the range."

"I keep my passport up to date!"

Philly, of course, had many civil rights and nationalist groups: the Black Panther Party, the Nation, RAM (the Revolutionary Action Movement), the Weathermen (for white folks), MOVE, the Moorish Science Temple of America, SNCC, CORE, the Urban League, the Black Liberation Army, and the NAACP, among others. Of course, every college/university with an appreciable number of black students had a Black Student Union, including Amir's school.

University of Pennsylvania at one time even had a dorm where almost all the residents were African American, a black dorm!

US Army field jackets, berets, buttons espousing many different causes, red-black-and-green items of many types, dashikis, kufis, garments with African prints (genuine or mass-produced), especially Kente cloth, were all quite the rage. Some wore a fifty-caliber bullet around their necks. One of the coldest buttons Amir ever observed appeared during the Nixon administration and read, "Lee Harvey Oswald, where are you now that we need you?"

When approached in the cafeteria at CCP that afternoon quietly as he was sitting alone at his group's table, Amir was informed he had been drafted into the RAM (Revolutionary Action Movement) organization, to be their political officer! They had watched and studied him and thought he was a good choice. He had no say in the matter, according to the messenger. Further, he explained, he would be tested, given a number of assignments and tasks to prove he was worthy of membership. This caused him some concern. He didn't really know these folks, their philosophy, goals, or plans.

Meanwhile, Leslie, an aspiring attorney, good-looking and very popular with the girls, had been arrested for allegedly trying to poison some of the water drunk by the Philadelphia police force! Amir and Omar were very similar in their analysis of the coming revolution. How could blacks, outnumbered, outgunned, and for the most part untrained really pull off a violent revolution in America? They were not in a colony like Jamaica, Haiti, Kenya, or Algeria. They lived in the belly of the beast! They were outnumbered by whites who were better armed and had shown a propensity for violence against blacks! Tarik was reading Du Bois's *The Souls of Black Folks*. A discussion ensued comparing and contrasting W.E.B.'s analysis of the struggle with Booker T.'s comments in his famous Atlanta Exposition speech.

It's a Family Affair

Amir had come back to his apartment for lunch on that spring Tuesday afternoon. Living so close to his job had its advantages. His workplace was only four blocks from where he lived. As he was eating his egg salad sandwich, the phone rang. It was his basic black landline phone. This was precellular/mobile phone. It was Mom. He became nervous right away.

Something must be wrong. Someone is in trouble or danger! Mom rarely called in the middle of the day. Over the years, Amir's experience had taught him that phone calls late at night or very early in the morning, unless from a lover, usually meant something was wrong. Someone had died or was dying, perhaps was very ill, had had a car accident, and so on.

"Your father is locked up!" Mom said.

Amir was shocked. Dad in jail? His father was a hardworking family man who paid his bills, almost never missed work, and was a solid citizen. Of course, he was a Teamster and must've known sketchy people!

The Philly police were in the habit of harassing black men. Maybe Dad, tooling around town in his deuce and a quarter, had somehow run afoul of the Rizzopo!

"Where do they have him?" Amir asked.

"He's at the Roundhouse," Mom said.

The Roundhouse was the common term used for the Philly police administrative building, largely due to its roundish architecture.

Already dressed in a suit, Amir told Mom, "I'm going right over!"

He drove over to the Roundhouse, probably violating the speed limit! When he inquired about Dad, they thought he was an attorney and asked, "Do you represent him?"

Without hesitation, Amir responded, "Yes." If it would help get information about Dad, why not? He was pleasantly surprised to learn he had been released on his own recognizance (ROR). It made sense, he thought. Dad had no record and was employed and a home owner. The charge had been possession of an illegal firearm!

As soon as he could find a pay phone, he called Dad.

"You're home?" he asked.

"Yes, I'm out," he said.

"What happened?"

"I called the Teamsters," he said.

"When do you have to go back for the arraignment?" asked Amir.

"I don't. The Teamsters told me to not worry about it."

"Wow, that's great, Dad," stated Amir. He let Dad know that he had been worried about him. Amir immediately called Mom and Melinda and gave them the good news.

When Amir was relaxing in his crib that evening, he pondered over the day's events and then felt guilty. Dad had been arrested while driving his deuce and a quarter, probably speeding. The arresting officer claimed he observed a thirty-eight special in the car. Dad did not have a permit to carry.

Amir was feeling guilty because a few months prior, it was he and his sister, Melinda, who had urged Dad to carry a gun if he insisted on traveling around with big wads of cash in his pocket as he routinely did. This was common practice for men of his generation. Having bankrolls, often fastened with rubber bands, was a status symbol, a class denotation. Credit and debit cards, while in existence, were not used nearly as much as they would be a decade or two later.

Melinda and Amir had felt they had had good reason for urging Dad to get and carry a gun. He had been mugged. Evidently some young boys from the neighborhood, two, three, or four of them, had jumped Dad and taken his wallet and money. He had fought back, of course. Luckily, he wasn't seriously injured—a black eye, some bruising, and so on. But a middle-aged man against three or four young boys was not a fair match! Evidently, Dad took their advice, and this was the outcome.

Love Is a Many-Splintered Thing

"Once you get past the smell, you got it licked," the naked, voluptuous, shapely brown-skinned girl with the pretty black hair and fruity smell had said as she placed herself over Omar in the bed.

"Yeah, and once you get past the head, you got it swallowed," he had retorted in his smallish one-bedroom bachelor pad in Center City. This was quite the topic of the day at that time.

Many brothers stated they didn't eat pussy at that time.

"I don't have to" or "I'm too much man" were typical responses. "White people do that" was another, as well as "That's nasty."

Amir's high school buddy Never was one of the few black men Amir knew who not only freely admitted he indulged but bragged about it! Amir's high school was a majority white school at that time, early to midsixties, with some blacks, a few Latinos, and a few Asians. Never sometimes walked the hallways of it with a napkin dangling from a rear pants pocket and a fork!

He earned quite a rep as a cunning linguist. He could often be heard lamenting, "I need some trim!"

An older brother, probably drunk, once uttered from his bar stool in a loud voice at the packed Trestle Inn late one frigid Friday evening as a particularly nubile and sexy young woman all oiled up and smelling great was dancing up on the stage, "There's two kinds of men in this world: those that eat pussy and those that lie!" Then, looking up at the dancer on stage, the same brother uttered, "Dat girl is sitting on a gold mine! Bend over and crack a smile."

Clearly, cunnilingus was something he felt should be added to his lovemaking skills. After the first couple of tries and seeing how women reacted to it, the die was cast! Of course, "nobody begs like a brother" had become one of Amir's favorite sayings, as epitomized in "'Cause I Love You" by Lenny Williams, a popular singer of the time. But then half of the songs by the popular black groups or solo artists were begging songs, songs about a man wanting to get with a woman, get her back, or have her leave her current companion for him.

Happy Holidays

Amir and most of his circle believed that a man should have more than one woman. Sure, you might have a main squeeze, but you might be seeing one, two, or even three others. This had several implications. You had to have skills. Lying convincingly was one of them. Calling all your female callers on the phone "hun," "sweet-heart," or "baby" until you caught the voice was another. Didn't want to call anyone by the wrong name! "What are you doing for Christmas or New Year's Eve?" was often responded to with "I'll be out of town." Some women wanted you to spend quality time with them during the holidays. When you had more than one, this became problematic.

"Have you seen Omar?" the beautiful young woman was asking him.

"He said he was flying to Detroit" was his rehearsed answer. They covered for each other. If you did spend time with one, you had to lie to the others.

It was also expensive, this being a playa, dates, dinners, movies, shows, trips, flowers, candy, jewelry, and so on cost money. Smokey's "Can You Love a Poor Boy?" became one of his favorite songs, along with "It'll Be a Sad New Year Without You." Of course, some of the honeys were playing you and seeing someone else. Fidelity was not a sign of the times. So many women, so little time. Unmarried and childless, this was prime time. Why shouldn't they sample many flowers? The thought that they might be hurting someone was not part of their youthful male arrogance. Eventually, Amir learned that all this lying wasn't necessary. If a woman really liked you, was drawn to you, or enjoyed your company, it was amazing how much some of them would tolerate! Of course, the old double standard applied. It was more acceptable for guys to play the field than for girls! There were names for girls who slept around.

"Where were you last night?" could be answered with "Don't ask" if you were bold enough and consistent. There were times when all women got on his nerves, and he would take a vacation from all of them and return to the game after convalescing. Managing multiple simultaneous relationships was work! But it was also fun, at least at times.

Pistons and Cylinders

Ever since he could remember, he had been fascinated by cars. Amir read books and magazines about cars. He liked and enjoyed them. Dad had studied auto mechanics at Lincoln Technical Institute but never really worked as a mechanic. He was constantly tinkering with cars, Dad and Skip or Michael T. or his cousin Bernard Lee in Deptford, New Jersey, who had a used car lot and auto repair shop there. The older brothers almost all seemed to be car guys, gearheads as some would say today. Slick, a cousin in Philly, had a tiny used car lot located near one of Amir's future work sites at Broad and Spring Garden Streets. He liked Slick, a plumb, good-looking, wavy-haired, clean-shaven, light-brown-skinned man who walked with a cane and a slight limp, and whose part Native American heritage was apparent when you looked at him. He had an infectious smile and loved to laugh. He had personality plus. A real salesman, he talked a lot of shit, like the time he was explaining to Amir that he had been at the emergency ward the previous night after kicking someone's ass. He explained, "The surgeon had to determine whether to cut off part of my foot to save his ass or part of his ass to save my foot!"

Slick allowed Amir to hang around his used car sales lot when he wanted to. Sitting there watching Shakey do his thing was educational. "As is, where is" was Slick's response when the prospective car buyer had asked him if a particular low-priced used car had a warranty. "Once you drive away, it's yours. I don't want to see you again!" was also among his quips. These were low-priced used cars after all. "That Negro wouldn't work in a pie factory!" was in his arsenal. As was "If I catch you with it, I gotta git it!"

"That girl is fine," he often observed as various women walked near or by his used car lot. At that time, hot pants and halter tops were in style, along with miniskirts and platform shoes. "I'd like to ride her to the finish line!" he sometimes said. "I'd be on her like a cheap suit," "like white on rice," or "like stink on shit." Amir liked Slick. He had personality; he had game. "I know Negroes. You see, I majored in Negroology and minored in Negritude," Slick was fond of saying.

Amir's first car in life was a used Chevy Impala SS. It was white with red interior. It had bucket seats and a console! It was sporty looking, he thought. Dad didn't like Ford products, saying *Ford* was an acronym meaning "fix or repair daily"! He was proud to be driving his Impala SS. When it was stolen some months later, he was crestfallen. Biggy had helped him buy the car. She, his grandmother, was his favorite in the family. Always in his corner, Biggy would come to his aid many times in his young life. Amir had saved a few hundred dollars, which was not quite enough.

"Get my grandson a car!" she had demanded of his dad. "Don't want him waiting for buses."

He had to love her. It was found some days later, by the Philly police, sans its red bucket seats and its radiator. Obviously, someone needed those parts. He picked it up and drove it home, sitting on a milk crate, as the bucket seats were gone!

Over the years, he would have many adventures while driving, like the time he ran out of gas on the Schuylkill Expressway while driving in the fast lane, the time a steering wheel came off in his hands as he was driving, or the time a car's engine caught on fire while he was driving it. He also ran into a brick wall once because of bad motor mounts in New York City. As he and Omar were motoring to University Park, Penn State's main campus, for a party, they ran off the road because of bald tires and a light rain on the Pennsylvania Turnpike! The car settled on its side, but neither he nor Omar was hurt.

"You okay, brother?" Amir had asked Omar as they sat in the car laying on its side.

"I'm okay, brother" was the response.

When the tow truck pulled them out of the ditch with a wench, the car was still drivable, so they continued on to the party! (Amir had written a bad check for the tow truck operator.) There were— they hoped—honeys to be met and romanced! Of course, there was the ever-present issue of dwb (driving while black) to be dealt with.

One time, for instance, he was headed to New York City on the New Jersey Turnpike with his African girlfriend, and the New Jersey State Police pulled him over for no apparent reason.

"Got any guns or drugs in the car?" the trooper had asked him.

"Not that I'm aware of," he had replied. He then added that his passenger was the daughter of the Ethiopian ambassador to the United States and that they needed to be on their way! Although he appeared skeptical, the trooper let them drive on without further hassle.

Amir had observed for years while motoring on the New Jersey Turnpike, black drivers were pulled over on the northbound side by the New Jersey State Police. Sometimes they were still sitting in their vehicles as he drove by and sometimes outside of them, on the ground or on highway guardrails.

He never observed a white guy or family pulled over and hassled in the same manner. This became so much of an issue in New Jersey that litigation emerged, and the US Justice Department and the New Jersey State Police actually joined in a consent decree for a number of years based on these discriminatory practices. Another time coming from CCP, he had accepted a ride with a guy he didn't know. So a car full of young black men with Afros, wearing movement badges and US Army field jackets was pulled over near Philly's city hall. They were boot cops, the highway patrolmen of Philly's Police Force. Their crushed hats and high boots reminded him of the Gestapo he had seen in pictures of and films about World War II. Their guns were drawn as they ordered them out of the Volkswagen Beetle. He was nervous. Philly cops were notorious at that time for brutalizing black and Latino males. Many were beaten, some shot, some killed! Fortunately, no drugs or guns were found in the vehicle, and they were instructed to take off.

He would always be hesitant and careful about accepting rides after the incident. Being pulled over for no apparent or legitimate reason was a common occurrence in those days for brothers. The fact that he was light-skinned and usually alone in his car probably lessened his instances of illegal stops, he always believed. He was obsessive about always having his license, proof of insurance, and owner's card up to date and on him. He didn't want to give the cops any excuse to hassle him.

All lights, turn signals, and so on would always be working or repaired or replaced very quickly. Still, for the rest of his life, whenever a police car was behind him, he would become a bit anxious, sometimes actually turning off his intended route to see if they followed! He resented this harassment, as he knew all his paperwork was in order and he wasn't up to any illegal activity!

A series of cars would become his over the years, some sporty, some not. He had a Pontiac LeMans, two customized VW Bugs, a black Ford Torino GT, two Mustang IIs (one a Mach I), a Cadillac Cimarron, and two Datsun 280 ZXs (one a turbo), and, in years to come, they would be followed by BMWs, Audis, a Porsche, and others. Amir liked fast cars that handled well.

When talking trash, Amir would sometimes say, "I like my cars like I like my women, sleek and fast, with plenty of horsepower!" He developed a penchant for road trips over the years, usually by himself. Destinations included New York City, Atlantic City, Baltimore, Washington, DC, and finally Montreal and Quebec City, Quebec. He often packed a bag and went to Montreal for long weekends. He enjoyed the sophisticated European atmosphere there. Amir knew only a few words in French, but that was never a problem. Up the New Jersey Turnpike to the Garden State Parkway to the New York State Throughway up into Canada was a beautiful drive when the weather was nice and traffic not too heavy.

There was the time he made the trip in a car with an oil leak and had to keep stopping to add oil! There was another time when once in Canada, the fog was so thick he had to pull off the road, put his blinkers on, and hope he wouldn't get rear ended. The Canadian women were more forward and aggressive than American women, he felt. At customs, he was asked by the young male customs agent, "Is the purpose of your visit business or pleasure?" to which he replied with a smile, "Pleasure is my business."

Back in the day, at least in Philly, the thing was to put hijacker shock absorbers on the rear of your hoopdi to raise the rear end, along with fat tires mounted on the rear. Often, Cragars or another kind of mag wheel was in place. Meeting at stoplights, one young guy would often look across at another in his ride and ask, "What you got under the hood, blood?" or words to that effect. It was a challenge. They then often raced to the next traffic light. Like many young men, Amir drove too fast in the city.

It was two or three in the morning that day when he went

through a stop sign and clipped the sedan on the rear quarter panel. His car kept going and was stopped by a telephone pole! He didn't have on his seat belt. It was not cool to wear them at the time and not a legal requirement. He felt the pain in his chest and right knee. One lens had popped out of his eyeglasses, and he had a real shiner. He also later learned the semicircle imprint of the upper half of the steering wheel was on his chest! As the police approached his driver's side door, he noticed the driver he had hit getting out of his car.

"Do you need an ambulance?" the officer asked him.

Right away, he was thinking lawsuit and money and said yes. "I can't walk." He would later learn that he had hit an off-duty cop! Amir got an attorney who sent him to a doctor who administered heat treatments to him every week during his rehabilitation. The bills were adding up, which of course was the point. For weeks, he walked with a cane and wore an eye patch over his left eye. He looked a mess! But there was probably money down the road, he figured. By the time the hearing or arbitration came about two and a half years later, the other driver had died—not as a result of the accident, thank goodness!

When his lawyer coached him on what to say, it was easy. Obviously, he would lie. "I was doing about thirty-five to forty miles per hour when the accident occurred." In fact, he was probably doing about seventy miles per hour.

"I didn't see the other car," he stated.

The other driver being deceased, there was no contrary statement. There would be a settlement. His lawyer would get about one-third. He would still have a few thousand left. *Greatest legal system in the world*, thought Amir as he deposited his settlement check into his bank account.

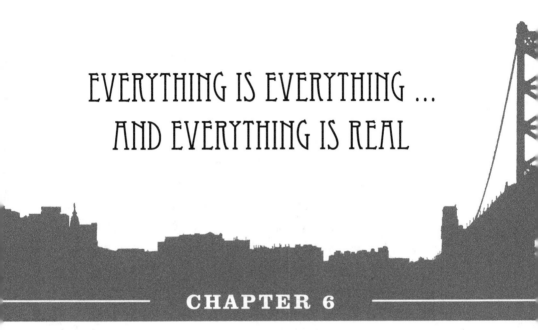

EVERYTHING IS EVERYTHING ... AND EVERYTHING IS REAL

CHAPTER 6

T hey're just titties," the tall, almond-colored young teacher with the great figure and huge breasts was explaining to Amir as they were petting on the love seat in her living room.

The dim light was on, and soft music was playing. He had been enjoying her mounds of delight and complimenting her on them.

"Gurl, to call these things you have 'just titties' is the height of understatement" replied Amir, "akin to calling Mount Everest just a hill! And I want to be Sir Edmund Hilary!" They then continued their dance of love. She was just a date to him, and he believed he was just a date to her. This was recreational sex to him and presumably also to her. No commitment, promises, or assurances had been exchanged. Few personal questions had been asked.

It was a typical Friday night at the Hippo.[9] "Shaft" was on the door. Big Eddy, one of the bouncers, was on duty. The bartenders were bartending, and the waitresses were waitressing. His friend Omar was spinning the records. Little Johnny didn't appear to be

---

[9] Discotheque where Omar worked.

around, but Fat Nick was hanging around at one of the bars, looking like he was expecting him.

The Hippo was a big spot—four bars, two dance floors, a DJ booth, and of course the basement, off limits to the customers, where Little Johnny's office was. The office was where Johnny and his associates discussed business. Often, they were Italians, but not always. A few blacks and whites of other ethnicities were often observed meeting with him, as were some civic leaders, politicians, and others. What would this night bring? Of course, he was hunting, hoping to meet some interesting woman and take her back to his Center City apartment or go with her to her place to make love. He was hoping for at least some pleasant conversation and her digits[10] at a minimum. Amir always got there early, usually around eleven o'clock. It was easy for him, as his apartment was only a few blocks away.

In fact, he and Omar were neighbors, both living in Center City Philly at a time when few blacks did, and they knew all of them! Life was good. They were "dressing fine, making time." They were part of the in crowd. "Oh, to be young, gifted, and black!" Amir usually hung around the DJ booth, where Omar was working. He truly enjoyed Omar's company. In addition, many of the foxes would gravitate to the DJ booth. The DJ booth was also generally a good location to view the pickings. As the night grew on, he would see a veritable parade of honeys on a good night—sophisticated, crude, fine, not so fine, low class, middle class, upper class, no class, locals, out-of-towners, occasionally foreigners. Of course, the later/earlier it got, the better looking the available females became. He thought the women were probably thinking the same thing.

"The black guys where I come from are not like you guys," the young, friendly, average-looking white girl was saying to him and

---

[10] Phone number.

SaRon that evening at the Half Moon bar in Center City. "The way they dress, wear their hair, and so on."

"We know, girl, but you're in Philly now. We're not farmers. You're in the big time now, girl. Enjoy," was their retort. "By the way, we take applications from white girls too!" was added as an aside.

After she walked away, SaRon said to Amir, "Maybe we can put her in a samich?" (ménage à trois). They didn't prefer white women. Good-looking or sexy ones were fair game, however. The common wisdom of the time was that white girls were freakier than black girls, that they would have sex more easily and didn't necessarily have to be wined and dined like most sisters. They would go dutch on dates and had better legs than sisters, but sisters had better butts. "It's all pink inside" was a common saying of the era. Of course, he also knew a few brothers who had more exotic tastes—Chinese women, dwarfs, the hunch backed, those with disabilities.

He and the fellows actually made up a sexual preference term for a few brothers who seemed to have no standards and for whom the usual sexual orientations and preferences—straight, gay, bisexual—didn't seem adequate or descriptive enough. For these guys, any warm orifice would suffice! They were therefore dubbed try-sexuals, meaning they would try almost anything!

AIDS was unknown at the time, and what guys usually worried about was crabs or gonorrhea. There was a clinic near the college at Broad and Lombard Streets where penicillin shots could be had. If greeted with "Didn't I see you at Broad and Lombard?" it conveyed an instant meaning.

The Dating Game

Amir didn't really start dating regularly until about twenty or twenty-one years of age. Sure, in high school and even junior high, he was attracted to girls. But he had to overcome his innate bashfulness and shyness. There would be many dates over many years. Amir wouldn't get married until he was middle-aged. He dated mostly African American girls but occasionally white or Hispanic women. He dated a Turkish one once. They were his same age, younger than he, and, in a few instances, older than he. There would be unemployed women, secretaries, a couple of lawyers, key punch operators, teachers, go-go girls, morticians, a doctor, an FBI agent, and so on. He would date single women, engaged women, and married and divorced or separated women. He had felt a little guilty about one married woman. She didn't wear a wedding ring, however, and by the time she clearly told him that she was married, they were already off to the races, knocking boots. Another married woman had explained to him that she and her spouse had an understanding. They both allegedly saw other people but showed each other respect, she had explained.

Some women he dated were very bright and articulate—others not so much. Most had class; a few didn't, like the date who took him to a function given by her company that included a buffet meal. Her coworkers and bosses were there. He couldn't believe that as they did the buffet, she was stuffing biscuits, pastries, fruit, and other items into her pocketbook and jacket pockets! When he could take no more, he sarcastically asked, "Do you have your own business, a food truck or something?" Then there was the young lady who liked to drink. He went to the movies with her and cringed as she talked back to the film in a loud voice! He never particularly cared for loud people, male or female. Not being embarrassed in public was always a thing with Amir. He didn't intentionally embarrass others in public and expected reciprocity. It would be their last date.

Some of these women were scary, like the incredibly shapely and sexy Latina who carried a knife in her pocketbook. She explained one evening after a wonderful session of lovemaking that if she ever thought he was cheating on her, she'd have to cut his throat. Of course, he was already cheating on her. It always amazed him that so many women thought their respective boyfriends or husbands were cheating on them because of some deficiency on their part, real or imagined. They didn't seem to understand that it had more to do with the man than with them, usually. Some of these women shared horrible stories with him of rape or some form of sexual abuse that had often occurred when they were little girls.

He genuinely felt sympathy for these women and realized even more how fortunate he was to have had a loving family with no outstanding issues, just the run-of-the-mill family conflicts and disputes. Neither he nor Melinda was sexually abused. Nor were they physically abused as far as he was concerned.

He had had a little help along the way getting over his natural shyness from a couple of assertive women. There was that warm summer night down south when one evening on a porch as the spanish moss was gently moving with the wind, a southern cutey he was necking with placed his hand on her firm, young breast. Her nipples were hard, and it felt good. She then started rubbing his penis while his pants were still on. This girl meant business!

Shame, he thought, that her mother was only a few yards away. They couldn't take a chance and go all the way. Then there was the girl from the neighborhood whom he never had paid much attention to. She was at the same neighborhood party one night and gave him a great grind. Of course, he popped a hardy. As they were grinding, she whispered in his ear that he was her type and that she would do anything. Amir didn't follow up. Her aggression must have been off-putting. But it sure felt good!

This was still the era of romance, wooing the girls. Black girls—at least most of them—wanted to be wined and dined. Most wouldn't just jump in the bed with you. Even after weeks or months of romancing them, it was not certain you'd get some. Amir did meet a few he considered nymphomaniacs. "Be careful of what you ask for," it is said. While he enjoyed the sex, they never got enough.

"Go to sleep, gurl. I'm tired," he told one consistently. She was insatiable. Might have to start sewing his zipper shut, he thought.

How to meet eligible honeys? If one waited to be introduced by family or friends to eligible honeys, one might wait a long time or not be interested in the offerings. In the words of Fredrick the Great, "L'audace, l'audace, toujours l'audace." In a couple of years, he would mostly overcome his innate shyness. He worked at it. Small steps. Nothing ventured; nothing gained. One yes makes up for a whole lot of nos. Along the way, Amir discovered something very interesting; the fine girls were no more difficult to talk to than the also-rans, as he and Omar termed them. Might as well go for the gusto! Just because a girl was good-looking didn't mean she necessarily had a boyfriend. Often, he discovered, the really fine girls were lonely. A lot of guys were afraid to approach them, fearing rejection, and didn't. Hence, many were lonely. But Amir learned that if you could got them to smile, moreover to laugh, you had a shot. A truism he came to believe in was that women are not as visual as men. Sure, they noticed and checked out the handsome guys but often ended up with a guy who didn't match them in the looks department. Were they less shallow than guys? Maybe. A man with money or celebrity or a nice ride or a sense of humor or all the foregoing didn't necessarily have to be good-looking. The dependable, reliable, hard worker, good earner, solid citizen type who seemed to have a future worked for some honeys.

Let's face it. When listening to a description of an unseen woman from almost anyone, what is the question most guys have? What does she look like? Whereas in similar circumstances, many women want to know "What does he do?" Amir, like many of the guys he knew, learned to always have his antenna up. In any situation where there was a woman or women, he was aware of and assessing them—walking down the street, riding the bus or subway, at the laundromat, at school, at the doctor's office, at the library, in the supermarket, in the post office, at church or the masjid, everywhere.

They would be evaluated—win, place, show, and also-ran. If so moved, he would hit on her. If rejected, so what? Next! The law of averages says that if you hit on enough women often enough, some will respond positively. You become impervious to the rejection with enough practice. "Her loss! I'm on my way to the big stuff! She doesn't know what she's missing!" etc. Some women, in the minority at that time, would initiate the flirting. They would send obvious signals to you. God bless them. You, of course, as did they, had veto power over their advances.

For dates, Amir would take them to a movie, often a foreign one, or to breakfast, lunch, or dinner, for walks, drives in the car, perhaps a concert, maybe a lecture, a play, a concert, or fishing, if the outdoor type. Some were impressed with his fairly educated palate and the exotic cuisine he was actually introducing some of them too—Lebanese food, Ethiopian food, Greek food, Moroccan food, and so on. One of his favorite places to take his dates in Philly was to the Moshulu, a steel-hulled sailing ship moored on Delaware Avenue, now North Columbus Boulevard. It was used in the first Godfather movie. You could have dinner or drinks there. Dinner was served belowdecks, and the ambiance was romantic and different as you gazed out on the river as you dined. One could also have drinks on deck, weather permitting. Gazing at the stars on a clear night and into each other's eyes was quite enjoyable and romantic. "In your eyes, I see what I was born to be." Marrakech, a Moroccan restaurant off South Street, was an interesting dining experience, akin to eating at someone's home. It was decorated Moroccan style, with cushions, pillows, and low couches to sit on. You would eat traditional style, with your hands, after washing them of course. The sweet mint tea that Morocco is known for would be served. There were several courses. The tagines were delicious. Meat and vegetable ones were on the menu. The desserts were sweet, particularly the baklava.

Some girls found him quite handsome and quite a catch, others not so much. The women who liked roughnecks or bad boys were not usually drawn to Amir. "Your hands are so soft" was a comment he heard frequently. Sometimes, it was simply an observation; at other times, it was a criticism or a compliment. He felt no shame to have soft hands. To each his own, thought Amir. He wasn't ashamed of or apologetic for not working hard manual labor jobs, of not having calloused hands. He liked wearing suits and sports jackets and working in an office setting. Of course, one's appearance matters in the dating world. You can be too light or too dark, too tall or not tall enough, too slim or too heavy, too well dressed or not well dressed enough, too smart or not smart enough, too talkative or not talkative enough, too middle class or not middle class enough, too sophisticated or not sophisticated enough, a good lover, not good enough or too good. You can't please everybody!

It was interesting that many darker-skinned blacks had no problem telling a light-skinned guy, "You're too light" or "I don't like light skinned guys." The reverse of course was unacceptable to say, "I'm not attracted to brown-skinned girls" or "You're too dark." Over time, Amir figured it out. Fat girls could talk about slender and shapely girls, short people could talk about very tall people, poor people could talk about wealthy people, but the reverse was not appreciated. That was just the way it was.

This dating game was full of contradictions and ironies: one got sharply dressed and groomed with the goal of hopefully getting undressed. Many women who said they didn't want to be wanted for just their bodies dressed seductively and provocatively while out, exposing breasts, legs, and so on. Most of us initially send a representative when dating a new person, afraid that if we are ourselves, we might be rejected or not make a favorable impression, so that it may take weeks, months, and sometimes years before the full person is revealed! Most guys, if they can get one, want a woman who is hot and sexy and whom other men will also find hot and sexy, respectfully. After they get her, however, many become unreasonably jealous. Many of the characteristics and traits that men and women initially find cute, magnetic, and attractive or charming in each other are the same ones they ultimately find intolerable and irritating: tardiness, being flirtatious, not managing finances well, drinking too much, taking too long to get dressed, shopping too much, dressing too provocatively, and so on.

Even though Amir and his associates spent innumerable hours in discos and clubs hunting in Philly, New York City, Washington, DC, Baltimore, LA, Camden, and other places, perched like birds of prey on bar stools, at tables, and standing. Very few of their long-term relationships evolved from such situations. Most women he met and developed serious relationships with were met at work, at school, or when just generally out and about. Clubs and discos were mainly about posturing and hanging out with one's friends.

Rarely did African American women of that day ask men to dance in clubs or discos. Some white girls would. One of the few times it happened to Amir, he would never forget. He was alone that night, and after he entered the disco and was there for about ten minutes, this sister rushed over to him and asked him to dance to a slow record. She held him tightly as they danced, explaining that he was her type of man. While this was flattering on some level, it was also disturbing. A little aggression was cool, but this much? Most guys of the time wanted a woman who was a good sex partner but who had not had too many sexual liaisons. If she had, then she was a ho. Most guys also demanded fidelity, while many were cheating on their partner. Men and women both have their crosses to bear in this dating game of course. If he tried to get a woman in the bed too quickly, he risked being accused of only wanting her for her body. If he took too long, she might wonder if he was gay or didn't find her attractive or sexy. Amir was sure there was a corresponding analysis among women. When or if to give it up? If quickly, would the man think she was a tramp, doing this with everybody? If too slowly, would he think she was a lesbian, or frigid, or that she didn't find him attractive? Over time, Omar and Amir grew to agree that as much as they liked women, all of them, no matter how attractive, sexy, or interesting could be pains in the ass, could get on your nerves, your last nerve. Amir would, in fact, take vacations from all women periodically too recharge his batteries. The dating scene could be fun and exciting at times and incredibly boring at other times. Amir always found the dates who talked about their so-called exes over dinner with him at length interesting. "He disrespected me. He cheated on me. He hit me. He wouldn't work."

After listening to a litany of such grievances, he would typically ask, "And how long were you with him?"

"Five years, eight years, or ten years" was often the response.

Also interesting was the list of traits and characteristics many women articulated when asked, "What do you want in a man?" Typically, it was good-looking, above a certain height, nice body, well dressed, drives a nice car, has a good job, is a good lover, is faithful, and so on. To which Amir would usually respond, "And what do you have to offer in return for this package?" The typical response was "Me!" Over time, Amir pondered on this dating game and dance. It was not universal. He had learned that in many foreign countries, it didn't exist, for the most part. There were arranged marriages, and when one reached the appropriate age, one married the arranged partner. The notion of being alone, man and woman, unmarried to do whatever, was prohibited in many cultures; others permitted some semidating with a chaperone. But males and females could not be alone.

He had heard that even in America, once upon a time, there had been chaperones, and boys and girls couldn't be alone without one. Obviously, protecting the female's virginity was the core of a lot of this. Maybe these foreigners with their arranged marriages had a point. He knew some South Asians, Arabs, and some Africans practiced arranged marriage. *Here in the West*, he thought, *we have this concept of romantic love.*

On a planet with billions of people on it, many of whom could not even communicate with each other because of language or distance barriers, one was to find that special someone, fall in love, and hook up. But wasn't love essentially an emotion? Were emotions reliable? Consistent? Permanent? Did they ebb and flow? Sometimes dissipate? Clearly, what many labeled as love was lust. Lust was an indispensable human characteristic probably grounded in our need to reproduce or procreate, to "be fruitful and multiply," but was it love?

Some anthropologists posit that it's smell, that we are actually attracted to people based on their respective smells, whether we realize it or not. People make determinations to partner up with other people for a variety of reasons: societal pressure, loneliness, the desire to have children, money, status, fear of being or growing old alone, shotgun weddings, to have regular and accessible sex, and religious reasons, among others. The entertainer Tina Turner once famously sang "What's love got to do with it?" Clearly, marriage developed to have an orderly and peaceful way to protect and transmit wealth and property. Amir concluded that maybe, on some level, love had nothing to do with it.

The ancient Greeks had several words for what they considered to be the different types of love, at least four. Some societies don't subscribe to the concept at all. Folks are matched based on their suitability, age, ability to earn an income, education, socioeconomic status, health, religion, tribe, family connections, potential, and so on. When one looks at the high divorce rate in America, one does sometime wonder, "What's love got to do with it?"

Give Me a Pig's Foot and a Bottle of Beer

Although Amir and Omar and most of their circle were fiercely proud of their black American and African heritage and ancestry, there were those aspects of contemporary black culture that they found embarrassing, reactionary, or counterrevolutionary. "Why do so many of our people just love eating pork?" he asked.

Omar and he were having a discussion at Bain's Deli that beautiful winter afternoon over french onion soup.

"I know that a high percentage of black folk have origins in the South, including my family," replied Amir.

"Pork is an integral part of the southern diet, I understand," said Omar. "Now, however, we don't have to eat slave food."

They agreed.

There was beef, lamb, chicken, turkey, duck, pheasant, venison, and other types of meat. Wasn't there evidence that pork played a major role in high blood pressure and other ailments? Also, Amir could not help but observe that in almost all bars he had gone to with a high percentage of black patrons, there would be for all to see a big jar of pickled pigs' feet on display. They were for sale. Often, there would also be bags of pork rinds for sale. If one had to eat pork, why wouldn't one want the better higher cuts of meat from the hog, not the feet? Pig tails were also eaten by some. Tails! Of course, hog intestines were also consumed (chitterlings), as well as hog brains. One understands that slaves often had no options in their diets, but slavery was abolished in 1865 with the Thirteenth Amendment.

What Omar and he were wondering was "Don't blacks know that one of the great things about America is reinvention?" Groups come here from around the world, often with unremarkable histories or histories of oppression, and reinvent themselves, accentuating the positive and deaccentuating the negative, putting their best foot (image) forward. Was there some romantic reminiscing about chattel slavery among blacks? If true, that would really be tragic, they agreed. Blacks should define themselves, name themselves, not be defined by others or remnants from a period of oppression and brutality. You don't define yourself simply by what has been done to you. Granted, their generation was asking questions and maybe coming up with some new and different answers. Many of them were drawn to Islam, but not all. Hence, a lot of folks had stopped eating pork. As a child, Amir had loved pork chops and bacon, the smell of them cooking being intoxicating. But upon reaching adulthood and becoming awake, he "put away childish things." Another puzzling and irritating trait many African Americans seemed to evidence was living up or down to stereotypes, or trying to. No, all blacks were not good dancers, and that was okay. No, all blacks were not athletic, and that was all right also. All black women were not loud, confrontational, and ready to fight. They were mostly not hos either! Yet some tried to live up or down to this stereotype. Then there were those reactionary phrases liberally used by some, such as "He or she sounds or talks white." It was usually used for those who were articulate and used good grammar and syntax. So then what was talking or speaking black? Being inarticulate, using bad grammar and syntax? Another favorite pet peeve was that so many brothers referred to black women as "mommie" or "mama," as in "Hey, mommie!" If black women were "mommie," and white guys were the "man," what did that leave for black men, "boy"?

The incredible naivete of some young African Americans was also shocking. Omar and Amir were history buffs. But even if you were not, just a cursory knowledge of the history of Africans in America had to make any reasonable person know and feel that they had been mistreated, brutalized, killed, exploited, and on and on. As Omar liked to say, "We're at war; there are lulls in the fighting, but we are at war!" Sure, some blacks had escaped, for one reason or another, the worst of it—who their parents were, where they grew up, their physical appearance, luck, happenstance, circumstance, and so on. But periodically, he or Omar would meet and talk to a black person who said unbelievable things. "I've never been discriminated against," "No one has ever called me names," or "Whites have never treated me in a hostile manner."

Omar and Amir found such statements unbelievable and lacking in credibility. "Were you raised in the woods? A cave? Are you in some kind of denial?"

Of course, even those who made such proclamations had to admit they didn't know how whites or others talked about them in their absence. Both Amir and Omar had white fellow students, friends, and colleagues and had enjoyed the company of some whites. They had dated some white girls. But growing up in Philly when they did and seeing and experiencing what they had seen and experienced and were still experiencing made racism very real for them, not crippling but real.

Prostitutes, Pimps, and Peep Shows

When bored with Philly, Amir and some of the crew or Amir alone would make the trek up the New Jersey Turnpike, I-95 N to New York City. It was about a one-hundred-mile trip one way by car, as the crow flies.

Omar had been traveling to the City often alone, since early in high school or before. During the late 1960s and early to mid-1970s Times Square was a modern Sodom and Gammorah! Probably worse! The ladies were out in force, standing on corners, in doorways, on stoops, under bridges and trestles, in alleys, or simply walking along certain streets. Their big-hat, maxi-coat-wearing, customized-Cadillac-driving, usually black pimps would be just around the corner or slightly out of view. So interesting, thought Amir. He didn't admire pimps, but brothers, hated and despised by many, were pimping an international array of women. Clearly in the pimp job description, there had to be a healthy dose of motivational acumen. Manipulating women, who did most of the work, to hand the money over to them, sometimes all the money, required skills, thought Amir, evil and negative skills, but skills nonetheless.

SaRon, who occasionally introduced sketchy friends of his to the crew, had brought a real pimp to one of their dinner meetings in Philly. He wasn't very good-looking, contrary to myth, and didn't come across as particularly charming. When questioned, he explained that one of the things he did to his stable members was to take all their money away, making them totally dependent on him. He also explained how he had a "bottom bitch," sort of a supervisor over the other stable members.

Back to Gotham

Some of the ladies were quite attractive with good or great bodies, others not so much. Black, white, Asian, Hispanic, and mixed race were all represented. They wore short, tight miniskirts or dresses, low-cut tops of one type or another, hot pants, and halter tops, even in the freezing cold! Some were actually wearing lingerie, negligees, baby doll pajamas, and, of course, the obligatory high-heeled shoes. Clear heels on the high-heeled shoes were quite common. Many smelled good, were well coiffured, and had applied their makeup with expertise, others, not so much. The gait, of course, had to be eye catching. They were working after all. Usually, it was slow and syncopated, and the hips and pelvic area were moved to entice. Some were so skilled it appeared to be an art form. If you are trying to get tricks, you should appear as desirable as possible. "Want a date? Looking for a date? Want some company? Want to go out? Want to party? Looking for a good time? Can I go with you?" The more assertive ladies would approach a man whether he was alone, with others, or even accompanied by a woman, whether he was walking or driving. Truck stops were one of their favorite areas.

Forty-Second Street itself from the Port Authority Bus Terminal and continuing for about three New York blocks contained all-night movie theaters, peep shows, adult stores, burlesque shows, a few cheap restaurants, bars, hustlers, con men, pimps, drug dealers, pickpockets, five-card monty dealers, and sidewalk vendors selling many different goods, including some West African brothers selling fake Rolex watches for twenty dollars. There were also civilians (regular people), who had come to view the goings-on, to be shocked and appalled by them, or to be part of them or who had to walk through the area to reach their respective travel destinations. As Amir and the fellows were walking up Forty-Second Street that freezing cold November night with the wind whipping around the tall New York buildings, it had a wind tunnel effect. Good thing he and Omar had their long maxi coats on. They both had purchased conservative maxi coats, nothing too flamboyant or wild; that wouldn't be stylish or cool. They were not pimps or hustlers after all. Nor were they tricks. But the extra-long maxi coat was quite the rage at the time. It was often double-breasted, made of wool, and had a lot of inside pockets—perfect for young men about town on cold winter days or nights. They stopped at Doc Johnson's Love Products. Doc also had a store in Philly in Chinatown they had been to. It was like a supermarket for adult products. Most patrons were male. They had edible panties, inflatable dolls with orifices in white and brown, handcuffs, creams, gels, lotions, whips, chains, masks, ben wa balls, dildos, vibrators, butt plugs, fisting devices, and so on, and there was sometimes live entertainment.

Among the other offerings were a series of booths with curtains for ingress and egress, where for a quarter, a small cover would lift to reveal a small screen. A porno film was the usual fare. For a few seconds, one could view heterosexual, homosexual, group, or interracial sex or bestiality. One had to have a lot of quarters to feed the machine. The attendant could make change, of course. The floor was often sticky from the ejaculate of previous viewers who had pleasured themselves in the small dark booths! There were also the live women sitting in a kind of telephone booth, which faced another booth where the customer would sit. A glass partition separated the two. The women would be seductively dressed, usually in a negligee or baby doll pajamas, often wearing fishnet stockings. For a dollar, one could sit there for a few minutes and flirt or talk dirty with the woman as she strategically removed various articles of clothing and tried to entice you to keep spending dollars. When you stopped, the entertainment stopped.

"The real show is in the back!" the middle-aged, sketchy-looking brother with the scraggly, unkempt beard had whispered to them. They passed through a curtain, and there was a young, attractive African American girl in a bikini and tall black boots whipping an older white guy tied to a post with a thick belt! He either enjoyed or pretended to enjoy the beating. They could only observe for a few minutes. It was not really their taste.

Back to Gotham, the crew was developing an attitude that evening. The ladies were soliciting white guys for sex but not them. What's up with that? They didn't come to New York City to buy sex. They were young and felt they didn't have to. They didn't have money for that either, but that wasn't the point. They weren't soliciting brothers! They would ask one why not—in a friendly, respectful way, of course. The answer was illuminating. "I can't make any money off brothers," the young, attractive light-brown-skinned sister with the pumpkin butt said. "They bring a jug and want to fuck all night!" Wow, interesting analysis.

Don't Call My Bitch No Ho!

As Amir came of age, he would experience many understandable disillusionments about life. There was no tooth fairy and no Santa Claus. The good guys aren't always as good as advertised and the bad guys not always as bad! Some politicians, judges, and police officers were on the take. Some ministers were drinking and sleeping with women or men or boys. There were no-show jobs with the city government, street money to vote a certain way, getting your traffic tickets fixed, folks paying for jobs under the table, beautiful women with sleazy men because they were drug addicted or money hungry, and so on. Another significant disillusionment he would become aware of as his nascent young sexuality started to roar was that African American women, in the main, were not the lustful, wanton, hot mamas, the jezebels of myth he had been led to believe they were by the larger society. Of course, most folks enjoy la petite mort, and he would occasionally meet a black nympho, but they were few and far between. There were black working girls, but broke young college students didn't usually patronize them.

No, most blacks, he was discovering, particularly the middle-class ones he tended to be attracted to, with their religious backgrounds, strong family ties, Southern roots, and generally conservative views on almost everything, added to by the scars and insecurities left by racism, sexism, and other forms of discrimination, were not sexual adventurers hopping from bed to bed. These were still the days of the good girls (not sexually active) and the bad (sexually active) girls.

He was already experiencing, while engaged in heavy petting with some of his dates and trying to consummate, responses such as, "I'm saving myself for my husband," "You may not respect me in the morning," and "I don't want to get pregnant." It was very frustrating when one's hormones were raging! Of course, what he did was what most other guys seemed to be doing—get to know some bad girls who would give it up! Oral sex had not really caught on with most of the sisters yet, unlike with the white girls, as he was told. A few would allow you to do them but then sometimes didn't want to return the favor! It would take a few more years before most sisters caught up in that area. Perception versus reality. Words like *ho*, *slut*, *tart*, and *loose*, he grew to believe, often had no basis in fact but were a cheap shot that could be pulled out and used against almost any woman. Interestingly, the old double standard still applied. Men were playas or lovers or playboys. The sayings were "Men will be men," "All men are dogs!" "They're sowing their wild oats," and on and on. There was the "he'd fuck a snake if you held its fangs" insult, and a few other male-oriented comments, but generally sexually active guys earned a wink and smile from others, often including young ladies. "That girl got more fingerprints than the FBI." "I wouldn't fuck her with your dick." "I've seen better heads on a mug of beer!" "Seen better legs on a table!" "She's so ugly she has to sneak up on a glass of water!" "You'd have to put a bag over her head!" "That's a two bag girl!" "She so ugly she'd make an onion cry." No, the digs and insults for women far outweighed those for men.

The insults for women were myriad and omnipresent. Amir rarely used them, however; he felt that his young male sexual behavior left him little room to criticize others, male or female. Amir felt that other than his quite normal, he felt, female conquest and seduction missions he had a fairly healthy respect for women. He had grown up around strong, decent, and good women—his mother, sister, grandmother, aunts, cousins, and so on. They were not perfect, not angels, but decent, strong, and good people.

Amir genuinely liked women, and not just for sex. But sex was a need, like eating, sleeping. It didn't have to be complicated, thought Amir. He at first naively thought that if a young or older woman agreed to go to the movies or dinner with him; it really meant she wanted to jump into the sack! Amir would be in for a rude awakening. Years later, he had painfully learned that to some, sex could never be just a need, a fun, recreational activity. They would attach more to it, no matter what discussions were held, no matter how frank and honest he was with them. Was this nature or nurture? Were most males and females fundamentally different that way? Most guys, he felt, could separate the sex act from love or commitment or some further expectation. Why couldn't more women? A date was sometimes just a date. The woman was curious, liked to eat, liked movies or plays, or was bored. She found the guy fun or interesting but didn't necessarily know if she wanted to sleep with him. One of the rare black nymphos he had encountered was insatiable! Amir thought of sewing his fly closed at one point. "They can look up, brother, longer than you can look down" was a common wisdom of the era.

A middle ground would be nice, he thought to himself as he walked along Chestnut Street that cold Saturday afternoon on his way to see Omar at the audio store where he worked, about three blocks from his apartment. During this period, a lot of brothers were referring to their girlfriends, fiancées, or wives as queens, certainly a positive if somewhat overstated term of respect for the sisters. Blacks seemed to have more regard and respect for each other during this era, he would conclude years later. Brother had more meaning, as did sister. There was more caring, more love, more of a sense of camaraderie and unity, as naive as some of the aspirations and goals of the movement would prove to be over time. The seventies era did not encourage or contribute to a heightened sense of monogamy, morality, faithfulness, or commitment, however.

Hedonism and bacchanalia were everywhere. The then popular culture was replete with sexual messages, such as in the popular songs "All I Want Is a One Night Affair," "Love the One You're With," "What's Love Got to Do with It?" "Strangers in the Night," "Love Don't Love Nobody," "Come and Go with Me (to My Place)," "I Be Stroking," "If Loving You Is Wrong, I Don't Wanna Be Right," and so on. "Your place or mine?" became a common catchphrase of the era. This was also the free love era! The pill[11] had liberated at least some women, for better or worse! "How many girls have you been with?" the girls would often ask him as they were about to make love. Another frequent query postsex was "Where did you learn how to do that?" At a fairly young age, he had figured out it did not pay to truthfully answer such questions. "You're the first" with a smile was his typical response to the former question and "I don't remember" to the latter one. Promises of "I won't hold it against you" or "I'll never bring it up again" were not to be believed in Amir's estimation. He never asked a woman how many men she had been with. He didn't want to know! He prided himself on the fact that he never told a girl he loved her just to have sex with her—almost anything else but not that! He would lie, be insincere, pretend to be something he was not, and feign interest in a variety of avocations, hobbies, and interests all in the name of cherchez la femme, but not say, "I love you," unless he meant it. It wasn't easy; as Omar said, "They come at you in waves" (women). There was a cacophony of cunt a plethora of pussy!

At one point in his young bachelor life, he received what seemed like a divine revelation. You don't have to tell a lot of lies to get the honeys! Like most guys he knew, he felt he was supposed to have more than one girl at a time, no matter how nice, how valuable she was. Many of the older men he had been exposed to growing up, black and white, had a wife and another woman on the side. Popular film, TV, and book idols, like James Bond, Shaft, Peter Gunn, the Troubleman, and the guys on *77 Sunset Strip*, all had or at least had sex with more than one! Our Man Flint and all the cool guys seemed to be ladies' men. Sure, you might have a main squeeze, but you had to have at least one on the side. Wasn't polygamy still practiced in many parts of the world? Wasn't it an African tradition for

---

[11] Birth control pill.

some Africans? How many wives did Abraham, Moses, Solomon, or David have? Wasn't there a surplus of women? What were these extra women to do? Why, a brother was just doing his part!

Maria and Nim

As far back as Amir could remember, there had always been Puerto Ricans, a.k.a. Ricans near or around him. Many had been living in the contiguous states for generations and spoke excellent English—hell, some didn't even speak Spanish! Philadelphia and its environs had a Puerto Rican population that often lived in close proximity to or with its African American population.

His dad, Bill, would sometimes be approached by a Rican speaking Spanish, who thought because of Dad's looks that he was a Rican, upon which he would usually become offended. Amir understood, however, Dad did look like he might be a Rican! To some Philadelphians and other Americans at the time, all Spanish speakers were Puerto Ricans, just as all Asians were Chinese. Some blacks looked down on Ricans. "The men won't work, run the streets, and keep the women on lockdown!" "They'll sleep with your women, but don't want you to sleep with theirs." Interesting, a black prejudice. Do all humans have to look down on someone to feel good about themselves? He and his buddies, however, couldn't help but notice how fine some of the Puerto Rican girls in Philly were! Their obvious mixtures and admixtures—black, white, Indian, and so on—often produced some good-looking, sexy women. They reminded him of a whole race or ethnic group made up of light-skinned black people! Or were they, as he would hear one black comedian say years later, "Black people who can swim!" Another one would opine that "sexy is a young Puerto Rican girl." He had to learn some Spanish so he could effectively flirt with these honeys. "Como se llama de usted? Donde vive usted? Da me un beso!" were the first phrases he learned, followed later by "Te amo" and "Quiero a usted." He occasionally would be mistaken as a Rican himself when pulled over by the Philly police while driving—usually for no legit reason. "A black? Uh … Puerto Rican guy just robbed a bank." Sure!

He and his buddies often referred to the Spanish girls in their code collectively as "Maria" after the beautiful and haunting song from *West Side Story*, "Maria," just as Asian girls were collectively "Suzy" from the motion picture *The Wonderful World of Suzy Wong*, whose main character was played by a beautiful Eurasian actress. These references weren't meant to be denigrating or digs, just descriptive and mildly humorous terms, like their buddy Never being named after the Fellini movie *Never on Sunday*.

He was a bit surprised on one lovely summer evening while sitting on the couch in his Center City bachelor pad with a lovely young caramel-colored Rican he had been dating when she explained to him that while she liked him, she could never take him home. It took him a minute to process, as he wasn't thinking of prejudice or color, and she was darker than he! In years to come, he would become more acutely aware of the color consciousness and outright racism and prejudice that were the dirty little secrets of many of the Hispanic/Latino cultures and traditions—and many of these folks obviously had African blood themselves! They tended to resonate to a European model, no matter how African or Indian they actually looked, with some notable exceptions. Some claimed to be Indio, sometimes as a way to avoid saying black or African, as an explanation for their person-of-color appearance. The radical Young Lords were obviously an exception. White superiority was a worldwide concept evidently! No one wanted to be black, or did they? It appeared that brothers were more popular in America and abroad with white girls than with Spanish girls. *Ironic when you look at history*, he thought.

What does a racially mixed person born in the Caribbean or

even South America really have in common with the inhabitants of Spain? Many of them looked like other Europeans and didn't necessarily relate to the South Americans or folks from the Caribbean. African Americans spoke English but didn't see themselves as English. Where did they think those hips, their coloring, and often their facial features come from if not Africa?

Didn't these Hispanics know about the Moors in Spain and Portugal, about how much of Spanish culture is really African in its origin, that after Nigeria in West Africa, the biggest population of persons of African ancestry on the planet is in Brazil, South America? Of course, many people, he felt, confused national origin or ancestry with race. Omar would sometimes say to them, "You're not Spanish but a victim of the Spanish much as we are victims of the English. Your slave/colonial master was Spanish! Mine was English, but mine won! Ouch!

In terms of the honeys, Amir would conclude that overall the mixes, so-called mixed race women, were often the most attractive, sexiest among women. You got the best of both worlds! Amir also grew to believe that the whole concept of race was man made. It did not exist in nature and was a social construct. After all, weren't we all *Homo sapiens*? According to what he had read, there were no subspecies in the human family. There really were no whites. *Europeans* was probably a more accurate and descriptive term. *Negro* was obviously another questionable term. *African* made more sense to him. The Lamb[12] had taught that the first people were black people since the 1920s and 1930s. Further, that whites and Europeans were essentially grafted from blacks and that blacks were the originators of civilization. Some mainstream (white) anthropologists, biologists, historians, and other scientists were starting to acknowledge the same.

Africa was the homeland of everybody. Of course, for the most

---

[12] The Honorable Elijah Muhammad.

part, the educational system, public and private, including colleges and universities, taught almost nothing about the pre-American/Columbian history of blacks! Black/African studies courses were just starting to appear in colleges and universities, usually, in part at least, because of pressure and demands made by Amir's generation at the various institutions. The Moorish Science Temple of America and the Nation of Islam were among the few groups who did teach this deeper knowledge, this science. Both existed and were active in Philly. So Amir and some of the guys went to the temple, the mosque, and the library. They bought the literature, albums, and tapes and studied. They sat around with some of the older brothers to absorb some of this science. "You were here before George Washington and 'nem. The Moors were here. The white man knows this but won't tell you."

He also studied entirely on his own, amassing a small library of black history books, authored by J. Kenneth Clarke, Basil Davidson, W. E. B. DuBois, John Hope Franklin, J. A. Rogers, Lerone Bennett Jr., Dr. Asante, Dr. John Henrik Clarke, Professor Ivan Van Sertima, Cheikh Anta Diop, Anthony Appiah, and Dr. Ben. He read about the West African Kingdoms of Ghana, Mali, and Songhay; ancient Nubia; Kush; Great Zimbabwe; Egypt; Kanem-Bornu; Timbuktu; Kilwa; Zanzibar; the Zulus; and ancient Ethiopia, among other kingdoms and empires.

In addition, he attended some lectures by Dr. Ben, Ivan Van Sertima, and Professor John Henrik Clark, among others. Shaka Zulu, Hannibal, Tarik (the general who led the Moors in their 711 CE successful invasion of Spain), Mansa Musa I, Abu Bakri II, the Mahdi from the Sudan, Yaa Asanteewa of the Ashanti, Nat Turner, Denmark Vesey, Gabriel Prosser, Charles LeLonde, Harriet Tubman, Queen Nzinga, Jomo Kenyaata, Patrice Lumumba, Kwame Nkrumah, Gamal Abdel Nasser, and Ahmed Ben Bella joined his list of heroes and heroines. Amir also began to read and view the Holy Bible, the Torah, and the Holy Koran with new eyes, realizing that many of the characters in same were blacks and Africans! He began realizing also that many of the events recorded in these holy books occurred in Africa or in an African context. A realization also developed that as long as more of this knowledge was not passed along in schools, blacks, whites, and others would not have an accurate and full understanding of the contributions of blacks in world and American history, which of course contributed to negative stereotypes, prejudice, and racism.

It was also a big factor in the self-hatred and low self-esteem that all too many African Americans apparently still suffered from to some degree, he felt.

Talk that Talk

That's a bad vine, brother! That brother is clean! That girl is a stallion! She's got big stockings. Let's go to Mary house. I'm headed to the crib. What it is? Right on. What's your bag? I feel like some shrimps. Party tonight, y'all! I want a fish samich. These expressions and many, many more were a part of the Black English of the time, which, decades later, came to be called Ebonics and was considered a controversial issue. Amir and some of his friends went back and forth between this Black English and standard English multiple times daily. It was not a problem, he felt, to switch back and forth. It didn't impede one's ability to articulate in standard English. It was fun, it was creative, and it was theirs! Unlike many other ethnic groups in America, who could lapse into their respective native tongues for enjoyment or better communication or to prevent others from understanding what was being said in their presence, most African Americans had had this ability taken away from them because of an institution called chattel slavery. Therefore, this slang, this talking jive, this Black English, made perfect sense to Amir and was justified. Of course, there were rules of grammar and terminology and vocabulary to be observed:

A *vine* was a man's suit.

Boss meant stylish or good-looking.

Clean meant exceptionally well or sharply dressed.

No apostrophe *s* was placed after people's names to show possession; for example, "Mary's house" became "Mary house."

The word *ask* was pronounced "axe" so that we said not "Ask Jane" but "Axe Jane."

The plural of *shrimp* was *shrimps*, as in "I want some shrimps."

The word *y'all*, which is really a southern word, was used liberally.

"Lawd ham mercy" was a commonly used expression, especially among older blacks, probably of southern origin, expressing joy, surprise, gratitude, or shock.

A *stallion* was a voluptuous female, not a male horse!

A *set* was a kind of afterparty, where the cool people went after the regular party was over, "dancing in their stocking feet."

A *one-* or *two-bag woman* was a woman so unattractive you'd have to put a bag over her head in order to have sex with her.

Bag, as in "What's your bag?" referred to one's passion, interests, and so on.

Big boned meant a husky or plump person, often a euphemism for fat.

One eats not a sandwich but a "samich."

Big stockings meant nicely shaped and substantial legs and calves on a woman.

Fine or *foxy* meant a pretty or good-looking woman.

A *dog* or a *skank* was an unattractive woman.

Pumping was a woman wearing high heels well.

Ho heels were the extremely high-heeled (spiked-heeled) shoes worn by some women.

An *all-night worker* was a sexy, nubile, sinewy, voluptuous-looking woman.

Trim, underplunder, stinky, ooooh wee, cock, p——y, and *fuzzy bank* were all references to the female sexual organ and/or having sex.

A *monkey hiney* was a term usually reserved for a woman with a pronounced butt that sort of jutted out, sat up. You could set a cup on it.

Behind meant after/post, as in "behind last night."

One's *nose being open* or *wide open* meant someone madly in love or in lust with someone.

P——y-whipped was an allegation that a guy was strongly influenced or controlled by the sex he was having or wanted to have with a woman.

Sang meant someone or the singing of someone exceptionally talented, as in "Aretha Franklin could sang."

Jive was something unapproved of, in bad taste, and so on, as in "That's jive!"

Hammer was a healthy, robust-looking girl.

Mack/macking was a pimp or pimping.

Drop a dime was snitching or telling.

Booga was an unattractive woman.

Puns, double entendre, witticisms, rhymes, repartee, and plays on words were constant, whether in the vernacular Black English or standard English. "If I catch you with it, I gotta get it!" "Mother born ya, mother feed ya, I never need ya!" "Bullshit the baker and you might get a bun, bullshit me and you get naree one!" "A stiff dick has no conscience!" "That Negro wouldn't work in a pie factory!" "It's my duty to get that booty." "Life is a beach, and then you die!" "Her troubles are all behind her!" "Behind every good man, there's a good woman, and behind every good woman, there's a behind." They played the dozens[13] a lot. The old heads seemed to also.

When Amir, Omar, Phil, and SaRon were together, few could match or keep up with their repartee, their wit and witticisms, like the time they were walking along the streets of Center City one evening after classes at CCP and an acquaintance was observed urinating in an alley. He retorted, "I am European," to which Phil quickly responded, "That's right; you are peeing."

There was the time a younger freshman at CCP who obviously looked up to the crew admitted he was a little overwhelmed and bemused by the black consciousness movement and its various manifestations—integrationists, black nationalists, Panthers, Moorish Americans, the Nation, the Black Liberation Army, RAM, and so on—and was told, "Don't worry; it won't last much longer, and you're still a Negro!"

Make a Joyful Noise

The family Baptist church where Mom was an active member and sang on the choir was a Southern Baptist church. She went almost every Sunday. She loved and proudly owned and wore many crowns (hats), big and small, plain and ornate, colorful and simple, which were a part of Southern Baptist, black female tradition. Dad didn't ever go to church and explained, "I don't need a man telling me how to live!" Amir and Melinda were required to attend Sunday school

---

[13] Interestingly, a term from slavery, disabled or less than prime condition slaves were often sold in lots of a dozen.

almost every Sunday as young children. Amir, Melinda, and Mom would get dressed, he in a suit and Linda in a dress typically. Linda was very pretty and looked quite attractive in her outfits. Amir also enjoyed getting sharp. A couple of his suits had even been tailor made! They typically would walk over to church, it being only a few blocks away and the era being much safer then for children to travel without adults than it would become in years to come.

Problem was there was a candy store between home and church. Amir and Melinda reasoned that God was in the sky and didn't really need money, so they could spend half of the offering money given to them for the church collection on candy! They usually did. The service was sometimes entertaining. A woman or two might get happy or get the spirit during the service.

Getting happy usually entailed the flinging and flailing of arms and legs, sweating, jumping around, and finally oftentimes fainting. One or more ushers grabbed the person and calmed her down. Men never got happy in that manner. It was usually a middle-aged or older woman. Sometimes their dresses flew up, and you could sneak a peek. "Any brother who looks up that sister's dress will have his eyes struck out!" said the minister as the old joke goes, to which one deacon said under his breath, "Well, I'm going to close one eye, but I'll take a chance with the other!"

Amir sometimes found the service to be spooky. Should one believe out of fear? Because Mom did? Because so many others did? Where were the young adult males? Most of the congregation seemed to be female, middle-aged and older, and older men. What wasn't resonating with the young adult males?

Amir also found it interesting that black folks spoke of Jesus as if they knew him personally! They called on him for almost every-thing! They talked about Jesus like he lived on the same street. Was Jesus a surrogate father, husband, boyfriend, or lover for some of these women? It was also interesting how obviously gay men had a place in the black church. Unspoken and unacknowledged at the time, gay men were many times the organists or had some role in the musical aspect of church services. Amir found this interesting because officially many church members were supposedly antigay. The presence of obviously gay males didn't upset or bother Amir, but he found it interesting. It was such an obvious contradiction to what he understood church doctrine to be. Religion, for some, was malleable. For others, it was very fixed and rigid. In later years, he would sometimes reflect on the history of the Catholic Church. Although not a Catholic himself, he was becoming a history buff. And what a history!

Folks were sometimes burned at the stake for deviating from church doctrine. Popes and priests used to marry. In modern times, of course, with vows of chastity, they couldn't. Indulgences used to be sold. Popes made war and led armies. As he grew older, Amir came to believe that all religions, particularly the Abrahamic ones, were guilty of abuses and excesses—the treatment of women, participation in the trans-Atlantic slave trade, teaching anti-Semitism, and so on. All three major faiths owed an apology and possibly some reparations to women and to people of African descent, he decided.

As he got older, the stained-glass windows of the church, decorated with white figures exclusively, started to bother him. The depictions of Jesus, for the most part, were of a fair, long-haired, and bearded European. In fact, he often looked Nordic, sort of like a then modern-day hippie, though he was a Jew. Buddha looked Asian, and Muhammad could not be depicted. If Jesus looked that way, then his father, God, must be a big white guy in the sky. Some argued that Jesus's appearance didn't matter. He disagreed. A people worshipping a God who looked like their oppressor couldn't be healthy, he thought.

The trend in the Baptist churches of the time had become to seek better and more formally educated ministers to lead the church or flock, as opposed to those who were simply called to preach. Rev.

Paul was of that group. A smallish, eyeglasses-wearing man, he was well dressed, very articulate, and gave a stirring sermon. He was also an NAACP official.

Years later, when it was discovered that he had been drinking alcohol and sleeping with women, he had to leave the church. These princes of the church got special treatment, it seemed to Amir. They had a direct line to God. They had privileges. Counseling and consoling the sisters was among their duties. Counseling evidently sometimes led to sleeping with! He occasionally visited Black Methodist churches or AME churches as well.

While women were generally the backbone of these churches, they clearly were male-dominated. The ministers and the deacons were usually the real power brokers. The extent to which religion aids in the liberation of a people is debatable, of course. Is it the opiate of the people or a change agent? Certainly, he came to realize over the years, the black church was a bedrock of the freedom struggle here in America. Dr. Martin Luther King Jr. certainly used the church as the centerpiece of his civil rights movement, as had others before him, such as Richard Allen of AME fame. Even during the days of Jim and Jane Crow, where was the one place blacks could control, be acknowledged, be respected, and hold positions of power and authority? The black church.

Of course, he and his black nationalist and white liberal/progressive friends and acquaintances weren't really MLK Jr. fans. They were more Malcolm (El Hajj Malik El Shabazz) fans, more W. E. B. Dubois and Marcus Garvey than Booker T. Washington or George Washington Carver, more Richard Pryor than Bill Cosby. It would take years for Amir and some of his associates to recognize and acknowledge the courage, genius, and effectiveness of King's movement with its nonviolence philosophy.

In their youthful arrogance and elitism, they saw MLK as country. They were big-city blacks who sort of felt superior to their southern brethren. They were snobs after their own fashion. They thought they were more sophisticated, better dressed, danced better, were better educated, and were more urbane than their southern brethren. They often referred to them as farmers or country. They "talked funny" and "dressed funny." The philosophy of nonviolence was not generally popular in the northeast. Part of the rejection or less than warm acceptance of King by the "young Turks" and many in the established black leadership was this snobbish northern versus southern black dynamic. The young and then media-celebrated King was also viewed as a johnny-come-lately by many in the Philadelphia, New York, and Washington, DC areas. Among established black elites and bourgeois, who had been struggling for civil rights for years, the Urban League, NAACP, and so on, MLK Jr. was sometimes considered too radical by the really conservative ministers and other establishment members. Jealousy over the attention this young upstart was getting was also probably a factor. MLK's Philadelphia reception had been somewhat chilly, and Amir would never forget what one Philly lawyer and activist said when he was assassinated years later: "I told that Negro that that nonviolent shit wouldn't work!" Amir would find it noteworthy that years later, many who would not have been caught dead in the same room as Rev. King at that time would be singing his praises and celebrating his memory, birthday, and contributions years later.

Philly had its own civil rights champions of the day, such as the Rev. Leon H. Sullivan of the Zion Baptist Church, the Lion of Zion, author of the "Sullivan Principles" for South Africa and Progress Plaza in North Central Philadelphia, among other achievements; Cecil B. Moore Jr. of the NAACP (for a time); Walt Palmer (black nationalist); Father Washington of the activist Church of the Advocate; Judge A. Leon Higgenbotham, author of *In the Matter of Color*; and Congressman/minister Bill Gray, among others. Aware Philadelphians were quite proud of Philly's progressive history and large black presence, which included both an established and a growing middle and upper class, with judges, doctors, lawyers, teachers, police officers, ministers, dentists, and businesspeople.

Amir and his crowd did participate in some demonstrations. He recalled walking down Fifth Avenue in New York City yelling, "Hell no, we won't go!" during the Vietnam war when LBJ was president, as part of a massive demonstration. Of course, although dressed casually, he and Omar had carried sports coats along with them so that they could go out clubbing in New York after the demonstration. They were for the cause but saw no point in not taking advantage of the NYC nightlife! The Philly Police had a Civil Disobedience (CD) Squad in those days, headed by a big, ruddy-colored Irishman named Lieutenant Pencil. Pencil had greeted Amir and his comrades one day near city hall with "As Salaamu Alaikum, fellas" as they gathered for a small demonstration. They, the CD Squad, took pics of demonstrators openly and secretly. Philly, he thought, was at its essence, still a conservative town in many ways, although every militant and radical group he was aware of existed there.

Even Philly's riot or rebellion in 1968 was still a conservative one. Some store windows were smashed, there was some looting, and there were arrests, but no one died—very unlike Newark, New Jersey, or LA rebellions. Maybe it was the Quaker influence or the basic conservatism of Philly blacks.

In a different context, there was to be no Playboy Club in Philly, although New York, Chicago, LA, Detroit, and other big cities all had them around the time. Amir figured the city fathers had probably put the kibosh on the idea. He actually saw the Playboy logo and sign that were to go up one day while walking in Center City. It never went up. A nationwide organization founded for and by well-heeled blacks in Philly in 1938 was considered bourgeois, or "bougys," by many. They had cotillions, coming out events for young ladies, and other functions and outings. The girls sometimes wore gowns, the boys tuxedos. Going to college or university was assumed and nurtured. Amir understood that back in the day, there were color issues with the organization. He often thought there were reasons why W. E. B. DuBois's classic *The Philadelphia Negro* was so titled! Amir himself, as a young boy, had been honored with a Boy's Award from a conservative Republican Philly organization. It was a prestigious, conservative, moneyed Philadelphia institution with an impressive location on South Broad Street. He would never forget the ornate look of the place—the dark oak paneling, chandeliers, carpeting, portraits of old rich-looking Europeans—as he entered the building along with other young men for their dinner and presentation of their Boy's Awards. Of course, he was one of the few black boys so honored at the dinner he attended.

Amir was conflicted over the black elites, the well-heeled folks. Sure, sometimes they overdid it. It was often exclusive, bourgeois, and too conservative. Membership, while limited, had its privileges and benefits however—jobs and positions, money, fine women, better homes, and cars. But in this radical black consciousness era, such traditional and often conservative organizations and groups were sometimes roundly criticized and lambasted as irrelevant, anachronistic, and part of the problem, not the solution. However, didn't white and Asian ethnics in America have their elites also? Didn't Africans in Africa? Why would American blacks be any different?

Thank goodness there were a few other African American boys at the old, stately looking building in Center City on Broad Street that cool fall night. Being the only one or one of a few blacks was a circumstance he would become all too familiar with as a black man at awards ceremonies, in a classroom, on an airplane, at a nice hotel or restaurant, at a seminar or workshop, and in many other situations. It was interesting; he was often the lightest-skinned or one of the lightest-skinned people when among blacks and often one of the few blacks when among whites! Some blacks seemed to get off on the only one thing, sometimes bragging about it, but not

Amir. He felt the pressure, felt he could not legitimately represent or speak for all blacks. "Blacks are not monolithic," he often retorted when others tried to maneuver him into that position. The "You're different" or "Why can't more of your people be like you?" comments and questions that he and other blacks often heard were insulting, he felt, and obviously stereotypical and racist.

So when, as a young man working as a job developer (only black there) for a big personnel agency in Center City Philly, he was complimented by a white coworker late one afternoon with the old "Why can't more of your people …?" question. He sarcastically replied, "You mean wear beards? Eat a lot? Wear glasses?" He then explained that both his father and grandfather were hard workers and probably worked harder than he and his white coworker!

Port, Cherry, Muscatel … Our High School Is Raising Hell!

His parents had given a different home address to get him into his high school. It wasn't in his district. So one gave the home address of a friend or relative to be in district of the school one wanted to attend. It was a common practice. They used a family friend named Madeline, who lived in West Oak Lane. He was supposed to go to a different high school, right across the street from his alma mater, a challenging junior high. He had survived junior high and didn't want to go to its high school equivalent. In those days, that high school was terrible! It had a lot of fights and other discipline problems, gangs, old and not enough textbooks and other resources, and new, inexperienced, or simply bad teachers, among other problems. Very few students went on to college. Amir wanted to go to college or some kind of post–high school education. Many years later, this school would turn around under the guidance of a black principal named Marcus Foster. Foster would be assassinated eventually in

California allegedly by the Symbionese Liberation Army (SLA), the same group that had famously kidnapped heiress Patty Hearst, supposedly because Foster was a fascist.

Both Amir's elementary and junior high schools were not only predominantly black but were 90 percent black. Amir's high school was mostly white. It was located in the mostly then middle class northeast section of Philly. It was supposed to be a good school, certainly more highly ranked than the high school in his district. They also had a fencing team! It was the only sport that really interested him. His district high school, in addition to all the other negatives, didn't have a fencing team. *Spick, kraut, guinea, frog, kite, polack, chink, heeb, mick, wetback, wog, gook, zipperhead,* and *dago* were terms he would learn in high school. He rarely used any of them, but you had to be able to defend yourself if insulted ethnically by someone else. He also learned *spear chucker, porch bunny, sambo, boy,* and *schwartza,* for African Americans. Amir took the Broad Street subway north several stops to Hunting Park Avenue and transferred to the R bus traveling on Roosevelt Boulevard in order to get to school every day; going home was, of course, the reverse. It worked out.

His high school was Amir's first racially diverse educational experience. Since there were a limited number of black girls there, the foxes were few and far between. There were some good-looking white girls, but he had never sought to date a white girl. He did not rank them as better or more desirable than black girls, just different, like a different flavor of ice cream. Neither Mom nor Dad had encouraged him to date or not date outside his race as he was growing up.

They didn't talk about race a lot in the family. He did hear that he shouldn't bring anything home with flies on it, according to Biggy, his grandmother and family favorite. Although not stated by Mom or Dad, Biggy seemed to have a color bias. Years later, she referred to one of his father's girlfriends as "Black Lily!" Blacks of her generation often displayed an unabashed color bias or prejudice and spoke in terms of brightening/lightning up the race or marrying up or down. Men, especially, could be too dark or too black. Women were often referred to as dark-skinned but pretty/ attractive/good-looking. Biggy herself was light-brown-skinned and good-looking with pretty dark-mixed-with-gray hair. Amir felt that all this colorism had to be the result of the intense racism and color prejudice that American blacks were constantly subjected to in their daily lives. Clearly, the closer to white, the better. Not that all blacks wanted to be white—they wanted the benefits and privileges that flowed therefrom, of course. It was well known among blacks that thousands of blacks passed for white. If you couldn't look at and discern that one was black, then with enough deception and subterfuge, one could live a white life. What a price to pay, however! Most black families, no matter how fair some of their members might be, had some darker-skinned members as well. They presumably would have to be kept away from and kept away. *How sad*, he thought.

There were books and movies about this tragic circumstance, this passing and its ramifications—*Pinkhy* and *Imitation of Life* and at least two other films of the same name, probably being the best known of the genre.

Of course, blacks were not alone in this passing. There were whites who got nose jobs, changed their names, or hid their Jewish or Latino heritage as well. Personally, Amir enjoyed being yella. He didn't think that being pasty and pale was a better look. He had seen many handsome and pretty dark-skinned and very dark-skinned people but didn't think that was a better look either. On balance, being yella wasn't so bad! A sort of compromise, as it were. Over the years, he did come to believe that lighter-skinned black people and darker-skinned black people felt the brunt of racism. Both, he felt, could make others uncomfortable, black and white. Both presented similar yet different dynamics of racism and colorism. Fair-skinned blacks often didn't look that different from whites in terms of features, coloring, hair, and so on. Dark-skinned blacks often presented in a way that emphasized the differences in appearance. Brown-skinned folk were in the middle and caught less hell, he figured. They didn't make people as uncomfortable and didn't necessarily put a lie to stereotypes.

Amir lived through an era when light-skinned guys with good hair were sought after and prized and when being light-skinned was passe and had to be defended against being labelled not really black or not black enough. This black enough period was notable. Black pride was a good thing, but more militant blacks competing on who was the blackest was silly and counterproductive, he felt. Vanessa Williams, the first black Ms. America was sometimes spoken of that way, usually by black women. In later years, he would wonder what stories Pop, his grandfather, could've told.

Pop and Biggy often babysat Melinda and Amir. He would never forget how, while he and Melinda were at Biggy's house, she would cook meals and say, "Don't get up from the table until you feel full!" Biggy was from Georgia, just like Dad, Mom, and Pop. She was a strong person but also loving and affectionate, especially to Amir.

Years later, he would learn that she married Pop as a young teenager, customary during that era, and that Dad was one of several children she gave birth to but the only one who survived! Dad had been an only child. Her words and spirit would stay with him forever. "Be proud." "Have your own." Biggy often worked as an office cleaning woman, like many black women of the time. It was probably one of the few jobs open to them. Amir would never forget the time he went to work with her as a little boy, at some company in Center City, and she proceeded to tell off the men in the office, one of whom had left a girlie magazine somewhere around, which she had discovered and construed as disrespectful! She would help him purchase his first car, when Dad wouldn't. Occasionally, she would loan him small amounts of money. She was always there for him. He felt obligated to her as a result and genuinely loved her. As she grew older and her eyesight began to fail, she would trust Amir to count her cash money for her. Pulling out a small purse that had been pinned to her bra as many black women of the time did, she would state, "Should be three hundred dollars there. Check and see if my red dress is upstairs in the closet. I think one of your father's cows[14] may have stolen it!"

Of course, he checked and assured her that her red dress was, in fact, there. Amir was proud of the fact he helped her secure the benefits the Commonwealth of Pennsylvania made available for those classified as legally blind. Amir often drove across town at Biggy's request, picking up dinners at various restaurants for her even when he really didn't feel like it or had just finished driving across town from the opposite direction. He owed her!

School Daze (Cont'd)—High School

The architecture was the gray stone structure common of the time. There was an athletic field sort of across and up the street. There were the student lockers in the hallways and of course a gym. Ms. Walsh, the principal, was older and had light-blue hair, probably, he thought, from attempts to get rid of the gray with various dyes. It had diversity. There were enough blacks to essentially keep things peaceful racially. You didn't mess with someone from another group for fear of retaliation from that group. In those days, vice principals were the disciplinarians. Often, gym teachers also were. Some of them were physically fit and tough. You didn't want to be told, "Go to the vice principal's office!" Teachers also generally commanded more respect during that era.

---

[14] Girlfriends she disapproved of.

Amir liked his high school. Occasionally, he would hear a fellow student make an overtly racist comment—like the time he was standing at the bus stop on Roosevelt Boulevard, waiting for the R bus on a beautiful spring afternoon, along with several other students. Suddenly and casually as a Cadillac driven by a brother stopped in front of them for a red light, a white fellow student commented, "Your people sure do love those Cadillacs!"

Amir's retort was "Yeah, and your people love to sell them to them!"

In the cafeteria one day, a white acquaintance used the "N word" while he was nearby. He immediately apologized and explained he didn't include Amir in that reference.

He would always remember Ms. Johnson, his twelfth-grade English teacher, for making him curious about and able to appreciate Shakespeare. She actually made reading the Bard fun! *Interesting*, he thought, *we remember two types of teachers—the very good and the very bad ones!* He almost didn't pass trigonometry in twelfth grade and would've had to graduate after his class in June. He had to get a paid tutor.

Dad wanted him to take a part-time job at a supermarket. He couldn't do both at the same time. He and Mom had a big fight over it. Dad didn't want him to grow up and be a bum. He wanted him to understand the value and meaning of work. Mom wanted him to graduate high school and also have a work ethic. They battled, and Mom won. Amir graduated with his class.

The class trip to Bear Mountain had been fun—the boat ride, the music. Amir had never been to Bear Mountain before. The senior prom had been fun. Amir double dated with his buddy Never. Dad let him borrow his Buick Electra 225, a.k.a. a deuce and a quarter. He was a bit nervous, knowing how meticulous Dad was about his cars. He joked that if he had an accident in it, he would have to leave the state! They went to a real restaurant in Center City for dinner and drinks. Amir didn't really drink but knew how to order a vodka martini, shaken and not stirred, from the James Bond novels he had been reading. The in thing to do after the prom was to drive to Atlantic City and get a hotel room for a few hours. He made the proposal to Ellen, and she seemed offended by the offer. Amir explained that she didn't really have to do anything, just stay in the room for a while for appearances' sake. She would not go along. Oh well. She really wasn't that much fun at the prom either. While many other couples were grinding and up on each other like cheap suits, like white on rice, she would not indulge. Amir still managed to enjoy the prom. After all, she really wasn't his girlfriend.

His graduating class was so big the ceremony had to be held at Philly's convention hall. Then Mayor Richardson Dilworth was the keynote speaker. His partner, Claudette, looked quizzical and empathetic when she saw a tear roll down his face during the ceremony as they walked down the aisle together. She said, "Amir, you're sentimental!"

He replied, "No, my dad told me I have to get off my butt and get a job now!"

"Invictus" was the poem recited at graduation. "Out of the night that covers me, black as the pit from pole to pole I thank whatever gods may be for my unconquerable soul!" Amir would find this poem motivational for the rest of his life as he faced certain of life's challenges. On another level, he also liked "Chartless" by Emily Dickinson. He became an Edgar Allen Poe fan in high school also—"The Raven," "The Pit and the Pendulum," "The Telltale Heart," and so on. Amir also learned of and developed a penchant for Langston Hughes, particularly the poems "Mother to Son," "The Negro Speaks of Rivers," and "Countee Cullen."

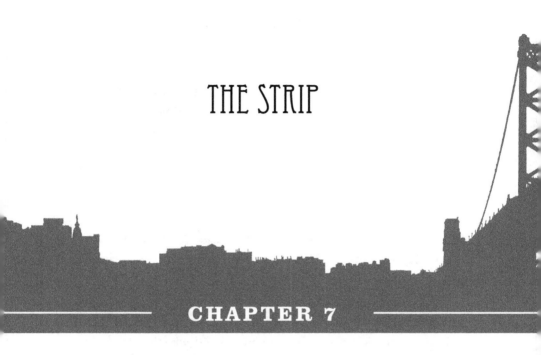

THE STRIP

CHAPTER 7

As SaRon, he, and Mike were walking along the Fifty-Second Street Strip, a section of West Philly that ran along Fifty-Second Street, starting at Market Street and continuing south for several blocks, they saw Omar coming out of Foo Foo's restaurant, home of the mammer jammer, a famous Philadelphia sandwich akin to a cheesesteak.

"Wassup, professor?"

"I can't call it, brother! Nothing shaking but the leaves in the trees, and they wouldn't be shaking if it wasn't for the breeze!"

"Let's go to Crazy Horse!" (a popular go-go bar on the Strip), and off they went.

The Strip was interesting. In addition to Foo Foo's, there was also Broughams', a big, popular club/bar/restaurant with live entertainment, including go-go girls dancing in cages above the bar. There was a stage. A fellow called "School Boy" or "Schooly," for short, was the emcee when live entertainment occurred. His intro for acts after intermission or a set was colorful. It went something like "And now it's time for you to powder your nose and paint your toes. Remember to stick and stay and don't go away, 'cause good God Amighty, from the looks of everybody, all you fine foxy mamas and bad daddy laddys, you shoo nuff came to party … Shoo 'em on!"

Acts were often just back from their European tours, where they had performed for the crowned heads of Europe. One afternoon, at Coupes' while seated at a small table with Omar, Mike, and a platonic friend named Dana, a fellow came in and shot a guy standing at the bar. The on-stage live band then began to play, "Hey, Hey, Gonna Be a Showdown!"

As he, Mike, Omar, and Dana had ducked under the table, Amir used the opportunity to get the phone number of the cute waitress he'd had his eye on who had also ducked under the table with them. Fortunately, they later learned, the brother was not killed but wounded. You could buy a Cadillac in the men's room at this place, as Amir learned one evening when he went in to pee and inadvertently heard a discussion in one of the stalls about what color interior the customer wanted in his Caddy!

The African Cultural Center was also on Fifty-Second Street. The scientific brothers and sisters could be found there, along with other intellectuals, Muslims, black nationalists, socialists, Garveyites, communists, pan-Africanists, anarchists, and revolutionaries. The muntu and mink (a phrase coined by Omar) set was also in evidence. These were the middle- or upper-middle-class blacks who pretended to be so radical when convenient or stylish. On the Strip, he had always noticed that certain guys would drive up in expensive cars, in those days Cadillacs and maybe an occasional Mercedes. These gentlemen would park their respective rides on the street and not even lock them. No one bothered their rides. These were men who got respect, or was it fear? Maybe both?

He and the fellas would visit, just as they visited Muhammad's Mosque or Temple, the Black House, the Church of the Advocate, the Moors, and Father Divine's[15] Hotel on North Broad Street for some free grub. A full meal at no cost! Places were left for the deceased Father and Mother Divine. Father Divine also had filling/gas stations. There was knowledge to be had everywhere! Christians, Muslims, Moorish Science, Masons, Black Hebrews, the Panthers—one could learn simply by osmosis! It seemed they all had a piece of the truth. Brother Daood, a force at the African Cultural Center, had yelled, "Allah!" as he was struck on the neck by a hatchet, the story went, and that was what saved his life!

North Philly, Philadelphia's version of Harlem, Chicago's South Side, the Bottom in other areas, was Amir's neighborhood. This area was duplicated all across America in urban centers—a section, mostly African American, in a city that had been comprised at one time of working-class folk and some recent immigrants from the South and that had been more prosperous in bygone days. It often had emerged from white flight. Usually, it contained many churches, bars, nightclubs, and stores of various kinds.

As industry had started moving away and the manufacturing jobs began drying up, employment declined, and crime, along with the drug epidemic, got underway. North Philly suffered greatly. The once-proud working-class owners of the often smallish row houses had started to move, those who could afford to, a migration to more aspirational neighborhoods, such as West Oak Lane, Germantown, and Mount Airy. Some even opted for the Jersey suburbs, Cherry Hill and Willingboro, New Jersey, in particular.

Philly had been a big textile industry center. The port of Philadelphia, of course, also provided some employment, but as America was becoming more of a service economy and less of a manufacturing one for a variety of reasons, urban blacks really suffered. It's difficult for unemployed or underemployed people to pay

---

[15] A popular and charismatic religious cult leader of the time who was quite prosperous, owning hotels, gas stations, and other properties.

their mortgage or rent, to maintain their property, to enjoy a decent quality of life. "Poverty makes a man a slave," Amir had read in a book of African quotations. People have to survive, so crime goes up. Citizens start preying on each other, and muggings, robberies, and thefts of all kinds increase.

Of course, the mass incarceration of blacks was well underway by this time as well. Incarceration of fathers, sons, brothers, and nephews weakened the family structure and obviously reduced the family or group's income. This prison-industrial system/complex provided employment and profit for others who lived in different areas, often white. Entire communities sometimes existed because of or profited from their existence. The government welfare rules of the time, such as a female recipient of AFDC not being able to legally have a man around her domicile to keep her aid for dependent children (AFDC) eligibility checks coming was also devastating to the family structure. Men had to hide or disappear if the caseworker was coming around! A popular movie of the time *Claudine*, with James Earl Jones and foxy Diane Carroll, illustrated this. Now the recurring theme was becoming, "Black men just make babies and don't take care of them!" "They are lazy. They are irresponsible!" all of which, ran contrary to his growing up experiences!

Most of the black men he knew worked! Most of the old heads he knew were married and had families. Some were taking care of multiple families! The more other blacks, often women, bought into these negative stereotypes, the more it hurt. Certainly, his father, Will, worked hard, as did his grandfather, Pop, and so did Whip, Flip, Slick, Michael T., and on and on. He couldn't relate! Most of these brothers worked at manual labor jobs, like many other brothers of that era—hard work—as truck drivers, auto mechanics, warehousemen, deliverymen, construction workers, and so on. They went to work early in the morning, sometimes working long days. They worked in inclement weather. They rarely were late or absent from work.

Of course, on the job, he was sure they were often subjected to unequal treatment, lower pay, to discrimination. They often endured slights, insults, and denigrating treatment on a regular basis. Very often underemployed, these brothers usually stuck it out to keep their jobs and to support their families. You never heard their praises sung! *Getting up every morning or night and going to a job you hate and get no satisfaction from, that's real courage,* Amir thought. Of course, many black women worked as well and endured their measure of discrimination also.

He'd never forget how in the evening, standing at the intersection of Sixteenth and Market Streets, waiting for the northbound Number 2 bus to get home, along with some black cleaning women freshly finished working at some Center City offices they had been cleaning, usually middle-aged or older, not particularly well dressed or in most cases attractive, never dressed provocatively, invariably some white guy passing in his car would pull over to the curb or slow down, thinking that these women were prostitutes, simply because they were standing on the corner late at night and were black women! The stereotypes about black women, however, in the main, were different. There were the mammy, the sapphire, and the Jezebel stereotypes, of course. But Amir had learned that many white men and others fantasized about sisters sexually in America and in Europe especially, Italy, France, and so on. Their womanhood, however, was not usually questioned. Their ability to be good mothers was not constantly held up for examination or derision. No, it was the black man's manhood in America that was always up for debate or derision by the larger society and unfortunately by increasing numbers of black women as well. Men in America are not usually the recipients of unconditional love. Women, children, dogs, and some cats are. This goes double for black American men. The exception is the son who is loved by his mother while his sisters are raised by her. This concept is a truism among some African Americans. Even the slang of the time reflected this. After all, wasn't the white man "the Man" and the black woman "Mama" or "Mommy"? What did that leave for the black man, "boy"? Amir grew to believe that there were forces at work to undermine the black family and black progress, either consciously or unconsciously, intentionally or not. This was particularly true of the black male. In the biblical story, didn't Herod Antipas have the firstborn male children of the ancient Hebrews slaughtered when he feared the coming of a messiah or king? Hadn't the Egyptian pharaoh before that tried the same thing, killing the firstborn male children?

Most blacks he knew had migrated or fled north or west or to the Midwest from the American South in search of a better life. They came from Georgia, Mississippi, Alabama, Virginia, North and South Carolina, and various other states with their accents and often little formal education but with strong work ethics, religious faith, strong family values, hope, and basic human decency, much like most immigrants from foreign countries who come to America. They were seeking better jobs, homes, and treatment; friendships in all walks of life; a better future for their progeny, and so on. He had learned that in the South, the work ethic was traditionally very strong, as were religious beliefs and family and community ties. This background was brought with them as immigrants. Omar's words seemed to ring true, "We [black people] are at war; there are lulls in the fighting, but make no mistake, we are at war." Another axiom was "Life's a struggle, from the womb to the tomb."

Amir had witnessed his own family more than once welcome new southern immigrants, sometimes relatives, sometimes not, as they assisted them in finding living quarters and employment and acclimating them to northern life. He would never forget the time that shortly after a visit by Michael T., a delightful cousin from Elberton, Georgia, two FBI agents came to the house asking questions about him. Mom was home and spoke to them. Of course, she denied any knowledge of his current whereabouts and having seen him recently as they all sat in the living room conversing. Michael

T.'s visit had only been a week or two before! Amir was a boy at the time and found the incident exciting, real FBI agents, like on television, with Efrem Zimbalist Jr. and company. He had figured out that something was up when he saw them.

Two white guys in suits was an unusual sight on Huntingdon Street unless they were insurance agents collecting premiums from residents or baseball fans (usually nonsuited) invading the neighborhood to go to close by Connie Mack Stadium for a baseball game. The roar of the crowd from the stadium could often be heard on Huntingdon Street! The husband of a cousin, Eddy K., a real baseball fan, actually took Amir to a couple of baseball games at Connie Mack Stadium when he was a young boy. Baseball wasn't nearly as boring in person, he thought.

The Uptown Theatre at Broad and Dauphin Streets was one of the highlights of North Philadelphia and Philly generally. It was Philly's Apollo. It was an old movie theater with a real stage, balcony, and curtains. He could believe that it had actually been a theater once upon a time. Of course, movies were screened there then. Periodically, there were, however, stage shows, usually put on by Georgie Woods, "the man with the goods," a local and very popular DJ on radio station WDAS AM and FM. A tall, good-looking, light-brown-skinned man, he was slender with a neatly trimmed moustache. He was an immigrant from the state of Georgia. Of course, he dressed immaculately.

Most blacks in Philly grew up listening to WDAS AM and FM, a radio station that catered to black listeners and was also involved in the movement. The programming consisted of rock and roll and gospel music. The DJs were local celebrities; they included Jimmy Bishop, Georgie Woods, Joseph "Butterball" Tamburro (a.k.a. Butter), Mary Mason, John "Lord Fauntleroy" Bandy, Jocko Henderson, and Louise Williams, among others. Back in the day, a black DJ located in Philly or New York had to talk in rhymes, talk a lot of shit, be a kind of poet, and dress well, and, of course, it didn't hurt if he or she were good-looking and played the hits. Some had a schtick. One of his favorites, the aforementioned Lord Fauntleroy (John Bandy) had a British accent—whether he was in fact British, he never learned. He dressed like an English country gentleman, in waistcoats, braces, Donegal tweeds, and jodhpurs. He had gray hair at his temples and drove a Bentley! This brother was bad! He would go on to have a few stints on TV, join management at WDAS, and marry Roberta Pew of the wealthy and famous old-money Pew family (Sun Oil) of Pennsylvania! A black radio disc jockey marrying an old-money white heiress—only in Philadelphia!

The stage shows were a who's who of music of the era—the Temptations, the Supremes, Four Tops, Gene Chandler, the Duke of Earl, James Brown, Smokey Robinson and the Miracles, Jackie Wilson, Gary "US" Bonds, "Little" Stevie Wonder, Mary Wells, Martha Reeves and the Vandellas, the Contours, and many others. Moms Mabley was often the comedian on the show. She was funny. "The only thing an old man can tell me is where a young man is!" "Old men give you warts!"

Amir and Melinda would walk over to the Uptown on a Saturday morning or afternoon, see a double feature and cartoons, and stay for the stage show for just a few dollars. Georgie Woods would host or emcee the shows. Standing on stage elegantly dressed and tapping his foot, he would introduce the acts. He was as much a celebrity as the stars he was introducing. There was a live band on stage, of course—horns, a piano, guitars, drums, and so on, a real band. He later learned that Philly was on the chittling circuit so that Motown acts and others came there regularly.

There were many churches and bars or beer gardens, as his parents used to call them in North Philly. An interesting dichotomy. There was one right across and up the street from the house. In the old days, however, even drunks hanging on the corner had a modicum of respect for women. Amir often saw a few brothers on the corner, having a taste, usually enclosed in a brown paper bag. Often, one or more in the group would be cussing, but almost invariably, if a female was approaching, one in the group would shoosh the ones cussing and say, "Here comes a lady!" Sometimes the patrons in a bar would spill out onto the street. Sometimes there would be arguments and sometimes fights but not that often really.

Of course, there were high-class and low-class bars. There was the one for instance downtown (Center City) that was a hangout for many lawyers and judges. Cops usually had certain bars they frequented as well. African American males who frequented these bars were known as sportsmen. There was an entire bar culture. Folks often got sharp—clothing, jewelry, and so on—and patron-ized these bars. Amir didn't desire to become a sportsman.

Mom and Dad were not nightlife or bar people, and he never actually saw either of them go into one. As a young man in his twenties, either alone or with one or more of his buddies, he would go to many go-go bars fairly frequently. That was because they had go-go girls dancing in them, not for the drinking or just to be hanging out in a bar.

Amir never became a real drinker, usually ordering ginger ales and paying the price of a real drink for them. He visited the Bird Cage, the Trestle Inn, the Pony Tail, Bob's Yacht Club, the Half Moon, and the Living Room, among many others.

There were factories and warehouses in North Philly during the era. Mom sometimes worked at a cigar factory nearby. PBM (Pincus Brothers Maxwell), a clothing and textile factory, existed. There was a whiskey factory not too far from the house; sometimes if the wind blew from a certain direction, the smell of whiskey wafted through the neighborhood. Not too far away, there was a slaughterhouse. If you approached it, the smell could be almost overpowering!

People thought to be lazy "wouldn't work in a pie factory." If one had no money, he or she "didn't have a pot to piss in or a window to throw it out of!" These southern immigrants tended to have a strong work ethic for the most part. "A man works," he had heard

Dad say more than once. Even though North Philly had seen better days, when Amir was young, it really wasn't that bad. Of course, like NYC, Chicago, Detroit, LA, and other big cities, there were the ever-present gangs and the danger they presented.

Young black men in Philly had to look out for gangs and the police. In those days, the gangs weren't as well armed, however, or as murderous as they would become in time. There didn't seem to be a lot of shootings. There was an occasional stabbing. Someone might get stomped or greased (beat up). Sometimes a tire chain or a switch blade was the weapon of choice. Philly also had fair ones (a fistfight between two males). "Can I get a fair one/box?" was usually a challenge to fight. There was somewhat of a code among gang members; upon seeing a young man they did not know on their turf, the challenge of "Where you from?" would be thrown down. If one replied, "nowhere," as Amir, not being a gang member, always did, you would usually get a pass, followed by "Go ahead. Don't let me see you around here again!" Occasionally, a gang member would respond, "Nowhere is getting kinda strong!"

Of course, his family and he lived on their street, and there was a gang there. He also respected and acknowledged them. *Wise*, he thought. One should try to respect everyone, if possible. But he never sought to join them. They, in turn, respected or at least didn't bother him. Whenever setting off on a journey as a young man, he always had to give some thought as to which gang turf he would be traversing or a guest on—the Diamond Street Gang, the Valley, the Zulu Nation, the Moroccos, the Klang, and so on. Years later, he would find it interesting, remembering that some of the gangs actually had Afrocentric names.

Mom had instructed him and Melinda back in elementary school, "If someone hits you, hit them back!" Biggy, however, had cautioned not to fight any people who were too ugly. Her wisdom was "they'll fight you all day, 'cause they got nothing to lose; they're already ugly! You're good-looking and don't want to get your face all messed up!" Out of context, she added, "Some of these girls want you to give them a baby. Be careful."

Upwardly mobile folks often moved from North Philly or South Philly to Germantown, West Oak Lane, Mount Airy, and Chestnut Hill, with their small, manicured lawns and sometimes porches, backyards, garages, and stone facades. Cherry Hill and Willingboro in the Jersey suburbs were also popular moves. He would never forget the evening Dad had the for sale sign in the vestibule of their Huntingdon Street house. Were they moving? Amir was excited. It turned out Mom didn't want to move!

Her network—that is, her church, friends, favorite stores, and so on—were important to her. They didn't move. Next door, there was a father, mother, and cute white girl living there about his age. Of course, being neighbors, they played with each other, he and Melinda and her. They played hide-and-seek, double dutch (the girls), and stickball and spent time just watching TV.

Jumping double dutch was a cultural thing for young inner-city African American girls. Some of those young women were really good! Amir would never forget being on Eighteenth Street one spring afternoon and observing Wanda, a neighbor, jumping double dutch. She was attractive anyway, with pretty eyes and a cute mole on her face. He had not seen those shapely yellow legs however! Wanda had big legs. As she jumped rope, he became transfixed by their musculature and shape. This girl was sexy! Aside from his neighbors on either side, everyone else in the neighborhood was black. There was a nice family right across the street with one son, a little younger than Amir. He would never forget the day Mom sent him to Jack's to get sanitary napkins! So embarrassing! Some of the neighborhood kids stole from Jack, but not Amir. It was wrong, and Mom would've killed him!

The barbershop was about two blocks up the street. It was a small shop with three or four barber chairs. It was a meeting place for the neighborhood's older brothers. It was stocked with magazines to browse through and had the obligatory television set placed high up on the wall so that all could see. Conversation, repartee, and trash talking were plentiful.

"I took care of your mom while you were gone," one guy said with a sly grin to another.

"Your wife is making my car payments!" another fella said with a smile to an acquaintance.

"What do you think of that Cassius Clay?"

"Did you hear the new Aretha Franklin album?"

Of course, there would always be the urgings to "get your lessons, son/boy," made to Amir and any other young guys in the shop. "Get your education, boy. The white man can't take that from you!" was heard frequently at the barber shop, the supermarket, the church, the playground, the garage, almost everywhere. Many of these older brothers were southern migrants to the North and only had a fifth- or sixth-grade education. "Had to drop out. Had to help on the farm," many would explain.

Some had actually picked cotton and tobacco! Many had been drafted or volunteered and had served in World War II or Korea, mostly for the army, some the navy, and a few the marines. Many had served in Europe or the Pacific.

"Dem crackers are no damn good!" would occasionally be heard.

At the barbershop, everyone laughed when one guy commented, during a group discussion about Islam, "I can give up pork and drinking, but I loves my white women."

Greetings of "you the man" were often heard, as well as "Hey, deacon," and "Hey, Doctor," to entering patrons.

Bragging about their sexual exploits, real or imagined, was also common.

"They call me Sweet Dick Tony."

"Women give me money!"

"I rode her to the finish line!"

"My father was a jockey; he taught me how to ride. He said, 'Son, you got to hit it from side to side!'"

"There are only two kinds of pussy, good and better."

Everyone guffawed.

Of course, the barber always cut off more hair than you wanted or had told him to. There never were any females in the barbershop in those days. This was a male bastion and sanctuary in those days. It would remind him years later, after traveling abroad, of the way men congregated in parts of Europe, the Middle East, and Africa in cafés and coffeehouses, where they relaxed, had animated discussions, drank tea or coffee, and enjoyed an all-male environment.

Cheerio, Old Chap

His hotel in London was on Kensington High Street. It was named the Royal Kensington Hotel. He thought this was probably considered Central London. Since this was a TWA Getaway Tour, a kind of unescorted tour, the hotels and flights had been arranged by TWA. His tour included a continental breakfast daily and a half-day of sightseeing along with transfers and a few other features. Then you were on your own. He had landed at Heathrow Airport but would be going on to Paris from Gatwick Airport when the London portion was done. He was excited. It was his first trip abroad! Several first impressions followed. Mostly, these were real white people; he didn't see too many dark whites or Southern European / Mediterranean types. These folks were usually pale to very pale and big, and many had, surprisingly, bad teeth! Most of the English girls he encountered looked okay but were not fine.

The fine ones stood out. London was somewhat like NYC but seemed to be more historical. Of course, the architecture was somewhat different. Nothing in NYC looked like the Houses of Parliament or Big Ben or the Tower! Everything was oriented toward the left, not the right, like in America. Better be careful crossing the street! He had always liked the English accents, especially on women. They sounded sophisticated yet sexy. He was pleasantly surprised to find there were so many blacks from around the world in London! They were from Africa, the Caribbean, and the South Pacific. Movies and television had not prepared him for this! He had some familiarity with English culture. *All Americans do*, he thought. *We speak English, after all. Don't many of our laws emerge from English Common Law. Aren't many of our traditions really English traditions? Didn't America actually emerge from England? Isn't English the lingua franca of the world? Don't airline pilots, regardless of national origin, speak English to the tower?*

The Magna Carta, Shakespeare, Keats, Shelley, Lord Byron, Henry the VIII, the Duke of Windsor, Queen Victoria, Queen Elizabeth, Prince Charles, high tea, James Bond, bobbies, Jack the Ripper, Sherlock Holmes, the little black cabs, the red double-decker buses, the red telephone booths, bowler hats, umbrellas, and on and on.

He had enjoyed reading most of the Sherlock Holmes stories but wouldn't be going to 221 B Baker Street. He knew it was just an address used in Conan Doyle's works of fiction. He would have to take the "Jack the Ripper" walk however. Had "the Ripper" been Prince Edward? Leather Apron? Aaron Kosminsky? Thomas Cutbush? Amir had always liked many of the English expressions or slang; an apartment is a "flat" and an elevator a "lift"; cars have "bonnets," not hoods; the trunk of your car is the "boot"; your windshield is a "windscreen"; a transmission a "gearbox"; a parking lot is a "car park"; a circle is a "roundabout"; a friend is a "mate"; you didn't *like* someone but "fancied" them; you had "bangers and mash" for breakfast; and so on and so forth.

He thought these expressions were the essence of communication, direct, concise, and conveying an instant meaning. Truth be told, even though he was aware of some of the horrible and bestial things the English had done historically, he felt they had more class than Americans. He was a bit of an anglophile.

Amir had a bit of jet lag due to the five-hour time difference between Philly and London (GMT) on his arrival. After checking into the hotel, he took a short nap in his small hotel room. He had read that European hotel rooms tended to be smaller than American ones. As he walked around the immediate area of the hotel, certain impressions started to form in his mind.

Every African American should travel abroad at least once. Because it is only after leaving America, if only briefly, that you begin to view yourself in a world context. These strangers don't know you and by inference don't know where you're from! One could be African or Middle Eastern, from the Caribbean, from a Spanish country, from an island, or from there. This land had similar yet different traditions and history than America.

He was not naive; he figured that racism must be ever present like in the States, but there was no legacy of lynching blacks, of the KKK, or, as far as he knew, of Jim Crow laws or white riots where numbers of blacks had been slaughtered like Black Wall Street, Rosewood, or the Red Summer of 1919. Sure, these white folk probably felt superior to blacks, but their racism, at least at home, didn't seem to be as vicious, as bestial, as in America. "Do you own a Cadillac?" "Are you rich?" He couldn't believe the naive questions some of the English girls were asking him. This was the 1970s, so many obviously still believed in the myths and stereotypes about America and Americans. He didn't lie outright but sort of didn't deny the myths either—at least the flattering ones. Of course, he wanted to impress the English girls, or birds, as the slang term for girls was then. This was still the Carnaby Street era, the Mod era in England, Twiggy and all that. Would he be able to shag one while there?

The tour of the famous Tower of London was fascinating. The crown jewels were quite impressive, huge diamonds, rubies, and other precious stones. The guards kept repeating as you looked, "Keep it moving. Keep the line moving!" Of course, England had simply taken many of these treasures from their native lands. The Greek government was still attempting to get the "Elgin Marbles" back from England. "The sun never sets on the British Empire" was once the case. Their influence and effect on world history was undeniable.

The Spanish, Portuguese, French, Dutch, and others had all vied for world domination. The British had ultimately won! The Beefeater who guided his tour was fantastic; he was so British with his lamb-chop sideburns, accent, and crisp Beefeater uniform. One of the things he explained to the assembled tour group was how there was a legend that said as long as the ravens were in the Tower, there would always be an England! "So we clip the wing that allows them to fly!"

The Jack the Ripper walk was a must. He had been fascinated by the "Ripper" story. Amir had read a few books about the ghastly murders. It was the "who done it" aspect that was really interesting to him—not the horrible, bestial things he did to his victims. Was it Prince Eddy, Leather Apron, Thomas Cutbush, or Aaron Kosminsky? White Chapel, Spitalfields, the walks actually went to the locations where the five canonical victims' bodies were discovered. Of course, since 1888, some street names had been changed, some buildings were no longer there, as was explained during the tour. It culminated at the Ten Bells Pub, for a drink, where allegedly one or more of the Ripper's victims had been patrons. This was allegedly one of the oldest pubs in London. Very interesting, they were selling Jack the Ripper sweatshirts, T-shirts, and coffee mugs at the Ten Bells!

Amir decided against purchasing a sweatshirt emblazoned with the words "Jack the Ripper" on the back of it. That would be too much! The Thames and "Cleopatra's Needle" (which had nothing to do with Cleopatra) were both quite interesting, especially the cruise on the former.

The British Museum was mind blowing! He headed straight for the Egyptian exhibits. Mummies in various stages of preservation, chariots, bows, jewelry, furniture, sandals, swords, daggers—it was amazing, room after room. While pausing in front of one mummy, he got this eerie feeling. Some of the hair and the fingernails were visible after thousands of years! He wondered if it was a violation of some kind to be staring at this long-dead human being in a display case! In one display case, in a distant part of a room, along with other artifacts, he saw little Afro combs! He thought those ancient Egyptians had been black.

Once he realized one could go to the top open level on the red double-decker buses and smoke cigarettes, he went up there almost all the time to smoke his Benson and Hedges menthols. He sat there happily puffing away as the bus passed Piccadilly Circus, Trafalgar Square, Nelson's Column, and many other London landmarks. While in London, although he was sure racism existed, he didn't feel as aware of his blackness. He didn't notice too many stares or hateful or disapproving looks from Londoners. At one of the outdoor markets, maybe Petticoat Lane, that only opened on Sundays, he purchased a sharply tailored but inexpensive black double-breasted blazer. It looked so English! A red tie topped it off nicely.

As he was just exploring London late one morning, he noticed her. She was on the opposite side of the street. She was fairly tall and sinewy and nubile looking. Was she African? Caribbean? From somewhere else? She was on the same side of the street now, so he smiled and said, "Excuse me. Can you help me? I'm an American tourist, and I'm looking for the queen."

She flashed a broad and beautiful smile.

Game on, he thought.

"Buckingham Palace is down that way a few blocks. If you're in time, you can see the changing of the guard."

"So what time shall we meet for lunch tomorrow?" he asked her with a confident smile.

She said around one in the afternoon would be fine. He had discovered that if a woman was attracted to you, or simply curious about you, it really didn't matter much what line you used, she would respond positively.

Over shepherd's pie and a ploughman's lunch the next day, she began to reveal some things about herself. Yes, she was born in London, but her folks had immigrated from Jamaica. Yes, she was single and unattached.

No, she had never been to America but was contemplating a trip in the near future, maybe during a summer. He hadn't fallen in love or even really in like; however, she was fun to be around and spend some time with. When they went out the next evening to London's Penthouse Club, it was like in a movie. She was looking sharp with her tight dress on, and she was pumping. Her long, shapely light-brown legs were sexy. As they were seated, Bobby Womack's cover of "The Look of Love" started playing. He had to get that slow drag. As they danced around the dance floor, her young, tight, sinewy body felt good. She smelled good also. She was throwing it back. London, a sexy girl, "The Look of Love" playing while they danced, it didn't get much better than this, he thought. It was like a movie. Zaats boogaloo!

This was the 1970s, and disco was king. He was never much of a dancer, however. He loved music, and his tastes were quite eclectic: Johnny Mathis, Bobby Womack, the Doobie Brothers, the Four Tops, the Temptations, Isaac Hayes, the Beatles, Chicago, Redbone, Lionel Ritchie, and the Commodores, the Average White Band, Jeffrey Osborne, Lenny Williams, Tom Jones, Jerry Butler, Smokey Robinson, and even Frank Sinatra and Tony Bennett. Hell, he occasionally even listened to music in other languages that he didn't speak—Arabic, Spanish, and Italian. He went to the discos basically in hopes of meeting women. He enjoyed being out and about, listening to music, seeing and being seen, but as he sometimes reminded friends, "I can listen to music at home." No, he was usually hunting, either alone or with friends. He used, "Give me those digits, girl. Just seven numbers could change my life," and other favorites if they were needed. Some girls didn't have to be asked. They volunteered their numbers. Others wouldn't give theirs or, worse, gave wrong numbers—numbers to laundromats, bowling alleys, stores, and so on. This game, this dance, played at clubs and discos, at least in Philly, was interesting. You'd get sharp (a nice suit or sports jacket and trousers), shave or trim your beard (almost all his male friends had beards), put on some cologne (Canoe, English Leather, Pierre Cardin, British Sterling, or some other), and go to the club or disco, sometimes with your buddies, sometimes alone.

At some point, you'd probably want to dance. Of course, initially, you had surveyed the scene. Any foxes and bad hammers about? Usually the fine women would be in the minority, but the older the night grew, the better-looking everyone got! Young women usually traveled in packs or herds. Rarely would you find one alone. If you were with your boys, this could be problematic, as good-looking was generally defined the same way.

"I saw her first!"

"I told you I wanted to talk to that one!"

Omar and SaRon often had this dispute.

"I had checked her out first," said SaRon.

"Yeah, but you didn't bust a move! You sat there staring at her for an hour!" Omar said.

All of this before any conversation with the young lady in question had even begun! Amir and Omar never had this issue. Upon entering a club, bar, party, or other social event and surveying the scene, one would say to the other while subtly pointing out the ones referred to, "That's you, brother," or "What you gonna do?"

They both seemed to think that there were plenty of girls around, no need for drama! At times, Omar would say, "They come at you in human waves. Don't know who to go after." Of course, he and Omar, as young men, had met almost all of each other's significant others. Omar had been accused of preferring light-skinned women, redbones, which he vehemently denied, offering up Valerie, an attractive, dark-skinned girl as proof.

Amir and Omar had rather catholic tastes. They didn't really have a preference as to color, height, hair length, or type. Suzanne was a light-skinned slender young lady from the Tioga section of Philly. She attended the college. She had been attracted to Omar and had pursued him. She actually attended a funeral of a relative of his whom she hadn't known and sat next to Omar at the funeral! She liked to wear the then popular wet look for women. a kind of shiny, plasticky look in boots, coats, dresses, and so on. She drove a VW Beetle that had been painted red, black, and green! Sometimes her nails were also painted red, black, and green. Amir was for the cause, but this seemed a bit much! Omar would later explain that Suzanne caught him on the rebound, that she "threw all that at him!" They would go on to have a lovely daughter together.

BLESSED EVENTS

CHAPTER 8

Back in the day, brothers, at least the ones he hung out with, and most sisters as well were not trying to make babies. Have sex, yes. Make babies, no! Amir often inquired if the lady in question had taken her pill before attempting any carnal activity. "I'm pregnant!" were not words he and most of his friends wanted to hear. Amir often, while in the bathroom of a young lady's apartment, would look into the birth control pill dispenser if visible, to see if she was taking her pills.

Meanwhile Back in London

They had a great time at the Penthouse Club. She was buying what Amir was selling. He had learned that he could be quite charming to the opposite sex, that he had game. Of course, not all women found him irresistible. For some, he was not their type (e.g., too light or dark, too tall or short, too cute or not cute enough, too polished or not polished enough, and so on). He had learned at an early age that "you can't please them all." Some thought he was a great lover, others mediocre, still others poor. Many remarked on how soft his hands were. In some cases, this was seen as a positive; in others, it was not. Some girls liked thugs or bad boys. He didn't generally appeal to that taste. Almost everyone thought he was well dressed, however. There was not much difference of opinion on that. At the college, SaRon had nicknamed him "British Peter" in part because of his sharply tailored English looking suits, sports coats, and wardrobe. After the Penthouse Club, they went back to the hotel for a nice evening together.

Westminster Abbey was very impressive, the architecture, all those famous people buried there—many beneath the floor you were walking on. Of course, the British monarch was traditionally crowned there. He liked the queen, always had. Prince Charles and he were about the same age. The queen had class, whether you agreed with all her actions or not. Some Americans, black and white, were puzzled by his fondness for the queen. He understood why. A black American who admired the queen?

This was his logic. Whites collectively had done terrible things to people of color over the past several hundred years. The British sometimes were among the worst! The Spanish, Portuguese, French, Belgians, and Italians, among others, including the Catholic church, all owed an apology and reparations in some cases to blacks and women as well. That being said, the balance was slowly, inexorably changing, the arc of history being long and all that—OPEC, African independence, control of their own resources, and rising education and income levels for at least some people of color.

Europeans hadn't come to dominate the world overnight, and it wouldn't change overnight, but it would change! It was cyclical he thought. Had the British not outlawed slavery before the Americans? Had the Prince Hall Masons (black Masons) not gotten their charter from the British failing to get one from the Americans?

Had the British not offered freedom to blacks in America if they fought on their side during the revolution? They weren't all bad. Besides, as an American, didn't most American stuff really come from Britain, from English Common Law to GMT to the way we celebrate Christmas, to the names of so many cities, villages, and towns across America, Elizabeth, Somerset, and Middlesex, New Jersey? Wasn't the melody of "My Country 'Tis of Thee" the same as the older British "God Save the King/Queen?" Didn't the founders of America initially and fundamentally consider themselves British up until the time of the American Revolution? Wasn't Great Britain still one of the largest foreign investors in America? Don't we, as Americans, speak English along with millions of others around the world? Hadn't English become the lingua franca of the modern world? Don't many Americans have English/British names? Aren't many towns and cities in America named after English towns, cities, or areas? If one is going to emulate some of the positive aspects of a culture, it seemed to him, one could do worse than the British! An IRA bomb actually went off during his stay in London. It was nowhere near where he was at the time. The bombers had phoned in a warning so that customers could be cleared from the store before it went off. Evidently, this was customary. He had to visit Trafalgar Square and Piccadilly Circus. He hung out for a few hours at each, wondering if Dad had hung out at the same places during World War II. It was fun. There were tourists from around the world, some fine women! Harrods was unbelievable. They sold everything! Of course, he could only afford a cheap ballpoint pen and a key fob. After bidding a tender goodbye to his newfound friend and exchanging phone numbers, he got ready for Paris.

At Orly, Amir saw gendarmes with automatic and semiautomatic rifles walking around and stationary. It was a first for him. *There must be a reason*, he thought. On to the Hotel Francois on Monmarte Boulevard. Transfers from the airport to the hotels were a part of his Getaway tour. As he queued up to register at the

Francois, he noticed that the concierge spoke pretty good English. He was asked at the desk if he wanted a croissant or a young lady sent up to his room.

As he was on a budget, he declined the young lady but heard the fellow behind him indicate yes. Once settled in his room, his curiosity got the better of him so he left his room door ajar to see if the guy who indicated yes had received his young lady. Sure enough, about fifteen to twenty minutes later, a cute little Frenchie was seen knocking at the guy's door! Europeans were much more open and casual about adult entertainment than Americans. In the bathroom of his room, he observed two toilets, one right next to the other! He knew the French had a reputation for romance, for being romantic, but his and hers toilets? Of course, he later learned one fixture was not a toilet but a bidet. Of course, Amir left his shoes out in the hallway. It was customary. Paris truly was interesting— the Right Bank, the Left Bank, the Louvre, Napoleon's Tomb, the Arc de Triomphe, the Eiffel Tower, and other attractions. Again, he was surprised by the number of people of color he saw on the streets. Movies and television had not prepared him for this! He saw Africans, Caribbean folk, South Asians, and more. It was an international city. Yes, Paris was romantic, people holding hands, kissing almost everywhere. Parisians walked along with their bread and wine. The boat ride along the Seine was interesting, so much history.

The French girls looked different from the English girls, physically smaller, more fashionable, and often more attractive. Those French guys were into fashion also, scarves, European-cut jackets, and suits; even their jeans were stylized. One of his stops was at Pierre Cardin's personal boutique. Communication became a problem though. He hadn't even tried learning any French phrases, wrongly assuming that cabdrivers, waiters, and so on spoke some English!

While there, he learned that many of the French take English in school, but like he had heard, not too many seemed willing to try and help non-French-speaking tourists and visitors get by, at least in Paris! Typically, as he was traveling alone, he would go to a café or restaurant, be seated, and be given a menu entirely in French. Amir would then look around at what others were eating, and when he saw something that looked appealing, he'd say, "Give me la that, si vous plais," to the waiter!

He had been really shocked one morning after hailing a cab. The driver was a big, dark-skinned brother with a huge Afro. *At last!* he thought. His "Hey, brother!" was met with a response in French. Identity, black, white, or whatever, he was learning, was not a simple or universal matter!

The person he encountered in Paris who spoke the best English and was willing to try to communicate with him the most was a very well-dressed (fur and pearls) working lady one evening as he was strolling along the famous Champs-Élysées, who inquired of him, "Are you looking for zee good love?" to which he replied, "Merci, but I probably can't afford zee good love, but merci anyway." He had to get to the Left Bank, the naughty side of Paris. He had heard of the famous Crazy Horse club, a kind of burlesque/exotic dance club. He went, and sure enough, it was interesting. Women, good-looking and sexy, black, white, and Asian, were scantily clad and dancing around everywhere! He ordered champagne and was joined by a black and a white woman at his small table. He knew the deal, that they probably wanted him to buy them watered-down, overpriced drinks with the hint of sex to come, either for real or a con, much as the bar girls had in Philly's Chinatown years before. He wouldn't buy sex, but he would play the game, for a while at least. He was on a budget after all.

He walked out of Crazy Horse with a woman on each arm and a bottle of champagne. *Life is good*, he thought. He felt more sophisticated in Paris, a world-class city, a fashion and food capital. All African Americans should have this experience, he thought.

America, alone, does not define you! He also learned that as a black American, he did have friends or allies, in spite of what he might be thinking in America or might have been led to believe. They were not alone!

He would never forget how while seated on the flight to London, two Kuwaiti guys had approached him respectfully and asked, "Are you an African American?"

When he responded affirmatively, one said to him, "We have read about your struggle and are with you."

He was a bit caught off guard by the comment but shook their hands and thanked them. Wow, he would have to tell the brothers when he got back to the States about that! He would also never forget how much the Europeans, particularly the British and the French, loved and appreciated American music, particularly black music. The English, in particular, not only knew about Motown for instance, they had fan clubs for particular Motown groups! When he landed in Paris, the first song he heard was "Everybody Was Kung Fu Fighting!" by American soul singer Karl Douglas.

French folks, some of whom couldn't speak English, were mouthing and singing the lyrics. Their fondness for American jazz was of course well known. Josephine Baker, the many black American expatriates—it was all starting to make sense to him now. Amir had gone to the movies in Paris near his hotel. He saw *Shaft* dubbed in French. What an experience. Richard Roundtree bursting through a door in Harlem, USA, yelling, "Que se passe-t-il!"

Black American culture truly is universal and appreciated worldwide, whether African Americans or white Americans know and acknowledge it or not! While flying back to JFK from De Gaulle Airport, as he settled in his seat and looked out the window at the beautiful sky, the clouds looking like giant cotton balls, his mind reeled with thoughts and memories of his first journey abroad. He would never be the same.

He had come to some conclusions:

- He was not simply who America said he was. He was, in fact, a world citizen. Accident of birth had labeled him, but he could've had several different identities.
- While white nationalism and superiority were a worldwide phenomenon, American whites were probably among the most racist whites on the planet.
- He could probably live in several different countries aside from America and be reasonably happy.
- He was, in fact, an American, and for poor and working-class people of any race/ethnicity, the America of today, even with its negatives, is probably the best place to be.
- If one has some serious cash, one can live well almost anywhere.
- Blacks generally have some allies; we are not alone.
- Black Americans get more deference and respect sometimes from foreigners than from their fellow white Americans.
- With the passage of time, politicians often become statesmen; hos and tramps, male or female, become respectable; old buildings become landmarks; and the biggest "devils" often find religion!

He was flat broke when the plane landed at JFK. Paris had been beautiful, romantic, interesting, and expensive. He had to take a bus back home because it was cheaper than the train. He realized that he was now a member of another minority group, Americans who had traveled abroad on their own, not because they were serving in the US military or because some corporation had assigned them to work abroad but simply because they went on their own. He was almost sure that the vast majority of African Americans and the majority of whites, for that matter, couldn't say as much at the time.

In years to come, when he would mention his European trip on occasion, some whites couldn't disguise their almost shock that he, a young black man, had traveled to Paris and London! Of course, none were stupid enough to explain that his race was the reason for their shock to his face, but what other reason could there be? Don't Americans fly to Europe as tourists? Didn't he have gainful employment? Did he come across as a rather parochial person with no interest in seeing any of the world? Didn't they know whites who had traveled abroad, or hadn't some of them traveled abroad themselves? Amir thought not. It was the *R* word (*racism*) once again.

Back in his small apartment, it felt good to be back home. He had called Mom to tell her he was safely back. In a few days, she would be advising him that someone had called from London, England, and left a message for him! As he walked along Chestnut Street that beautiful winter day, he passed the Countess. He didn't really know her, but she had been pointed out to him by Tarik and Omar, both of whom said she had money. A tall, sort of husky European woman of middle age, she wasn't particularly attractive; she dressed in a unique style of her own. Maybe she was a countess? It seemed that Tarik was trying to play her, trying to get some money out of her. Was he talking black and sleeping white? None of his business, he concluded.

Later that afternoon, he also saw "I'll Take Sweden" on the street. She was a young, red-headed, Swedish airline stewardess, or so she said; he never saw her in uniform.

She didn't have a beautiful face, but she had a curvaceous body, which she was obviously proud of, showing it off regularly. She clearly liked brothers because she was always with one. This particular day, she was rocking her hot pants, go-go boots, and halter top. He was learning that some white girls, not all, had a preference for brothers. Those women tended to be fanatical about it and aggressive. They were often exploited by brothers who took advantage of their preference by not working while they worked, blatantly seeing other people, or verbally and physically abusing them! "Once you go black, you'll never go back" was a saying of the time. He found the whole phenomenon very interesting and complex. What were the reasons? Opposites attract? Forbidden fruit? Revenge against the system, the man? Rebellion against one's family? Obtaining and possessing one of the larger society's true status symbols, a good-looking (preferably blond) white woman, meaning that you had arrived? Just sex? Loneliness?

He decided to do his social experiment once again that day. He would walk along Chestnut Street or Market Street alone, dressed business casual, and respectfully smile and say good morning to an equal number of black and white women as they passed each other on the street and note their respective and collective responses. Invariably, more white girls would speak back to him than black girls. Interesting, what did that mean? Was he more attractive to white women than he was to black women? Were black women more guarded than white women? If so, why? All these black women who didn't speak back couldn't have been the victims of disrespect or abuse by black men, could they? If not, why were they responding in this manner? He spoke in a respectful manner; he didn't try to carry on the conversation or follow them along the street. He called no one out of their name. He couldn't figure it out!

"The two freest people in America are the white man and the black woman," the older brother had said. "We catch the hell! Wars have been fought over white and black women," he went on to explain.

Amir listened respectfully but wasn't buying it.

"White women want you because you're black; black women are with you in spite of the fact that you're black, and therein lies the difference." Black Eric from NYC was explaining one evening in a small restaurant in Midtown Manhattan to Omar, SaRon, and Amir. "I'd rather have a white woman tell me no, than a black woman tell me yes! All I want for Christmas is a white woman!" Eric had a decided preference for white girls and bragged about it.

As he turned to two seated strangers at a nearby table, he smiled and said to them, "Shake your hair for me like in the Prell commercials."

One of them sort of sheepishly did!

"You crazy, boy," SaRon uttered. Thought provoking!

He drove Omar to Powelton Village that crisp, rainy autumn evening. Omar didn't drive at that time. He was making a delivery of stereo equipment to a fellow, an African American songwriter and producer of some note who had gold records displayed on his living room walls. He had an apartment there. A good-looking blond white woman opened the door, let them in, and made them comfortable. She then served them tea.

"I'll get Joe," she said.

Omar softly whispered, "See? You can train those white women."

His young female white neighbor, a coworker at the authority with an MSW degree, lived about two blocks away in a large walkup apartment, which she shared with her live-in boyfriend. He was black and tall. Amir would occasionally give her a ride home from work, they being neighbors. He had no ulterior motive. She wasn't his type. One day, while he was giving her a ride home, she invited him to come up to her flat for a coffee. He accepted her invitation. As he climbed the stairs to her second-floor flat with her, he was greeted by a large oil on canvas painting of a black man. When he asked, "Who's that?"

She nonchalantly replied, "My man."

Okay, he thought, a little different. While seated on the couch having coffee with her, she explained he wouldn't be meeting her man because he was currently incarcerated. She then proceeded to show him the Afro wig and sunglasses she had worn on her recent visit to the big house so as not to embarrass him, as she was white! On another occasion, while he was driving her home, she yelled, "Stop!" and bolted from his car. The reason was that she had observed her man panhandling on the street. He was talking to a young woman, and she got jealous. They were arguing loudly.

People were staring, and Amir got embarrassed, so he drove off, leaving the two of them!

In almost all the situations he encountered, the black man seemed to be exploiting or using the white woman. Black women, at least most of the ones he knew, did not approve of or like this race mixing, for the most part. "There are not enough good brothers to go around, and now the white girls are taking them!" Amir had different thoughts. Could it be that love is where you find it? Could it be that many men take the path of least resistance? Sex with a white girl certainly might beat no sex at all. Most sisters of the time wanted to be wined and dined. The word on the white girls was that you didn't necessarily have to wine and dine them. He had learned from personal experience that the white women who liked black men were often superaggressive. "I'm looking for a brother!" more than one white woman had shared with him. "I prefer brothers," others had declared. Amir, himself, was not in high demand by white women. Too light-skinned, he often thought. Hell, he didn't look that different from some of the white girls, color-wise and feature-wise, aside from his hair. Still, he occasionally was approached by those seeking that black experience.

He was at the party alone in Powelton Village that night. It was a diverse mix of blacks, whites, and an Asian or two. He was aware that a kind of attractive white woman was checking him out. When she came over and started a conversation, he wasn't totally surprised or shocked. White girls were often more aggressive than black ones. "You could be my pimp," she said with a smile. "You're so good-looking!" He was flattered and cautious at the same time. Pimp?

He would briefly date a couple of white girls during this era, not because he thought they were better or superior to black girls but out of curiosity. What was all the hubbub about? Invariably they would ask him, "Am I the first white girl you've dated?" This question always irritated him. What was the purpose of asking such a question? Then, of course, there were the stares from time to time from blacks and whites. Black women and white men were the worst. The looks could be quite nasty. "If looks could kill …" Some of these sisters who stared at him with such hostility would not give him any play but resented his being with a white woman! The conclusion he came to after dating a few white girls was that he was underwhelmed. They were just people like anyone else, no better, no worse. The one difference he came to believe was that because of societal disapproval and the fact that some families actually disowned their daughter, sister, or mother when she became involved with a black man, it meant they had to be committed to the relationship to stick it out.

When working for the government, he actually had a white female coworker who seemed nice enough. She was dating a black guy, and she was not allowed to visit her family's home! She was declared persona non grata. Of course, he was starting to believe generally that the tension in America between blacks and whites was largely sexual in nature anyway. White males because of their privileged position in America had had sexual access to all women, including black women from the beginning. Black women, on the whole, with notable exceptions, weren't attracted to white men. Black men, however, being canine, like all men, were usually attracted or at least would mate with any type of woman, causing much chagrin to many black women! Payback or revenge against the system or the man was the rationale many brothers articulated, sincerely or insincerely, when queried about why they were with or attracted to white women. Considering that in America, the white female was constantly being projected as the very essence of womanhood, sexuality, femininity, class, and all things female in print and visual media, it was a wonder that more brothers didn't end up with white women, Amir thought. The majority of blacks, like the majority of whites married within their respective groups, however. Why did such a high percentage of highly paid black professional athletes and other celebrities seem to marry white women? Could it be in part because the higher they climbed, the fewer the black people they were around or exposed to? Could it be because these white women and others sometimes threw themselves at these highly paid brothers? The lure of easy sex could be quite difficult for men of any race to resist! This debate, this discussion, would go on and on, he concluded.

Generally, Omar and he were fairly successful with the ladies. No man got all the women he desired, no matter how good-looking, well off, bright, well built, or charismatic. Neither did Amir and Omar. But on the whole, they both tended to get attractive, intelligent, sometimes exotic, interesting women. Both he and Omar were fairly articulate, could rap, and had game. Some other brothers had a Saran or weak rap. The honeys tended to like brothers who could rap, generally. Of course, being silver-tongued was a red flag to some young ladies, made them uncomfortable. How many times has he said this? How many women has he said this to? You couldn't win! If a man was shy and introverted or inarticulate, many women weren't interested. If he was articulate and suave, somewhat sophisticated, had some personality, then he must be a playboy/playa!

Later that spring day, Amir and Omar would go to Macy's. Omar explained he needed to purchase some shoes, some ho heels, for his current friend. They both had developed a bit of a foot fetish. They loved women in heels. "Leave 'em on, gurl," meaning have sex with her heels on. As they walked through the shoe department, Omar would periodically pick up a shoe and lightly tap himself on the chest with the heel of it. "These will do just fine," he finally said, selecting a pair of heels. He paid for them. They were actually quite proud of their shared fetish. A man should have at least one, thought Amir.

"Meet me at the eagle, brother," said Tarik to Amir. In Philly, the Eagle was a popular meeting place for Philadelphians of the time. It meant the big, larger-than-scale brass bald eagle in John

Wanamaker's Department Store in the street-level lobby. Friends, parents and their children, people who had made dates, and so on often chose this locale to meet up. It was inside, out of the elements, it was safe, and you could easily spot each other. It was a Philly tradition.

The crew was having dinner that evening in Philly's Chinatown. In the old days, Chinatown was seedy. Of course, there were the omnipresent Chinese restaurants, but on Race Street, there was also Doc Jonson's Love Products, a kind of adult store supermarket. It had live women sitting in a kind of telephone booth in various stages of undress trying to be sexy whom you could converse with, for a price, of course. They would seductively start removing some of or all of their clothing, maybe masturbate in front of you. You and they could talk dirty—no touching, however, as there was a glass partition separating you. There were also the expensive magazines with pictures, nude and seminude, sexual tools like dildos, vibrators, cock rings, butt plugs, ben wa balls, edible panties, inflatable female life-sized dolls with orifices sold in a box (hot water to be added) in different colors, handcuffs, black leather articles, masks, whips, chains, cat-o'-nine-tails, and so on. There were also the dirty films one could view in a booth, for a price, usually quarters. You had to keep feeding the machine, or it would stop. It was dark in those booths, and the floors were often sticky with come residue from customers who had rubbed one off, beat their meat, or choked their chickens while viewing films.

There were also some cheap bars with bar girls, usually middle-aged white women who had seen better days, who sat around trying to look alluring and sexy and who flirted with customers to get them to buy overpriced, watered-down drinks for them while the customer got a real drink. They often approached you with lines like "Hey, sexy," or "What's a good-looking man like you doing in here?" They usually attempted to get you to think they would leave the bar with you for sex but usually didn't. Of course, it was about money, about business. They worked in conjunction with the bartender or bar owner/manager.

Of course, there were also a few members of the oldest profession around as well, black, white, and an occasional Asian. SaRon enjoyed going to the area and observing them, which was curious, Amir and Omar thought.

Never and he had been advised, after sneaking into a club in Center City, as underaged high school seniors, early one Friday evening by a healthy white hammer that she was having a special that evening, a two-fer. She'd take on both of them for fifty dollars! While intriguing, the issue was moot in any event, as the two high schoolers had no money to spend on sex. It was exciting though! As they were enjoying their Chinese food in a small booth, the guys noticed a dark-skinned brother with a hat on eating alone. He looked familiar. It was Billy Paul of "Me and Mrs. Jones" fame, a Philly guy, as far as they knew.

Over the years, they would see or meet or actually interact with numerous celebrities in Philly—Sammy Davis Jr. as he was marrying Lola Falana, a Philly woman; Sidney Poitier, in town filming *The Lost Man*; William Marshall; Liberace; Sonny Liston; Muhammad Ali; Randall "Tex" Cobb; boxer Pinklon Thomas; Joe Frazier; Jim Brown; Sister Sledge; the Three Degrees; the Delphonics; the Stylistics; Chubby Checker; and many others. The reasons were many. First, it was Philadelphia, the nation's then fourth-biggest city and a Mecca for jazz and rock and roll music. A popular TV show, *The Mike Douglas Show*, was also being broadcast from Philly at that time, and Mike usually had celebrity guests. *American Bandstand* was also being broadcast from West Philly. Philly International Records was churning out the hits. The O'Jays and Dionne Warwick and others were recording in Philly.

A constant stream of R&B luminaries appeared on Dick Clark's TV show—James Brown, the Four Tops, Mary Wells, and so on. Amir first saw Sister Sledge as they were making a name for themselves at a subterranean club in Center City. It was a club with a bar and stage that actually looked like a cave. You even walked down into it from street level. One night, while he was sitting at the bar drinking his usual ginger ale, Sister Sledge was announced and performed on stage. These young sisters were literally sisters and fine! One particularly so to him—that Joni was sexy and fine. He hoped for the chance, no matter how remote, to possibly meet her one day and put his application in. Omar knew one of the Delphonics from high school. As Amir turned to glance at the brother who had just sat down next to him at the bar, he had a feeling this was someone he had seen before. He was dark-complexioned and muscular. He was maybe six feet tall. He wasn't particularly distinctive looking, and yet … It was Joe Frazier! Damn, the world's heavyweight champion was sitting at the bar next to him! Although Ali was his personal favorite and the one his inner circle liked also, Joe's gym was in his old neighborhood, around Broad and Glenwood. He had seen Joe before, walking along the street, riding motorcycles, singing, "Joe Frazier and the Knock Outs." They, Amir and his friends, all thought, *Keep your day job, Joe!*

As they were walking along Walnut Street that lovely winter afternoon, they passed one of their favorite eateries and meeting places, a kind of pub they frequented for dinner. SaRon would always be late no matter what time they agreed to meet, because he'd park blocks away to get away from the Center City parking meters or parking lots to save some change rather than park at the reasonably priced lot a short distance away from the restaurant. Omar would say, "He never met a check he liked!" They casually glanced through the large-paned glass window that looked out on Walnut Street and instantly knew who it was they were observing enjoying a burger there—the actor William Marshall! He was a tall, distinguished-looking man with a baritone voice who was in *The Robe* and some other Biblical-epic-type films as well as the recently released *Blacula* (dumb title, interesting concept). He was an actor, director, and opera singer.

An African prince had been bitten by the count and now was in present-day LA doing his vampire thing. Two fine women were also in the film, Denise Nicholas and Vonetta McGee. Vonetta was so sweet and those eyes. Why did he have to be called *Blacula* though? Marshall's acting was first rate, however. He had chops. They all smiled at Marshall as they walked by and called out, *"Blacula!"* He nodded and smiled back at them. They didn't want to go in and disturb the brother's meal. Marshall, like many other blacks in Hollywood, never got the roles his talent and body of work deserved.

The so-called black exploitation films were an interesting phenomenon. Many of the studios were in financial trouble at the time, and after seeing the success of Melvin Van Peebles's *Sweet Sweetback's Badass Song*, a little film Van Peebles had written, produced, directed, starred in, and whatever else, which had made substantial profits at relatively little cost, studios wanted to cash in on this black audience, thirsty to see themselves on the silver screen in a heroic, strong, sexy, and winning way, not simply as victims but also as agents!

Shaft in 1971 was revolutionary! Based on a novel by Ernest Tidyman, the author of the screenplay for the highly regarded film, *The French Connection*, it was directed by the renaissance man Gordon Parks Jr. What a brother! He was a photographer for *LIFE* magazine (first black one), artist, writer, and film director! The *Shaft* soundtrack was electric. Isaac Hayes (Black Moses) won an Academy Award for *Shaft*. He was the first African American to win for a film score! *Shaft* was a black man without angst.

Amir didn't see *Shaft* as a black exploitation movie, however; *Shaft* was simply a detective, not a pimp, not a gangster, not a black militant or a drug dealer, who operated in a black and white world.

He was pro-black but espoused no particular nationalist philosophy. He also had sex in the movie with a white woman.

A western, *Buck and the Preacher*, was entertaining as well, with Sidney P. and Harry Bellafonte. *Three the Hard Way*, with Jim Brown, Jim Kelly, and Fred Williamson was entertaining. *The Learning Tree*, directed by Parks Jr., was good. *JD's Revenge* with Glenn Turman was entertaining. *Cooley High* was the inner-city version of *American Graffiti*. A young Glen Turman was excellent in the film. Of course, Pam Grier's *Coffee*, *Foxy Brown*, *Friday Foster*, *Sheba Baby*, *Black Mama*, *White Mama*, and anything else she was in was mandatory viewing. What an exotic and sexy woman! Amir refused to pay his money to see *Nigger Charley* with Fred Williamson, however. A film with the "N-word" in the title, shameful! *Superfly*, although its main character was a drug dealer, was a good movie and had a great soundtrack. *Troubleman* was good (good soundtrack). Its star, Robert Hooks, was a Philly guy. *Across 110th Street* was another great soundtrack. Many didn't seem to get it. Blacks needed to see themselves as strong, as heroic, as winners. Sure, many of these films were unrealistic, but how realistic were the Bond films and many other majority motion pictures? Many had stereotypes, pimps, hustlers, gangsters, and so on but not all. Blacks were usually the good guys and whites the bad guys. Blacks often won in these movies. They defeated the white bad guys, kept their money or wealth, or successfully defended themselves. There was a need, a hunger, to see that and to see good-looking, well-dressed, smart, sexy, tough black protagonists, male and female. It was about time!

All the guys were in love with or lusted for Pam Grier. Vonetta McGee and Denise Nicholas were hot also, as was Brenda Sykes, Tracy Reed, and Jayne Kennedy. The singer Freda Payne of "Bring the Boys Home" fame was gorgeous and classy! In years to come, he would learn about early black filmmakers, such as Oscar Micheaux. Amir saw a couple of restored Micheaux movies in Philly at a retrospective put on by a local university. One was titled *Murder in Harlem*, or something like that. He couldn't quite remember.

What he could remember was that these movies were made by blacks for blacks and interestingly had normal or real African American characters in them, for the most part—police detectives, postal workers, lawyers, doctors, nurses, homemakers, teachers, and so on.

They weren't caricatures, not all maids, butlers, or chauffeurs, and reminded him of relatives, acquaintances, neighbors, and people he had met. He felt it was almost criminal that his generation had not been told about these movies! This history wasn't taught in the public education system by and large. Older blacks didn't always pass on this history either. Amir was beginning to figure out that blacks had to tell their own stories. We must all to some extent be like the African griots, he decided. Others could not be counted on to teach the true history of African people. Some Jews attended Hebrew school. That was an example, he thought, or the Sister Clara Muhammad Schools of the Nation of Islam.

"Young blood, I keeps me a white woman, love 'em, but when the revolution come, she gonna be the first to go!"

Amir was standing at the bar at Dade's Place in Center City talking to an older brother he didn't really know. Dade then sauntered over.

"Hey, brother, what's happening?"

"Say what do you think about this eggs epidemic?"

"Eggs?" Amir repeated with a quizzical look on his face.

"You know, *eggs*!"

"Oh, AIDS, I see."

Oscar, the owner, then stated, "I think it's just an attempt to keep us from getting them white women!"

"Ain't that a bitch," Amir responded.

"Yeah, catch you later, brother," he said, as he turned and walked out into the busy Center City streets. He was headed for the college.

Another thing Amir was learning was older black men had a deep distrust of white people and a lot of anger, often skillfully hidden or suppressed out of necessity. It was not hard to understand when one looked at the history of American race relations!

In the lobby at the college, one of their usual gathering places, Ahmed, Phil, Omar, and the Other Man were conversing. Amir joined them. Fat Frank was walking up also.

"Shiver me timbers, mateys, wassup?"

"Just traveling to and fro, brother, seeking whom I may devour," one of them said.

Then he noticed her. Margaret was walking across the lobby floor. She was pumping and had on a beautiful dress. Her caramel-colored shapely legs really stood out with the light-colored pumps on. Her hips looked like two mounds of pleasure as she ambulated along. "Yum, yum, give me some" came to mind, but it couldn't be said. *Too silly*, he thought.

"That's all beef, brother, no filler," Fat Frank said softly.

Yeah, they all sighed.

"You hitting that?" the Other Man was casually asking Mike about Sanaa.

Mike looked embarrassed.

"Dude," SaRon said to the Other Man, "you ain't had no pussy since pussy had you, boy!"

Everyone guffawed.

"Let's get some grub," Omar said.

They were off to Bains, a deli just a couple of blocks from the college. It was great for cheesecake and french onion soup.

Fat Frank volunteered, "I need some trim!"

"You look like you need some trim, brother. Good luck!" said Omar.

They all laughed.

A few white fellow students at the college were selling Israel Bonds on campus, openly. What about their Palestinian and

Muslim brothers in the struggle? They had to do something. The crew started selling Egyptian Bonds! Where would the likely paltry sum collected be sent to? They'd figure that out later. For now at least, someone was standing up for the Palestinians! Sure, they got some looks and stares, and there were only people of color at the event, but who cared? They had juice at the college! They weren't concerned about the JDL (Jewish Defense League), the militant Jews running around with baseball bats. Muslims, including the Nation, were strong in Philly at that time.

The nation had the FOI. Those brothers were serious, disciplined, and organized. They attended the program about Israel with Arab headdresses on and sat in the front of the auditorium. Amir, Omar, Phil, and Idress went. When Idress came along, they were never worried. Idress was a scary-looking brother with piercing eyes. Although a nice guy and not particularly big in size, he had an edge. He looked at you like he could rip your head off without hesitation. They behaved at the meeting, but they made their point—solidarity with their brothers and sisters in the struggle. Oppressed peoples can't just be victims; they must be agents! They had to seize the time!

A Man's Home

The house Amir, Mike, and Phil shared was in West Philly. West Philly, other than the Fifty-Second Street Strip, was like a different, yet familiar, city to Amir. Philadelphia was a city of neighborhoods: North Philadelphia, West Philadelphia, South Philadelphia, the Northeast, West Oak Lane, Overbrook, Mount Airy, Germantown, Kensington, Manayunk. There were subsections, Nicetown, Fishtown, and Tioga.

Center City/Downtown was a neutral zone, of course, made up largely of businesses, stores, restaurants, city offices, banks, office buildings, and theaters. Each Philly neighborhood was different, yet similar. Amir's, North Central Philly, was Philly's version of Harlem. In the main, row houses, from small ones with two stories, a small backyard, a single bathroom, and a basement to big three-storied ones with porches, basements, sometimes garages, and a little and maybe a larger backyard grass in front. Many had a brick facade, some a stone facade. Some were wider, and some were longer and deeper in layout. Many had fireplaces, working or nonworking. There were often mantels in the living room. Some city streets were tree-lined in those days, even in North Philly.

Fairmount Park was the largest city park of any American city park. Parts of it were in North, West, South, and other parts of Philly. At one time, there was an amusement park in Fairmount Park, named Woodside Park, complete with rides! The right trolley would take you directly to Woodside Park. The family went there when Amir was very young.

The Schuylkill River ran through Philadelphia and continued on to Norristown and further. The view of it from behind the art museum could be breathtaking. Amir would remember fishing from there as a youth, sitting high up on walls, not even a swimmer, to catch catfish, an occasional bass, or sunfish.

The two-story row house shared by him, Phil, and Mike was typical of West Philly. It was close to University City, the University of Pennsylvania area, where mostly white students lived. It was a gentrified area. It was called University City. Bars, restaurants, and stores catered to the Ivy League U of P clientele. There was a living room, dining room, and kitchen on the first floor. There were three bedrooms and a bathroom on the second floor. Mike had the bedroom facing the street with two large windows. Phil had a bedroom down the hall, as did Amir. The place was sparsely furnished. They generally kept little food in the fridge. But it was fun and exciting living with two college chums on his own, most of the time. They had lots of parties! They provided the music and pretzels and potato chips. Omar, who was originally from West Philly himself, was their most frequent visitor.

That cold winter afternoon, Phil was wearing his maxi coat when he arrived home. Omar, Amir, and Mike were there.

"You guys hungry?" Phil asked.

"Yeah, but broke," Mike said.

"Not to worry," Phil responded as he yawned. "I'll go to the supermarket."

There was one a few blocks away.

"Sandwiches?" Phil asked.

"Yeah," they all agreed.

"Rye bread? Mustard? Corned beef? Pastrami? I got it!"

They all knew what that meant. Phil would go and liberate those items from the market! Phil, an excellent and bold thief, manifested the era they were living in. Young folk, often college students, didn't see themselves as stealing but as appropriating or ripping off the system. To take from an individual was stealing; to take from a big corporation or the government was liberating.

Famously, during this era, hippie/yippie leader Abbie Hoffman wrote a book titled *Steal This Book!* Several of Amir's acquaintances promptly went out and stole/liberated the book! Amir and Omar were not thieves, but Phil was—from overcoats for winter wear obtained from restaurant cloakrooms, to food from the supermarket, to mail-ordering items from the Spiegel catalog and other catalogs and having them delivered to a vacant house or other blind address where he would later pick them up, to liberating items with White Mary from Wanamaker's Department Store near the college and returning to the college to sell them, to obtaining copies of exams and selling them to students. Amir never worried that Phil would liberate anything that was his. He never did. Phil was one of the most intelligent people he would ever personally meet. He had no compunction, however, about taking in life what he wanted, no matter the circumstances. A Gemini, he was fun to be around and never boring. Phil also used to do his meal thing. Not everyone could pull this off. Phil could. They would go to a restaurant, typically in Center City, and typically one that was busy. In the middle of a meal, Phil would place a tack, nail, or dead roach in his food.

"There's something in my food!" he would exclaim loudly, indignantly, and convincingly.

Typically, he would be offered a free meal as compensation by the manager. Phil did this often. He was not embarrassed to do this or any other get over device he used. He was ripping off the system. He also taught the group how to create a wallet full of fake but useful and valid looking IDs, useful for writing bad checks, checking into hotels, obtaining credit cards, or other situations where one's true identity could be a problem.

"Step one, go to a cemetery, find the grave of someone about your age who died as a child. Step two, write away for the deceased's birth certificate." In those days computers were not as widely used and birth certificates not typically cross-checked with death certificates. "Step three, once in possession of a birth certificate, go about getting a driver's license, some form of government ID, Social Security card, open a checking account, and so on." Before long, one had a wallet full of fake but useful and authentic-looking ID. Good for many situations!

Particularly during the ubiquitous paranoia of the late 1960s and '70s among conscious black and white people, the possibility of undercover and double agents and spies for the government or police were imagined everywhere as they carried out their important revoluntionary activities. Sometimes, they were correct, as evidenced by the government's admission of the FBI's Cointelpro program years later! That program's purpose was to surveil, infiltrate, disrupt, and discredit political organizations.

Years later, Amir would see a *60 Minutes* episode on how to accomplish this false ID thing with the same steps they had used successfully. Many years later, Phil would become a public school

teacher for a time in Washington, DC—a scary thought! Phil helping to shape young minds? Phil often referred to young blacks as
miscreants.

"You don't know who your father was, do you?" was one of his
favorite questions for young blacks.

Amir often said to Phil, "You should be a politician. You have no
ethical standards and will do anything to accomplish your goals!"

Some of their fellow students did not like Phil. Some thought he
was gay, which was not acceptable to many at that time. Guys often
referred to gay men as do-do chasers or do-do bandits. Amir wasn't
sure what Phil's sexual orientation was. Phil was wild. It wasn't an
issue for him, however. As long as a gay man didn't hit on him,
who cared? Even when he was hit on from time to time by gays,
it was usually not really threatening, just a little uncomfortable.
He never saw any clear evidence of Phil's possible homosexuality.
Phil would periodically go into heat and start saying, "Gotta find a
woman." Then he would go about doing so. He never indicated he
was in love with anyone, male or female. There was an air of mystery around Phil. He was older than the rest and from West Philly;
it was apparent he had done some traveling, possibly internationally. He appeared to possibly be a former member of the Nation
or some other black nationalist group. He was always receiving
grants, scholarships, and loans for school. He really knew how to
manipulate the system monetarily. Was Phil some kind of agent or
double agent or simply a well-traveled, sophisticated, amoral, kind
of weird and eccentric but fun to hang out with brother?

I'M IN A NEW YORK STATE OF MIND

CHAPTER 9

The guys would periodically get bored in and with Philly. "Let's go to New York," Omar, suggested. By New York, they usually meant Manhattan, Lower, Midtown, and Uptown. Sometimes they went by bus, Greyhound, or some other carrier but most often by driving up the New Jersey Turnpike, Route 95, and through the Lincoln and occasionally the Holland Tunnel, a trip of close to one hundred miles. Amir, Omar, SaRon, and sometimes Mike were the usual cast of characters. Amir was the one who drove his car most often. Omar might offer to help pay for gas. SaRon, a.k.a. Cheap Ron, never volunteered to help pay. Of course, they were headed for discos and clubs. Usually, there was the flavor of the month. Some nightclub or disco would open up, be popular for a while, and then lose its popularity. Some of the discos were huge with more than one floor and a series of rooms. Some were quite unique, with themes.

An admission charge was usually present and typically higher than Philly club fees, of course. They went, not so much to dance, but to meet honeys and get numbers. Philly women had a rep of being difficult to talk to. New York women seemed to be more forward, more aggressive, easier to talk to. Amir would never forget the night when he, SaRon, and Omar were seated at a table in a disco talking, and an attractive young lady at the bar across the way caught his eye. Game on, except she appeared to be with a guy. He didn't want to start any trouble. They were a long way from Philly. The young lady, however, must have been feeling him because at one point in the evening, she brushed past him on her way to the ladies' room and inserted her phone number written on a small piece of paper into his pocket very stealthily as she did so!

There was also the Macy's Harold Square incident. This had been like a movie. While in NYC alone one Saturday afternoon, he noticed a good-looking, well-dressed girl standing near the Harold Square Macy's entrance crying. He respectfully approached her and asked what was wrong. She explained that she worked at Macy's and had left her pocketbook in her car, and someone had broken in and taken it. She lived in Brooklyn. As he had driven to NYC on that occasion, the least he could do was offer this damsel in distress a ride home. He did, and she accepted. She was really cute and petite with freckles and auburn hair. They exchanged phone numbers and subsequently actually went out on a few dates. Periodically, Omar would actually rent a limo, specifying a white chauffeur, so the guys could go club hopping around Manhattan. Omar liked attention, liked being noticed. It was also a chick magnet, they all thought.

As he and Omar sat in the Midtown Manhattan luncheonette sipping coffee, they were tired. It was about three in the morning, and they had discoed the night away.

"Boy, if you were in the Sahara Desert in a sandstorm and a woman was around, you'd spot her!" Amir said to Omar with a smile. "It's uncanny, this ability you have."

Everyone knew it was true. Omar could be like a bird of prey gliding on the wind drafts and surveying the area, looking for prey! They both laughed.

"Let's go home," they agreed.

They walked back to Amir's car and climbed in. Amir inserted an Isaac Hayes eight-track, and they started the long trek back to Philly. It was approximately one hundred miles from Philly to NYC, as the crow flies. And at three to four in the morning, it seemed like much more. Trying to keep one's eyes open as one navigated the New Jersey Turnpike in the wee hours, heading home, was a challenge. Open the window and let cold air in, drink coffee, play the radio loudly—he tried them all at one time or another. In spite of these efforts, on more than one occasion, Amir caught himself nodding and drifting out of his lane on Route 95 South, headed back to Philly, waking up just in time to avoid an accident! During this period in his life, his favorite songs included the late Bobby Womack's "Daylight Is Gonna Catch Me Up Again" and Junior Walker's "Road Runner." The former was a song about someone who had been clubbing and discoing all night and was coming home as the sun and the regular people were just getting up, and the latter about a man who wanted no commitment.

Their youth and arrogance meant they didn't consider themselves to be average or typical, for blacks or whites! Young, intelligent, single, no kids, with at least some income, they could and did go out anytime they chose. They didn't have to wait for the weekend! They considered most holidays, like St. Patrick's Day or New Year's Eve, to be amateur nights! They usually had gainful employment or some other means of income but still went out frequently. They had all become fairly skilled at using or ripping off the system—collecting UC benefits, getting free passes for SEPTA, sometimes not paying rent knowing full well how long the legal eviction process would take, getting extra grants and loans for school, and so on. For a precious few years, when he and Omar both lived in Center City, they, the crew, were living the life, going to clubs and bars and not having to pay the cover charge or get in the queue like the regulars, because of who they knew. They were getting deals and discounts on quality merchandise, again because of who they knew. They made it a point to cultivate cordial relations and friendships with members of the Nation, the Italian Mob, musicians, black and white nationalists, and politicians all across town. They sometimes hung out in places that blacks didn't typically hang out. They refused to submit to the rules and assumptions that led to a kind of segregation of the races in Philly. They patronized predominantly black and predominantly white as well as mixed clubs, bars, and restaurants.

They were able to be in hostile territory and not be overly concerned. They became romantically involved with whomever they chose regardless of ethnicity or race. So when Amir learned that Tarik was after the Countess or that Omar was out showing off a beautiful blond white woman in all the right places because of a business deal he was working on, he was not surprised!

Forty-Four Caliber was going around to his ladies picking up envelopes from them, containing money on that beautiful winter afternoon. They were gainfully employed; he was not. "Shiiit, gurl," he would say with a big grin as he was handed the respective envelopes.

Amir ran into him in John Wanamaker's Department Store while Forty-Four was picking up one of his famous envelopes.

"Fat Frank is in the hospital," he told him.

"Wow, didn't know that," Amir replied. "I'll spread the word, Forty-Four."

SaRon hated Fat Frank. About a year before, Fat Frank, whom Amir and Omar never really trusted but periodically partied or hung out with, had come to Amir, Omar, and SaRon with an AC (Atlantic City) scheme. He would put on a cabaret in AC. The guys would be part of it and get paid. Tickets/shares were to be sold. Exactly what they were expected to do was not clear. They also didn't trust Fat Frank. Omar and Amir both demurred, but SaRon did not. Tickets were sold and money collected. The cabaret never occurred. It had been a scam. People who had bought tickets were upset.

Several guys who apparently couldn't find Fat Frank came down to the college looking for SaRon one evening. Neither Amir nor Omar were there at the time. Word got out to SaRon. He went underground for weeks. When he finally surfaced, he was mad. He could've gotten hurt. He blamed Fat Frank. When told that he was sick and hospitalized, SaRon said, "Good, I hope he dies!" Fat Frank, who was probably morbidly obese, did die!

Amir would never forget the time, months before, on their way to a party, Omar had composed an "Ode to Fat Frank, Lord of Fat and Funk," which he promptly delivered to Fat Frank in the presence of others once they arrived at the party. He prostrated himself in front of Frank and said, "O Lord of Fat and Funk, it is thee we praise, farting and belching the day away, wouldn't work in a pie factory ..." Frank laughed but probably was insulted and offended. Amir thought to himself, *I know some bold Negroes!* Amir liked Frank on one level, with his "Fat Albert" laugh, but felt he was "greasy," a term he used for people he thought were unethical, sneaky, and not to be trusted.

La La Land

Amir was sitting in his cubicle at work and bored but working when the phone on his desk rang that sunny Wednesday afternoon at about two o'clock. It was Omar.

"Ever been to California, brother?"

"No" was his response.

"Well, I'm out here on business in Beverly Hills. I'm staying at the Beverly Wilshire Hotel."

At first, Amir was stunned. Was Omar kidding? Not like him. Omar had always dreamed big, so it was possible.

"Call SaRon. There are tickets at Newark Airport for the redeye out here, waiting for you. Meet me in Beverly Hills. I'll give you the location to meet me."

Amir smiled and said, "Okay." A chance to go to Cali and stay at the Beverly Wilshire, how could he say no? Amir had a civil service job. He'd call out sick for the balance of the week from California. He'd go to Stu, his supervisor, right now and feign illness.

"I'm going home early today, Stu," were his words. No time for leave or vacation requests and all that. Amir's apartment at that time was only a few blocks away from the job, on Spring Garden Street. When SaRon picked up the phone, he sounded sleepy.

SaRon had never been to California either.

"Let's go, Brother," said Amir. "This chance may never come again!"

After quickly packing and meeting up with SaRon, he took the train from Philly to Newark Airport. SaRon, who owned some fashionable clothes, was wearing some unstylish, farmer-looking outfit. When asked why, he said he was saving his good clothes. Amir didn't understand. It was showtime! All those California girls. As they settled into their seats on their redeye flight to LA, he noticed the sexy flight attendant.

"Can I change my seat?" he asked. "I want to sit over the black box!" She looked quizzical and then smiled. He continued, "'Cause the black box almost always survives intact." He was warming up. She was just target practice, as Omar used to say.

"You're too much, boy," said SaRon. "You're starting already!"

"That's right. You bet your bippy. Wait till I get to Cali. I plan on doing some damage, brother. Hopefully you do too!"

Sure enough, after landing at LAX and taking a cab to the meeting place, they found Omar there waiting with a sly smile. He looked very comfortable and quite at home there. Palm trees, boulevards, multilane highways, tons of traffic, homeless people, neon signs everywhere—LA was interesting, a big sprawl. Beverly Hills, of course, was like a movie set—Gucci, Fiorucci, Versace, Rolex, and on and on. They saw mansions and cars you rarely or never saw on the East Coast like Ferraris, Lamborghinis, Bugattis, Rolls-Royces, and so on. SaRon, who lifted weights, couldn't wait to get to Venice Beach. Amir, who drove a VW Beetle at the time, wanted to get to a VW accessory and aftermarket parts store in Santa Monica, which he had been ordering aftermarket parts for his VW from.

Of course, the Beverly Wilshire was impressive—the poshness, the luxury, the service. They drew quite a few stares. Who were these young black men staying at the famous Beverly Wilshire Hotel? Blacks, particularly young ones, were not often seen there in those days, as guests. Omar had invited a business partner Amir and SaRon didn't know, a dude. Amir also didn't know what the business Omar was attending to was. Nor did he ask. He also didn't know how the two suites they were sharing were being paid for. He assumed it was by Omar's or someone else's corporate card? Guess he trusted him. Omar had always been pretty sophisticated and knowledgeable about business and financial matters, always wanted to do his own thing and be his own boss. So anything was possible. He had also taken a stab at the music industry, forming a band and going out on the road for a brief time. He had a photographic memory and was an avid reader. He had a way with people as well that inspired confidence. He was conversant on the stock market, mergers, IPOs, business trends, foreign affairs, and so on.

LA had a sort of cheap, plasticky look. It was not a city like Philly or New York but a big sprawl. LA and the whole California scene were different, not like the East Coast. The guys, for the most part, didn't seem as hard. The clothing styles and sometimes the hairstyles were different from those of the East Coast. Amir and Omar had commented to each other after viewing them that the so-called bad areas of Watts and Compton had palm trees, drive-ways, and garages and didn't look like the worst parts of NYC, Philly, or Newark! They didn't look as poor, depressed, forlorn, dangerous, or abandoned. Years later, after visiting San Francisco, Amir would decide that he liked San Francisco better than LA.

Frisco reminded him more of the cities he was used to—Philly, NYC, Baltimore, and so on. It seemed to have a center, an old part, grand old houses, buses, trolleys, traditions, history, and so on. Of course, they concluded that the LA brothers, like the brothers almost everywhere else, with the possible exception of NYC or Chicago, were not as fashionable, as stylish, as clean as Philly broth-ers. In fact, some of them dressed like farmers! No, Amir didn't conclude he'd ever want to necessarily move out there to Cali. He liked the change of seasons, the history present in the Northeast, the pain. Like in the Star Trek movie when Captain Kirk explains to another character, "My pain makes me who I am!" But visiting was fun and educational, another slice of life. He'd never forget sitting at a bar at the Hollywood Hotel with the late actor Herschel Bernardi or seeing the actress Yvette Mimmeaux in a hotel lobby. She was fine.

The concentration of wealth in Beverly Hills was obscene on some level, however. Some had so much, and others had so little. Early one beautiful, sunny morning while cruising in their rented convertible, the Chic hit "Good Times" came on the radio. They pumped up the volume. "Clams on the half shell and roller skates." *Life doesn't get much better than this*, Amir thought as they slowly motored around Beverly Hills and its environs.

By accident, they saw the mansion once owned by the Saudi prince who had been in the news for painting the humanlike stat-utes on his property anatomically, pubic hair and all, causing some controversy and alarm to his neighbors! Later, a fire occurred at the mansion.

Of course, they had some good meals while in Cali—Tex-Mex

or Mexican food in particular, which made sense as there were so many Mexicans and Mexican Americans out there. Carlos and Charlie's was one of their stops. They visited the Polo Lounge in the Beverly Hills Hotel, as well as Grauman's Chinese Theatre. It became quite obvious that even more so than on the East Coast, in Cali, your auto defined you. The climate in Southern Cali, at least, being what it was, cars didn't tend to rust as quickly either, as they sometimes did in the Northeast. Amir assumed the lack of road salt, winter temperatures, and so on were also reasons why antique and classic cars were big out there.

At some point during their stay, there was a dispute between hotel management and Omar about their bill. He had faith in Brother Omar, however. He was a good talker and could always think on his feet. So while SaRon got quite nervous, almost embarrassingly so, Amir was cool.

Over the years, he and Omar would find themselves in and get out of a lot of tight spots, monetary and otherwise! They had been to California, another dream fulfilled! On the long flight back to Newark Airport, among their discussions was how they really needed a fashion police, authorized to arrest on sight those folks who dressed like farmers, who committed major fashion faux paus—those women, for instance, with buffalo butts who insisted on wearing spandex pants! Amir recounted that while inadvertently following one the other day, the view of her gluteus maximus reminded him of two midgets fighting to get out of her pants! Or those folk, male or female, who wore clashing patterns and colors, plaids with stripes or checkered other garments or high water pants, black sandals with white socks and shorts, or extremely loud colors (often clashing). They concluded that the best-dressed black folks, with notable exceptions, of course, lived in Philly, NYC, and DC. Most California brothers didn't make the cut.

The Lone Ranger

Patricia was a beautiful and a genuinely nice person. This tall Piscean, as Omar was prone to say about such women, was "bursting with health." They had fun together. Amir genuinely cared for her. She lived with her mother and sister. Patricia's smile was warm and radiant and lit up her entire face. Her mother seemed to really like him. Her sister, not so much, he surmised.

They lived in a big three-story row house on Diamond Street, a few blocks over from Broad. That area has now been absorbed by Temple University. Frat houses and dorms now sit where the big grand old houses on Diamond Street once stood. College students, mostly white, now walk dogs, live, drink, party, and mill around where the once predominantly African American neighborhood use to be, where the Diamond Street gang was supreme. Temple was bound to expand and did. Was this also urban renewal / Negro removal?

Once after taking Patricia to a grand old movie theater on Market Street in Center city one cold winter evening, one of the guys at the college asked him some days later, "Who was that white girl I saw you with on Market Street?"

Amir had replied, "Not that it's any of your business, but she's not white!"

Patricia was very fair-skinned, and in the winter, she became simply pale. Evidently, there were still color issues in the black community! They were both so young, twenty-two and twenty-three. Amir would have married her, if possible. Years later, he would reflect that it was probably good that they didn't get married. It wouldn't have lasted! They didn't know who they were yet! Of course, Omar knew of the Lone Ranger, just as Amir knew of Omar's current and past loves.

Movies, walks, dinners, car rides, museums, picnics, spending time together just conversing—they did the kinds of things folks did during that time. Gradually, however, her availability lessened. Can't make Friday night? How about Saturday night? Next weekend would be better! He felt that something was wrong. Like David Ruffin sang in the Temptations' hit, "Losing You," "Your love is fading. I can feel your love fading, away from me. Your touch has grown cold as if someone else controls your very soul." Of course, he had seen other people. That was different, he was a man! Men were entitled to have more than one! The song lyrics sung by the Main Ingredient, "Everybody Plays the Fool," seemed relevant and largely true. "Loving eyes they cannot see a certain person wasn't meant to be!"

He would finally ask her. One night, seated at the dining room table across from her at her big Diamond Street house, he prefaced his question by asking, "Please tell me the truth." Was there another man? She lied by saying, "No." His suspicions were confirmed early one Sunday morning at the Stenton Diner, in West Oak Lane, one of the few diners in Philly, located on Stenton Avenue, a popular hangout for folks who had been out discoing or clubbing and were hungry and eating in the wee hours. He was there with the crew, Omar, Phil, SaRon, and Mike. As he surveyed the diner, he saw her, seated with a group and next to an older man. Amir was upset but wouldn't make a scene.

He walked past her booth on the pretext of going to the men's room. When their eyes met, he said, "Hi, Patricia." She looked clearly uncomfortable and nervous. He had accomplished his goal. He continued to the restroom. Over the years, his anger, hurt, and disappointment changed to friendship. A bond had formed between them. She apparently didn't really know what she wanted in life, he decided. She was conflicted. Years later, she joined the US Army and then became one of Philly's Finest. She would be married and divorced twice. Can one really blame someone for not giving what he or she is not capable of giving? They remained friends for decades. She would be dubbed, however, forevermore "The Lone

Ranger." A period of depression followed. Even his Dad on a car trip with him asked, "What's wrong with you?" as they drove down the highway.

"A girl," he replied.

Dad nodded in understanding.

Over the years, he would break a few hearts and have his broken a few times as well. "Everybody plays the fool."

EEO—Affirmative Action

That Friday night, when he walked the few blocks from his Center City apartment to the Hippo, he was feeling good. He was wearing a black-and-gray glen plaid Pierre Cardin suit and a black turtle-neck. There was a red handkerchief folded neatly in the outer jacket pocket. He knew he looked good in his clothes because people were constantly telling him so.

He had some money in his pocket, but it wasn't necessary. He wouldn't have to pay the cover to get in like most folks did or pay for drinks sometimes. Amir would leave generous tips, however. He didn't see Big Eddy on the door. Big Eddy was one of his favorites. He was a tall, brown-skinned strongly built brother with a thin moustache. Eddy had always been nice to him. Eddy didn't look like someone you wanted to mess with. He was therefore an excellent choice for a bouncer. Little Johnny was smart. Almost all the bartenders, waitresses, bouncers, and so on at the Hippo were black, as were most of the patrons! He generally stayed in the background. Interesting, the mob was practicing EEO and affirmative action! One learns not to ask a lot of questions when around certain kinds of people, particularly people who might be involved in illegal activities. They didn't like it. So he inquired about Eddy very delicately.

"Don't see Brother Eddy tonight," he stated very nonchalantly.

"Eddy's away" was the response.

Sometime later, Amir would learn that Eddy was doing time for someone else, an Italian mobster. He would be compensated upon his release and protected while inside. Part of the way of life! Sure enough, a couple of years later after Amir entered and had been seated at an unfamiliar go-go bar in Center City, Eddy had approached Amir and asked, "Like my place?"

"Wow, brother, it's good to see you!" was Amir's response.

Eddy knew Amir worked for the government.

"Say, brother," said Eddy. "Let me run something past you. Two guys from the IRS came by here and wanted to know how I could afford to pay cash for a Rolls Royce?"

"Wow, that's not my area, Eddy, but I'll see what I can find out," said Amir.

This was just like in the movies! *Interesting*, he thought, in the movies, *the Italian mobsters are usually portrayed as virulent racists, hating blacks, like in the Godfather*, but in real life, he was sure some were not haters, clearly, not all. Up in NYC for instance, "Crazy" Joey Gallo was known for working with blacks. Clearly, Little Johnny did also.

Amir would hear the famous Louis Armstrong on an old radio interview once explaining how when other whites would not book or hire black jazz musicians in their nightclubs back in the day, mobsters sometimes did! It made sense. How could Italian gangsters do business in black communities without the cooperation and participation of blacks? Life! Did it even seem believable that big black gangsters didn't work and cooperate with the mob? "Don't believe half of what you see, and none of what you hear!" Amir had noticed the new restaurant opening off Market Street near Delaware Avenue. It would be nice. The name of it sounded Italian. When it opened, he couldn't help but notice all the high-end cars in the parking lot, late-model Jags, Corvettes, Mercedes,

Porsches, Audis, Caddys, and so on. He figured it was probably a mob-owned-and-run place.

When he asked Little Johnny about it, Johnny said, "Go over there and use my name, and you won't have to pay!" Johnny often told him and Omar to go to certain bars, clubs, and restaurants and mention his name, which they sometimes did. It worked! Either the meal was on the house or they received good seats and the best of service in these frequently almost all-white establishments. Johnny was a "Sigi," as he called himself, a Sicilian. He encouraged them to call him that also, but it never felt comfortable to Amir to say that. He had offered to make them honorary "Sigis" as well! Amir had come to believe over the years that urban Italian American males and urban African American males were really quite similar. Many of both groups hung on the corner, liked dressing sharp, liked women, liked luxury or status cars, liked music, and had a kind of macho cultural ethic.

Of course, Sicilian Americans were descended from a place, Sicily, that was more Mediterranean than their neighbors to the north. Sicily was, in fact, at a period in history, known as the Emirate of Sicily. They had contact with the Moors and the Arabs. Could this historic cross-cultural pollination explain, in some small part, the present-day similarities between Italian males and black males? Food for thought.

It Takes a Fool

Mike was looking kind of sad as he, Amir, and Omar sat in his West Philly apartment discussing the woman he was currently playing house with. First, it was surprising that Mike was cohabitating with any woman! He had no history of doing so. While the crew all liked Mike, he had a cross to bear, the awful skin condition (keloids) he had been unfortunate to have all his life. It was difficult to overlook it unless you were his friend. The keloids were large and formed a kind of beard around his face. Amir and Omar liked him; his skin condition never affected their friendship. The ladies, however, were a different matter. Philly women were known to be difficult to talk to. Even good-looking brothers with game complained about it. And Mike didn't have much game. Starr W. seemed attracted to him, but did he act on it? After years of being overlooked, rejected, or stared at, was it any wonder Mike seemed to have little confidence as far as the honeys were concerned? You couldn't be heavy handed with him in terms of female advice or tips. Amir had tried to set him up once with a cute, dimpled waitress at Dewey's. Mike's response had been "I can find my own women." We all have an ego and, one hopes, some pride! Mike's female *roommate*, according to him, was being picked up and dropped off by other men at the place they shared, at all hours. She would also disappear for long stretches of time with no explanation. It didn't sound good. Bitch!

They didn't want to lecture Mike, however.

"Damn, brother!" was one response.

Amir had not met her. Neither had Omar. Bitch! Mike was their boy. Both Omar and Amir sympathized with Mike. Both had been done wrong themselves more than once but not so blatantly—Omar and Gina the nurse, Amir and the Lone Ranger. Of course, they were being hypocrites. It was okay for a man to have more than one but not for a woman. Ye good ole double standard was very useful. Years later, Shaharazad Ali, another Philadelphian, would argue in her controversial book, *The Black Man's Guide to Understanding the Black Woman*, that the black man had no history of being with just one woman, either in Africa or America! Certainly, this double standard worked to Omar's and Amir's advantage and every other man's. It was work, however, successfully juggling two, three, or more women at the same time. It could be complicated and very stressful, as well as quite expensive.

In addition to the telling of the usual lies, one told one woman in order to be with another, for example, "I'll be out of town for a few days" or "I'm not feeling well"—or mentioned the death of a relative, occasioning attendance at a wake or funeral, being out with the boys, and so on. Holidays were particularly challenging. "What are you doing New Year's Eve, around Christmas …?" One's friends also had to lie to cover for one.

"Have you seen Omar?"

"He's in Chicago."

"Where's Amir?"

"Traveling for work."

Sometimes you went on one date, feigned illness, parted, and then went on a second date. No matter how much of a catch one woman was, the thinking was there would be an even better one just around the bend. Of course, this sometimes backfired and you were left alone for a time. But there seemed to be so many. "They come at you in human waves," Omar was fond of saying. You thought you'd always find another!

"Aren't I enough?" she asked through her tears.

"I'm not a one woman man," was sometimes the arrogant and insensitive response.

Of course, some women played this game also. It was youth. It was the time, the social mores. Drugs, sex, and rock and roll or free love were often the battle cries of the time. AIDS was unknown then, and any possibly contracted venereal diseases that they knew about could be treated with penicillin.

They were at Amir's crib. He and Omar shared a fondness for the late actor Richard Harris's songs, though he was really not a singer. "Dancing Girl" and "A Tramp Shining" were two of their favorites. These were love songs and poems, somebody-done-somebody-wrong songs. In spite of all their bravado, they were romantics. They liked falling in and out of love, having one's heart broken, or breaking someone else's type songs, unrequited love songs, and so on. Omar particularly liked the line "It's so sad to belong to someone else when the right one comes along!" They used women sometimes, and sometimes women used them. But they did love, often speaking of the one who got away. Sometimes they loved and lost. Amir would never forget for instance the time he and Omar went to the Spectrum in South Philly to see Isaac Hayes. They had both recently been hurt by love. As Hayes sang one of his lesser known love songs, "Your Loving Is So Dog Gone Good," they must have made a sad-looking pair, sitting there looking depressed, periodically shaking their heads as Black Moses sang the lyrics.

Gathering in one or the other's apartment, they would play some Joe Cocker. They both liked the Righteous Brothers, Bill Medley and Bobby Hatfield, Tom Jones, Hall and Oates, Chicago, and the Average White Band. That was real blue-eyed soul, as was Lulu. Omar had been a Dionne Warwick fanatic years before, constantly traveling around with some of her albums under his arm. She and Burt Bacharach together were *awesome*, they agreed. They also loved the Four Tops, the Temptations, and Bobby Womack—"Ain't no cross over in him." They loved romantic, poetic, and creative lyrics. They were lyric men. They both loved to play with words, with language. "If I catch you with it, I got to get it." "If it's not here when you unpack, it won't be here when you get back!" "Body by Fisher, mind by Mattel." They were both cunning linguists.

"Heard from the Lone Ranger?" Omar asked.

"Not in a while," Amir replied. "How's Gina?"

"Nurse, I'm getting worse!" was the answer.

"Met this big-leg girl yesterday," stated Omar.

"Is she qualified?" asked Amir.

"If I can fit her in my schedule," was Omar's casual response. "How's your trainee coming along?"

"She's coming," Amir replied with an impish smile.

"If anyone asks, I'm out of town this weekend, akhi," Omar had mentioned.

Women Omar had broken up with or with whom he had had a

big fight sometimes sought out Amir for consolation, since they almost always knew they were close friends and neighbors. Through a veil of tears, they often cried, "He promised me ..." "He told me ..." They were always beautiful. His tastes ran to the exotic, and although they were somewhat vulnerable at the time, Amir never sought to take advantage of the situation as he attempted to console them. Omar was his boy, and he didn't want his sloppy seconds. They both shared this code: you don't mess with your boy's women! This code, over the years, meant that Omar was one of the few males he felt that he could trust with his girlfriend, sister, daughter, or wife if necessary!

Amir had been out discoing the night before and was tired and sleepy as he ate his pancakes and eggs at the local restaurant on the corner a couple of blocks from his crib. It was not unusual for him to be out, alone or with the boys, during the weekend or during the week. He was living in Center City and several clubs and bars were within walking distance from his apartment—the Hippo, the Funky Donkey, the Cave, The Fox Trap, Bob's Yacht Club, the Trestle Inn, among others. He was the only African American in the restaurant at the time, not unusual in Center City Philly during those days. So he noticed the tall, heavy-set brother standing in the doorway who seemed to be noticing him. He didn't look familiar. As he approached Amir's booth, Amir slid the butter knife and the fork over within reach of his right hand. Sure, it was only a fork and a butter knife, but it was better than nothing!

The guy politely asked, "May I join you?"

Amir's antenna immediately went up. Was he gay? Did he have some sort of beef with him? "Are you Amir?" the fellow asked.

"It all depends. Who's asking?" was Amir's response.

"I want you to stay away from my girl, Cathy!" was the retort.

Through a half smile, Amir said, "Brother, I don't even know who you are talking about! I was just out last night trying to collect phone numbers. Do you have a picture or something?"

Amir had already imagined stabbing this guy in the eye with the knife if he made a move. With that comment, the big guy shook his head, smiled, got up, and walked away. *Good, this could've ended badly*, Amir thought. He also thought, as in the Stevie Wonder song, "All in love is fair. Love's a crazy game." He hoped to never get into a fight over a girl. For what? Unless kidnapped, don't people usually chose who they want to be with?

People who were content in their relationships, he believed, were not necessarily looking to cheat. Then, of course, there was the other song lyric, "If you can beat me rocking, then you can have my chair!"

As Amir was walking on Twenty-First between Market and Chestnut in Center City, he heard the yell of "Sonny!" The voice was very familiar. It was his sister, Melinda. She was driving her new Mercury Cougar XR7. Melinda had grown into a very pretty young woman. She was well dressed with good makeup, hair, and so on. A lot of guys had always been attracted to Melinda. His sister was a fox! Once they had both moved out of the ponderosa, they didn't see each other very often. She had a house in West Oak Lane, he an apartment in Center City. Two active, busy young people, they were both on the go, working, dating, traveling, and so on.

Of course, as little children, they fought a lot. He was nineteen months older—not really that much older. But as toddlers and young children, she would often break his toys, particularly his extensive toy gun collection. As they grew older, they got along better.

Her high school sweetheart had been Donald. In her early twenties, she had married him. He seemed like a nice guy. Could he handle this smart, determined, strong, quick-witted, high-energy, beautiful Gemini woman? Amir had wondered.

Melinda never expressed a desire to go to college but had a strong work ethic and typically worked two or more jobs at a time. In fact, between him and Melinda, she was the first to buy a house and a brand-new car. Amir laughed to himself when he remembered how when he moved out of the family home, it was fine. He was being a man. But when Melinda expressed a desire to do so, the issue became why? Was she to become a fallen woman, a prostitute?

Did she want to have orgies in her place? Mom and Dad were traditional and old-fashioned in many ways. Their concerns, however, did not prevent her from moving out! They were like ships passing in the night at this stage in their young, single lives. But they did love each other.

As Omar and he were strolling through Center City that crisp autumn afternoon, they passed a brother at the intersection of Eighteenth and Chestnut Streets. Of course, he was selling *Muhammad Speaks* newspapers and bean pies.

"Salaam Alaikum, brothers," he said. "Get your *Speaks*."

"Sure, brother, wa alaikum salaam, and two bean pies please," replied Amir.

Bean pies kept them going through college, it seemed. Cheap and tasty and this was a holy pie!

Meanwhile, word was out that "Flash" a.k.a. Super Negro/ Nigger, a.k.a. the Black Spasm, had pimp-slapped Marsha. Marsha seemed to be a very nice, classy girl Flash was dating from the college.

Macho asshole, thought Amir.

"What's wrong with your boy?" Amir asked Omar.

Omar had been told Flash and Marsha had been play fighting, and it got out of hand!

Amir's African girlfriend, Nadia, was to meet him at the crib that evening, so he parted ways with Omar. "Catch you later, brother. I have a pressing engagement," he said to Omar with a grin.

"Salaam alaikum, akhi. Handle your business, brother," replied Omar slyly.

Amir readied the apartment for her visit. Incense would be burning, the lights would be dimmed, and soft, romantic music would be playing. He loved atmosphere and ambience. She was beautiful, a kind of café au lait color, with big, dark, round eyes and thick dark hair worn kind of long. She was keen featured. Her cheekbones were prominent, and she was slender and sinewy looking. She had class, dignity, and was still sexy at the same time. And that accent! She was his personal Queen of Sheba.

As she made herself comfortable in his smallish one-bedroom apartment, he was glad to see her. She visited often, and that was okay with him. He cared for her. As long as he kept his schedules straight! Seeing more than one at a time (creeping) was work! She was in the bedroom when she asked him in her charming accent, "Amir, what is this?" She was holding up a woman's earring in her right hand. It was apparent she had found it in his unmade bed. Amir thought that to lie in such a circumstance would be silly. Of course, he was nervous yet arrogant when he responded, "Looks like an earring to me."

It was not a good answer, but he couldn't think of a good cover story at the time. He ducked to his right like a boxer trying to avoid a punch as the heavy glass ashtray came whizzing by his head! She was understandably furious with him. She stormed out of his apartment. Not good! He would wait a couple of days, apologize profusely, send her some flowers, talk to her best friend, tell her it would never happen again, and probably get her back. Of course, he had been cheating on her. *One woman, probably not possible*, he thought. He hadn't realized though how some women leave things behind, mark their territory as it were! Leave their scent. From then on, he would scour his apartment after each visitor left, looking for articles left, intentionally or unintentionally!

Back at the college, the Forty-Four-Caliber Dude was explaining to the fellows gathered in the cafeteria at their table how his latest conquest had a biting pussy. Forty-Four Caliber was *different*. He had taken to wearing a T-shirt with an image of a forty-four-caliber pistol on it and the designation "Forty-Four" indicated. Amir sure had a diverse group of friends and acquaintances, he thought to himself as he smiled and shook his head! An obsession with pussy seemed to be part of young male bravado, hormones popping, and culture. "Young and dumb and full of come"—many of their discussions were about it. The old brothers said that "Asian women had slanted pussy," "slender girls often have the best pussy," "if you're good to pussy, pussy will be good to you," and "if God had not meant for man to eat pussy, why did he make it look like a taco?"

Looking at and staring at nude pics in *Playboy* and later *Penthouse* and other even more graphic pictures in other magazines and periodicals was a constant. "Look at that! Do you see that? Damn!" they said as they looked at, smelled, touched, rubbed, and sometimes licked some of the pictures! Amir was certain that some of this was posturing for the other guys around at the time—much like male behavior in the go-go bars, a lot of which was not to really impress the dancers, he was convinced, but the other male patrons, like the guys who instead of tipping with one-dollar bills, like most did, tipped with tens, twenties, fifties, and so on, or the fellow that time at the nightclub in Center City, who, on Men's Night lay supine on the floor after arranging a trail of dollar bills leading up to and terminating at his waiting crotch! Some of the male patrons at the Center City nightclub actually performed cunnilingus, in front of everyone, on some of the dancers! He and Omar would not go that far!

"You see, brothers, between cognitive dissonance and natal alienation, we, as a people, are fucked!" the heavy brother shared with him and Omar that night during the intermission at the Living Room.

They both smiled and nodded. They hadn't come for intellectual discourse but for pure lust and entertainment. They understood these ladies were working. They wanted tips. Fantasies about taking one home with you or dating or simply having sex with one were usually not realistic. The dancers, at least the good ones, were expert at getting you to feel that they were dancing for you, had noticed you, and that you had a chance. Amir would date a dancer casually. It didn't get serious. He didn't know whether Omar ever had. But some of these ladies were exceptional! They had great bodies, seductive dance moves, makeup, hair, nails, shoes, oils, perfume, and so on.

Amir figured that when the job was to look seductive and alluring, some would become expert at it. Flirting was an art, of course. Omar and he were not slouches in that department! But some of these women had it down! Some would get guys to spend significant amounts of money on them without ever actually going to bed with them. Some received gifts of clothes, cars, jewelry, drugs, furs, their rent/mortgages paid, and so on.

It's Just Business

Phil and White Ann had just returned from John Wanamaker's Department Store. They had liberated several items from there. Wanamaker's was only a few blocks from the college. It was one of Philly's upscale department stores back in the day. They would sell their goods to some interested students. Phil was wearing the handsome camel-hair polo-style topcoat he had "liberated" from the coatroom at an upscale Center City restaurant a few days ago. Phil was also selling a copy of a midterm test he had appropriated from the trash a day before. It was selling like hot cakes! Phil had threatened to spread the word on one professor he had discovered was gay unless he received a B in the course. Phil got his B. Amir and Omar had recently wired chocolates and flowers via Western Union to girls they had met. They both fancied themselves as being romantic. In those days, they had discovered, one could charge them to almost anyone listed in the phone book by simply providing that person's phone number and street address! The girls were impressed. How thoughtful and romantic!

Only the Strong Survive

When hungry, they would often travel to a busy big restaurant in Center City, preferably crowded, with sections, including a counter. They would order coffees from the counter, get a check, and then go to the dining area, eat a full meal, and get another check. When leaving, they would present the cashier with the checks for the coffees, pay them, and exit the restaurant. Phil often went to good restaurants, walked around picking up cash tips from the tables until he had enough to pay for a meal, and then dined, paying with his collected tips! Periodically, Phil would do his "there's something in my food" routine, often a tack, nail, or roach that he, of course, had brought with him to the establishment. Usually, it worked; he would be offered a free meal and an apology. Phil was proof positive that presentation was everything. Not just anybody could have pulled off some of Phil's routines. You had to look and act the part. You had to be convincing. Of course, there were also the weekend shopping sprees.

Armed with wallets full of fake IDs, they would open checking accounts at banks on a Friday, depositing a hundred or two, be given a few checks, and then go shopping on Saturday. They would pay for their purchases by check, producing driver's licenses or other forms of ID requested, and leave the stores with their purchases. Back in the day, banks were generally closed on weekends and couldn't be contacted by merchants to verify anything. Sometimes they'd return to the bank on the following Monday and withdraw the funds originally deposited in the checking account, thus recouping their original investment and having their purchases as well. These and other schemes allowed the fellows, although poor college students, to have a decent quality of life, money in their pockets, and nice clothes to wear. Companies, corporations, and the US government were fair game. Technology has, of course, made such schemes much more difficult to pull off subsequently.

It was not uncommon for a guy back in the day to be receiving at any given time, welfare checks, food stamps, unemployment compensation checks, a paycheck from a job he was actually working, student loans, scholarships, and grants. The code seemed to be you could rip off the system, but you didn't steal from an individual brother or sister—a kind of reparation.

Amir learned that one also had to learn how to carry oneself. You had to know how to play the part/role. Scared- or nervous-looking people are not generally successful at pulling off such deceptions. You also had to know how to dress the part. You had to look and act like you belonged in a particular setting or place. If you could do all that, Amir learned, it was amazing what you could pull off! If one acted like one belonged somewhere, many wouldn't question your presence.

As a boy, Amir had witnessed his own father bribe Philly cops more than once. Typically, Dad would be speeding, get pulled over sometimes by the police, and when asked to produce his driver's license and registration, there would just happen to be a twenty-dollar bill inserted behind the license. The offer was obvious but unspoken. Many cops took the twenty and admonished him to slow down or be more careful. A few asked if he was trying to bribe them, to which he said respectfully, "No, officer, but of course I have money in my wallet!" If the worst happened and Dad or he got a ticket, they'd call Sam, who for a modest fee of ten dollars would yank your traffic ticket out of the files at traffic court and no more ticket! Sam got a box of liquor every Christmas. When it was time to get your car inspected, by either the state or a private mechanic, Amir would go to a particular mechanic's garage, a cousin, he believed. He would pull the garage doors down, ask him if the car was all right without looking or checking anything, and then slap a sticker on the windshield and say, "Give me twenty dollars."

"Right on."

"Catch you later!"

It's good to have a network! One could ride SEPTA buses almost for free if one knew where to get on and off and where to get transfers, another saving. The subway could be worked as well if one knew how—certain exits, transfer points, and so on.

Till Death Do You Part

Mom and Dad had been married for a long time. They both grew up in the same area in Georgia. Close in age, they were both good-looking, intelligent, decent, and hardworking folk. Dad, the Aquarian, was more outgoing, gregarious, more the social butterfly. Although born and raised in small-town Georgia, he had served in World War II. He had been to Europe—Paris, London, and somewhere in Germany. He actually knew a few French and German phrases. Amir could only imagine some of the experiences, female-wise, Dad had had in Europe as a young, single, good-looking black American soldier. He had heard the stories about how some of the British, German, and French girls went mad for the black American GIs, who freed, to some degree, from America's race and caste system took advantage of the circumstances.

Of course, there were not usually any black women around in any event. So their options were limited. Some of the white American GIs, of course, resented the popularity of the black guys with the European women and their newfound freedom, and there were racial incidents. Of course, some of them encountered racism in Europe also, but it paled in comparison to what was going on back home.

The British had a saying about American GIs stationed in

England, "Oversexed, overpaid, and over here!" Amir could only imagine the cultural shock the black troops, especially those from the American South, like his father, must have experienced coming from the brutally oppressive segregation, Jim and Jane Crow systems then in place in America once landing in France or England! Some probably thought they had died and gone to heaven! Some of these men simply had sexual encounters with the European women. Others had relationships that ended in marriage and everything in between. Sometimes, the GI stayed in Europe after the war or brought his German, French, English, or Japanese wife or fiancée back to the States. One of Omar's great loves, Miho, part Japanese, part black American, and all gorgeous, was the product of such a union.

Mom, a Virgo, was an attractive woman from a fairly large family, two brothers and three sisters. Her father, James, had been the patriarch of the clan. She was the second oldest. Smart, hardworking, proud, and tough, she was essentially conservative. Amir didn't remember ever seeing her have a drink, curse, or gamble. She was sociable enough but rarely loud or the life of the party. She loved her crowns, the hats black women wore to church in that era. They ranged from simple to ornate, rather large to small, feathered and not feathered, all colors, inexpensive to expensive. She had a lot of them. Almost an entire room in the house was filled with Mom's hat boxes. When she got sharp, she was sharp! Basically a homebody, one of her few outlets was the church, Southern Baptist, of course. She sang on the choir and was active in some church activities, such as various bus trips, dinners being sold, and so on. One of her sisters, Aunt Maggie, had moved to Philly also and had a family.

Amir's aunt's husband was fun, very outgoing, and had a great sense of humor but enjoyed drinking and playing cards much to her chagrin. "The only things that get old are clothes and jewelry," he had heard him say once at a party as he was dancing. Like Dad, he had personality plus.

Mom and Dad had Amir and Melinda only nineteen months apart. Amir was born after they had been married for six to seven years. The firstborn and only male child, he was destined to be spoiled and was. They had built a life together. She worked some years at a cigar factory, and he was a long-distance truck driver. Dad made what was then considered a decent salary, and as a Teamster, he had benefits as well. The family's quality of life was not bad. They had a single-family home, vacations, good clothes to wear, and food to eat.

Fortunately, they never had to go on "the welfare." Amir couldn't remember Dad ever having to collect Unemployment Compensation benefits. He always worked. Amir and Melinda received allowances, good toys at Christmas, birthday presents, and so on. They probably were living a lower-middle to middle-class existence for the time. They occasionally fought, Mom and Dad, in an obvious way, like the time Dad had wanted him to get a paper route to earn money, and Mom was against it, thinking he was too young. Mom won. She was very protective of Amir. Dad wanted to make sure he had a work ethic and would grow up to be a man.

Since boyhood, Amir had heard females, young and old, comment on how handsome his dad was. It was true. He had to admit to himself, his dad was probably better looking than he. This was an explosive mixture, however, a good-looking man with charisma, for this was the era when the good old double standard was in full effect, pre–women's liberation, the pill, and so on. And many married men had an outside woman or women. Some had whole families across town. To their credit, many did support these families financially and emotionally—much like the natural children many famous Europeans had historically. Mob figures, for instance, often had a gumma. Having a mistress seemed to be a cultural phenomenon in many cultures.

It was a fact of life. Black men of the era were no better or worse than other men, he thought, many of whom had this practice as well. Women of the era, who Amir was sure didn't like this state of affairs, often could be heard saying things like, "At least he pays the bills," or "At least he comes home," or "Men will be men," or "I'm his *wife*!" Their grudging acceptance was in part economic. Females of the time could not make incomes even approaching what some men made for the most part. Could there also have been a surplus of females? Not enough men to go around?

Over time, it became apparent to Amir that Dad had other women. The signs were usually pretty easy to see, changes in behavior, wardrobe, the phone rings, no one picked up; he then left almost immediately and stayed out very late when out. There were strange scents and smells. Amir figured that if he observed this, so did Mom. They had been married for twenty-odd years! How could she not know! He decided to stay out of it. It was between them, he thought.

It was an ordinary night at the Hippo, and Amir was in the DJ booth with Omar and a couple of honeys. As he surveyed the rather large floor in the dim lighting, he thought his eyes were playing tricks on him. Was that Dad seated at one of the tables looking sharp?

Who was the woman seated next to him? She didn't look familiar, and it wasn't Mom! What to do? Pretend he didn't see him? Suppose he saw him? Confront him? He was his father after all in a public place! He didn't want to make a scene! Mom must know already. In most respects, he was a good father. One never really knew what went on between a man and a woman, even one's parents. He didn't think this was the first time. He sent a drink over to them. He then walked over to their small table. If Dad was embarrassed, it didn't show. The brown-skinned woman sitting with him was of average height, medium build, and not particularly attractive. She was also not particularly well dressed. She seemed a bit nervous.

Amir smiled and said, "Hello." They exchanged pleasantries, and then he left them. Wow! Life! Should he tell Mom? Keep his mouth shut? Bring it up later with Dad?

Amir decided on keeping his mouth shut. He loved both his parents. They both had been good parents. Mom had to know already. The bearer of bad tidings was sometimes resented. No, this was between them to resolve or not resolve. He would stay out of it. Yes, he was hurt, disappointed, but how many wives did Abraham, David, Solomon, and Muhammad have? If all of history's greats were judged by their marital faithfulness, how many would be left as greats? Wasn't polygamy practiced in many parts of the world even now? When he weighed all the good things his father had done—work to provide a good home for them to live in, food to eat, clothes to wear, vacations, gifts, and presents; never leaving the family without a father; showing them love in his own way; providing him with an example of manhood—they outweighed this one bad thing!

Things were rapidly deteriorating between Mom and Dad, but at least they had waited until Amir and Melinda had grown up before seriously contemplating divorce. The tension between them was palpable. It was sad. Dad would move out of the house and into his own place.

The family home would be left for Mom and him and Linda. Dad would keep the car, but Mom didn't drive anyway. Biggy would live with Dad. Biggy did not like his intended and referred to her as "Black Lilly!" The divorce rate in the country at that time was about 50 percent, Amir had read somewhere. Many folks, particularly the young, were just choosing to live together without benefit of marriage, at least for a trial period.

Amir would always have the memories of better familial days, family gatherings, fishing trips, picnics, vacations, Christmas mornings, going to work with Dad. Interestingly, years later, Mom and Dad were getting along fairly well. Should unhappy people stay married? If the love has died, what should people do? The Catholic church, of course, was against divorce. They were not Catholics, however. When Mom's second husband needed a car, years later, it was Dad she called, and he sold it to him. "Bring a good one, the one you're driving!" she had cautioned.

When Amir's daughter was born years later, in another state, after he was married, Mom accepted a ride with Dad and his second wife to the hospital to see her granddaughter! Dad's second wife used to call Mom for advice on how to handle him. Life is "a puzzle wrapped in an enigma!"

Over the years Omar and Amir would get involved with and break up with a series of girls, some because they wanted to end it, and some because the girlfriend wanted to, some because they simply drifted apart. Amir had learned that tactfully ending relationships could be difficult. Did one just stop calling the person? That seemed rude. Tell the person that you're busy whenever they suggest getting together? Be never available? Have a heart-to-heart talk where you tell the person you don't wish to be with him or her anymore? Most of us don't want to unnecessarily hurt the person's feelings. Amir had tried each, with varying degrees of success.

Je Me Souviens

He was off to Montreal again. He liked Canada. It was vast, scenic, and clean. Going to the French province of Quebec was almost like being in France. It was different enough for you to know you had left the United States, yet not so different that you felt alienated or lost. He usually made the trip alone. Only once did he not. The drive, on a nice, clear day, was beautiful, particularly once you reached Upstate New York, with its flora and fauna.

There were lots of places to stop and take photos, eat, gas up, and rest or stretch your legs. The trip was also good for people watching, as you mixed and mingled with a cross-section of Americana, the young, the old, white, black, Hispanic, Asian, South Asian, doing the American road trip thing. The first thing Amir had noticed about Canada was how clean all their cities were—Toronto, Montreal, Quebec City, all were cleaner than any American city he had visited.

While Toronto was nice and he could see why so many TV shows and movies were filmed there, he seemed to prefer the French province, Quebec, La Belle Province. These Frenchies knew how to live—good food, wine, fashion, art, a sense of history, and, of course, the French language sounded so sexy, you could say "I have to go to the bathroom" in French, and it sounded sexy!

He was laughing to himself as he sped along the New York State Throughway with the T-tops off on his Turbo 280ZX, thinking about the college and how he gave some of his boys "Spanish lessons" so that they could game the Puerto Rican girls in Philly—"el dicko," "el somo," "Yo quiero somo." Deep in his heart, Amir knew the laughs, joy, camaraderie, and good times he experienced with his boys would not last forever. Life would happen. They would graduate or leave school, get older, get real jobs, settle down, and have families. Some would move, some far away, and some would die.

The women up in Canada often seemed more aggressive, more forward, than their southern neighbors too! He would go to a bar or pub and have a seat, and often, a cute Frenchy would start a conversation with him. "Are you here alone? Are you American?" That was all right with Amir. He never understood the men who were put off by females who were a bit aggressive. They would often say, "I wonder how many other guys she has approached?" or words to that effect. Amir's thinking was she's making my job easier! At least you knew she had noticed you, was curious about you, or was simply on the prowl. You were at first base already! Yep, he thought, *I could probably live here.* He often sped because he didn't usually see a lot of highway patrol officers pulling people over or hiding so that they could give out tickets. Stops when hungry, to stretch his legs, or simply to drink coffee to stay awake were frequent. He was on no schedule, not in a road rally. Crossing the US-Canadian border in those days was a breeze. Show your license and answer a question or two, and you were off.

"Is your visit for business or pleasure, monsieur?" the young French customs guy had asked.

"Pleasure *is* my business," he had responded with a smile.

"Have fun, monsieur," was the agent's salutation with a grin as he sped off, the turbo spooling up.

During this particular trip, the song "A Horse with No Name" by America was popular, and he heard it so many times he thought he'd go crazy. He inadvertently learned the lyrics. Of course, he brought along his own recorded eight-tracks, later cassettes or CDs as well. He had an eclectic mix of R&B, Broadway tunes, jazz, and blues. The ride was long, and he loved music—B. B. King's "The Thrill Is Gone," Isaac Hayes's "Shaft" and "Your Loving Is So Dog Gone Good," as well as "One Woman." He also had Bobby Womack's "If You Think You're Lonely Now," "California Dreaming," "Across 110th Street," and "That's the Way I feel about Ya," along with "Daylight Is Gonna Catch Me Up Again," "Camelot" from *Camelot* (the Broadway show), and "The Impossible Dream" from *Man of La Mancha* (although David Ruffin's cover of it on the Temptations' *In a Mellow Mood* was awesome)! Even some of *South Pacific* was cool, "Some Enchanted Evening" and the oddly placed "You Must Be Carefully Taught." He listened to Smokey's "Oh Baby, Baby," "Give Her Up," "Bad Girl," "Cruising," "Fork in the Road," "I'll Try Something New," and "We've Saved the Best for Last"; the Bee Gees' "Love So Right"; Tom Jones's, "She's a Lady," "Green, Green, Grass of Home," and "It's Not Unusual"; Curtis Mayfield's "Superfly"; Marvin Gaye's "Troubleman" and "What's Going On"; Johnny Mathis's "Maria" and "When They Begin the Beguine"; among others. He even included a little Sinatra, "I've Got

You under My Skin," "Strangers in the Night," and also some of his Bossa Nova numbers done with Antonio Carlos Jobim, "Once I loved," "Quiet Nights and Quiet Stars." He also had some Ray Charles and even the soundtrack from *Lawrence of Arabia* with the London Philharmonic. He added "Let's Go Get Stoned," "I Can't Stop Loving You," and "I Got a Woman" by Ray and Stevie Wonder's early songs, before he got deep, like "My Cherie Amour" and "I Was Made to Love Her."

Hips, Lips, and Fingertips, Parts I and II

Amir thought he was developing some understanding of black American expatriates, because every time he left America, even for a brief time, he felt different—he felt freer, more liberated somehow. Sure, he understood that xenophobia, ethnocentrism, and racism weren't just American and were, to some extent, worldwide, but he rarely felt the palpable tension and prejudice or hate abroad that he sometimes felt in America. Amir now saw himself as a world citizen who happened to be born in America. Over the years, he would come to feel that he was lucky to be born in America, in most ways, as were most Americans, of whatever race or ethnicity. America was kind of like the uncle who paid your college tuition but who had molested you!

Montreal and Quebec City had fashions galore for men and women. He had noticed some really stylish men's shirts. He didn't see many like them in the States. He'd have to buy one or two on sale. He'd eat some good food while there—crepes, pheasant, venison, duck—things he didn't usually eat in America. A waitress, a little Frenchy in the restaurant of the hotel where he was staying, seemed to be flirting with him. She had long, thick, jet-black hair; a nice round butt; and those sturdy peasant legs, and although pale, she had a cute face. He wasn't sure she was flirting, however.

Sometimes people noticed him because he had a different kind of look, he had been told. Some people said, "They were probably trying to figure out what he was."

He also seemed to be one of only a few blacks around at that particular time. He had grown to realize that it could be difficult sometimes for him and men generally to really know when women were flirting with them or just being friendly or professional or had some other motive. It could be embarrassing to assume wrongly and act on it! Men, Amir concluded, were not always attuned to female subtlety. He would do nothing. The funicular in Quebec City, the Plains of Abraham, and other tourist draws were enjoyable. The old walled city, where he was staying, was so picturesque. Of course, the grand old Hotel Frontenac dominated the Quebec City skyline. Right beside the St. Lawrence River, there were even tours of this historic hotel given by costumed guides and a hotel mascot, a big St. Bernard, who could be walked by appointment. Sidewalk cafés, the French cuisine, artists painting and selling their wares, musicians playing on the street, tourists from all over the world, and so on—he was enjoying himself. He bought two beautiful dress shirts while there, slim fit, with widespread Windsor collars, one a pale blue with a kind of rust-colored grid pattern and the other a solid light-blue color.

The trip back home, when driving, always seemed longer than the trip there when one was on vacation or a pleasure trip of some kind, even if one followed the exact reverse route by which one had come, he was thinking as he motored out of Quebec City. During the long drive back to Philly, he was thinking that he'd had a good time but did miss Mom, Dad, and his boys and girls. They really were, for the most part, a great group of young men and women, bright, witty, and fun to be around.

Back at the college, SaRon was telling Amir and Omar about a party he had recently gone to. He added that there were some fine babes there. Of course, Amir and Omar looked at each other. *Why didn't you tell us about the party before it happened?* they were both thinking. SaRon had done this before, gone to some social event that they might want to go to also without telling them until it had already occurred! Could it be that SaRon saw them as competition and therefore didn't share this kind of info with them? Was he ashamed of some of his other associates? SaRon, when first encountered, seemed like a really interesting, cool brother. He was a jazz aficionado who smoked a pipe, played billiards, and was a good conversationalist. He was so good with the honeys, he was scheduling them, actually giving them appointments for when they would get together. They arrived to see him in the office of one of the staff at the college, a fellow named Hank.

He and Omar would never forget the day they went up to Hank's office at school to hang out, and SaRon had Melanie, a cute and curvy young tenderoni up against a file cabinet grinding on her while they french kissed and he made lustful, sexual sounds. SaRon was always good at making lustful, sexy noises and sounds.

SaRon was a lusty dude! Over time though, he seemed to become less interesting. Was it possible that a guy could lose his game, his mojo? Initially, he had game. A couple of years later, he didn't. What happened? He had, as we all do, certain quirks. He explained, for instance, that the reason he was involved with his attractive older woman girlfriend, Maddy, was simply because she did his hair for free (he was wearing a kind of jerry curl at the time). Further, that when he made his impending move to Florida in the near future, he wasn't taking her with him! He maintained that she couldn't keep up with him sexually as well. Of course, SaRon consistently opined that various women couldn't keep up with his sexual appetite. "I think some of these broads suffer from cherophobia; wouldn't know happiness if it walked up to them and slapped them!" Evidently, he saw himself as a sexual giant. The guys weren't sure of that or simply didn't care one way or the other!

The smell of the chittlings (chitterlings) cooking was

overwhelming! Mom didn't usually cook them at home for Melinda, Dad and him. She knew they didn't like or want them. On this occasion, she had let cousin Thelma Mae come over and cook them in her kitchen. This was when Amir was about twelve or thirteen years old and had not sworn off the eating of pork yet. He did like pork chops and bacon. But he was learning that some folks ate pigs' feet—often pickled—pigs' ears, the brain, almost everything, including these disgusting intestines (chitterlings). "Ma!" could be heard all over the house as Amir and Melinda protested this assault on their olfactory glands! They were city kids, born and raised in Philly, and of course, spoiled at that. These southern delicacies were generally not their cup of tea. Jars of pickled pigs' feet could be found at bars. The feet were for sale, of course, along with pork rinds in small plastic bags. *Yuck!* thought Amir and Omar in later years. "Slave food!" Why would one choose to continue to eat the scraps once given to slaves when good beef, chicken, lamb, duck, steak, pheasant, and other meats were available?

Law and Order

Most Philadelphians, including Amir, didn't really know much about what the MOVE organization actually believed or stood for. Sure, everyone's last name was Africa. Many wore dreads, and this so-called back-to-nature group was apparently against the system. Members gave speeches in public laced with blunt and often profane language. Their presentation was far from warm and fuzzy. They often used megaphones and loudspeakers. They spoke whether you wanted to hear it or not. The media did a job on them, saying that they homeschooled their children, rather than send them to public school, and that they didn't bathe. They said that here were outstanding warrants for some of them and that they had a veritable arsenal in their MOVE house. They seemed to be headquartered in a black working-class neighborhood in West Philly (Overbrook); formerly, they had been located in the Powelton Village neighborhood, where there was a confrontation with the Philly Police under former mayor Frank Lizaro Rizzo.

There had been one casualty, a Philly police officer. Amir could believe that many of MOVE's neighbors probably didn't want them there and found them a source of irritation. They purportedly would do things like lecture their neighbors, whether they wanted it or not, over megaphones and loudspeakers at all hours of the day and night with their political messages. Some demanded that the city do something! In 1985, the MOVE situation came to a climax, when eleven MOVE members, including men, women, and children, were killed in a firefight and actual fire with the Philly Police and Fire Department.

The entire neighborhood surrounding the MOVE house was burned down, because an "explosive device" was dropped on the house they were occupying, a fire started, and a decision was made to let the fire burn supposedly in hopes of forcing the MOVE members out of the house! This decision resulted in the deaths. Two MOVE members escaped the house, a woman and a then little boy. They said the Philly Police were firing on them, and that was why more did not escape or try to from the house! Of course, the Philly Police said MOVE had fired first, starting the battle. Only a few rifles and a couple of handguns were found in the MOVE house. The media had said they were heavily armed.

"Lawd ham mercy!" some Philly residents decried. Others said the MOVE members wanted to die! Amir would recall watching this battle scene on TV, Philly Police versus the MOVE organization. It looked like a scene from Vietnam, and his father's reaction as they were watching together when it was announced that among the firepower brought to bear by the Philly police against MOVE was a fifty-caliber machine gun was, "That's what we used during the war!"

The city administration promised an investigation. No one was ever blamed for the decision to let the fire burn. Thus Philadelphia, often a city of firsts, became the second city in American history to bomb itself (the first being the famous "Black Wall Street" white mob riot in the Greenwood Section of Tulsa, Oklahoma, back in 1921). Of course, one of the surviving MOVE members sued the city, and they settled for millions of dollars!

The neighborhood, of course, had to be rebuilt as well. Many wondered if this had been a working-class or middle-class white neighborhood, would the decision have been made to let the fire burn?

Amir thought, *If you live long enough, you'll witness some strange and ironic shit!*

Meanwhile Back at the College

"As Salaamu Alaikum, brother. What's new?" Tarik asked that afternoon in the lobby of the college as Amir and Omar were sitting near the escalator, a good vantage point to check out all the ladies walking by.

"Al hamdu lilah," replied Amir. "Just the usual."

"Just got back from Egypt," stated Tarik. "Had a blast. Beautiful Habibis there."

"Wow," replied Amir. "Got to go one day, in sha Allah."

Tarik then began to share photos of his Egyptian journey with them. He had photos of pyramids, camels, and the Egyptian friends he had made. Tarik was typically attracted to dancers, the Dance Theater of Harlem dancers, Arthur Hall's dancers, dancers from Philly, and so on. It was not hard to understand why; dancers were usually very shapely, lithe, and sinewy. They were some of the best-conditioned athletes, he thought. They were usually artsy in their presentation. Tarik said he was seeing one that night.

"Awesome, brother," said Amir. "Have a good time!"

"Give her a stroke for me!" cried Omar.

Amir reflected on the time Tarik had said he was going to travel to Bryn Mawr College, out on the Main Line, to try to meet Sheik Yamani's daughter. They understood she was a student there. Sheik Yamani was the then current oil minister of Saudi Arabia and was shown on TV a lot at OPEC meetings, news conferences, and so on.

He and Omar had cautioned him about his idea. Surely she would have security and bodyguards, and they wouldn't appreciate a "trifling Negro" hanging around campus or her! Many of Amir's friends and associates had traveled to Africa, during this black consciousness era. Ghana, Sierra Leone, Ivory Coast, Nigeria, Egypt, and Morocco were among the most popular destinations. Many folks were wearing dashikis or kufis. Kente cloth was everywhere; garments, including neckties, hats, scarves, and cummerbunds, made of it were seen all around.

Of course, Omar and Amir had to be different. They often wore kufis or red fezzes, the Moroccan kind, and a vest but not the kente cloth. The bejeweled vests from Afghanistan with embroidery and little mirrors on them were handsome, Amir thought as he purchased his first one. Amir and Omar related to the warrior, businessman, trader Africans, like the Tuareg people or the Afar from Ethiopia.

They particularly related to the Moors, who had conquered Spain and Portugal and had made inroads into France. They had universities, public paths, paved streets, and libraries at a time when Paris was a backwater town and London a village! They were the civilized Africans, the ones who had fought with Europeans and transmitted culture to them. "We tried to civilize them [Europeans]," Amir and Omar would often say, "but they were slow."

It was 1975, and America's Bicentennial was upcoming. The guys were discussing it at the College. Money would be made in Philadelphia as anticipated large numbers of tourists, American and otherwise, would hopefully be coming into town. Perhaps they could make some of the money! Their first idea was to sell small leather pouches of "soul soil" to be worn around one's neck or on one's belt. They would go to Fairmount Park and load these pouches with soil. They would be advertised as containing genuine African soil!

"Carry the homeland/motherland with you" would be the catchphrase. Costs would be relatively low, and they should sell, particularly with young people and with, as Omar used to call them, the "Muntu and mink crowd."

Their other idea was Ghetto Tours. They would rent or lease a couple of school buses, drive tourists through certain parts of North Philly, the worst-looking parts. There would be a security guard on each bus. There would be prearranged fake gang fights with the local brothers, who, of course, would be compensated. They would provide them with realistic-looking rubber knives and toy guns. They would also hang out on certain corners, looking menacing and hostile and be given brown paper bags they would drink out of (soda would be in the bags) as the buses came by. Some would nod and act unsteady like they were high on drugs. The bus would then return safely to Center City. People from Oklahoma, Idaho, Wyoming, Iowa, Montana, or other such places might pay to see such sights, they thought, if in town for the Bicentennial! They would have stories to tell when back home! Their racist stereotypes and prejudices would be confirmed! Why should white merchants and contractors make all the money? After more reflection, they decided not to act on the two ideas. The then current Philly mayor had sort of poisoned the atmosphere for anticipated bicentennial visitors to Philly anyway, forecasting trouble and unrest in town during the bicentennial. Of course, there was none!

Nadia, Amir's African girlfriend, looked beautiful as she stood in the early-morning sunlight, her café au lait color sort of glistening in the sun filtering through the blinds in his smallish bachelor pad bedroom that morning. Her dark thick hair cascaded around her narrow, attractive face as her big dark eyes stared at him. She was different from African American women he had known and dated. It was almost like dating outside his race. She had a soft and tender female voice. She always deferred to him in public situations, something as simple as going through a doorway for instance, became problematic. She'd let him go through first, even after he positioned himself to allow her to enter first! She never raised her voice in public. She almost seemed to try to walk behind him at times on the street. She was never flashy or loud in public situations.

He always did most of the talking in public, as she typically demurred to him. In private, however, if she had an issue, she raised it. If she was angry with him for some reason, she showed it. She was not a doormat! *Must be her African upbringing*, Amir thought. He both liked and didn't like this different behavior. It did make him feel more protective of her, more manly at times. At other times, it could be irritating. How would she respond to situations if he happened not to be around at a particular time? People could be devious. Could he trust her instincts, her street savvy, when he was not around? Was she a wartime woman? She was intelligent, educated, and well traveled. Her folks were Christian, not Muslim. Her country, of course, had both. Her dad was a businessman back home. He had been imprisoned for a time by the new regime. He was not executed, however. Emperor Haile Salasie was not killed by the revolutionaries either but deposed. Based on photos she showed him, they lived at least a middle-class or upper-middle-class life in the old country. If he were ready to get married, she'd probably make a good choice for a wife. Of course, he didn't speak Amharic or Tagrenya, and when she and her fellow students were speaking their native tongue, it made him feel left out sometimes.

Would she want to return to her country to live one day? If so and if they were together, how accepting would her people be of this American, this foreigner? Like most of his male friends, he seemed to think there would always be a better woman around the bend, more attractive, sexier, more fun, and so on.

They were in the school cafeteria at their table—Omar, Amir, SaRon, and Breeze a.k.a. Cool Breeze. They were enjoying each other's wit.

"It's not the size of the ship; it's the motion of the ocean," SaRon had added to the repartee.

Breeze contributed, "It's not just the motion of the ocean, but the potency of the depth charges."

"Girl, you talk a lot of shit!" Omar said.

"I can back it up too!" was Breeze's response.

"Young girl, I'd make your knees freeze, your bladder shatter, and your liver quiver."

Breeze countered with, "Possibly, but I'd put more pep in your step, more glide in your stride, and more dip in your hip!"

"Zaats, boogaloo," Omar said. "A standoff!"

They all laughed heartily.

THE OLD NEIGHBORHOOD

CHAPTER 10

I
f it weren't for the fact that Mom still lived there, he would rarely
go back to the old neighborhood. It had deteriorated badly. It
was depressing. There were always the gangs, but now there were
actual shootings! Amir could remember a time when young men
didn't steal cars but took them for joy rides and then parked them,
when hubcaps might be stolen. Years later, his stepdad had gotten
bullet holes in his Buick while parked in front of the house. Young
men in the pharmaceutical trade were everywhere. Amir didn't
know any of them, a different generation. Openly selling pharmaceuticals wasn't as popular when Amir was growing up. Gangs also
weren't doing drive-bys or killing each other nearly as much.

The guys he had been friendly with growing up in the old neighborhood had either moved away, were guests at state institutions, or
were deceased. When he parked his customized VW Beetle in front
of Mom's, he really wasn't worried about the car. He would walk
down Biggy's street to visit Biggy before stopping in to see Mom.
Biggy greeted him with a broad smile and a hug.

They had a bond that was still unbroken. She said she was doing fine as he settled into a chair in the living room. She looked good, for her age, still a proud, good-looking black woman. He was embarrassed to ask her, but he needed forty or fifty dollars until payday. She reached into her bra and unpinned the little black purse where she kept her money. She handed him two crisp twenties. He was sincerely grateful and thankful.

"You better start saving your money, boy. One day, old need mo is gonna hit you."

He said, "You're right. I'll do better."

"Need mo" was one of the southern/country phrases Biggy would use from time to time, along with directly, as in "I'll be there directly."

Some of Biggy's phrases were actually quite funny, such as if angry with someone, she would say, "I'll slice him too thin to fry!" She was legally blind at this point, and he had tried to help her by securing homeowner rebates from the state and goodies for people who were legally blind. Biggy had always done so much for him. He had to return the favor. With a hug and a kiss on the cheek, he bade her farewell.

As he walked up to his Beetle, he noticed right away that the Porsche-style wheel covers he had special ordered for it and which he rarely saw on other Bugs were gone!

Just then, a young man in T-shirt and jeans approached him very casually and asked, "Aren't you from the neighborhood?"

Amir replied, "Yes, I am."

The young man smiled and said, "I saw who took your hub caps and where he put them."

He gestured and led Amir a few yards away to the alley near Mom's house. There, stacked against one of the walls, were his wheel covers!

"Thank you, brother," said Amir as he collected them and placed them back on his wheels.

As he looked over at Mom's house, he realized it was choir rehearsal night. She wouldn't be home. He drove off in his Beetle, enjoying the sound of the little rear engine and shifting his auto stick transmission. As he drove off, his mind went to the changes in the old neighborhood. More folks were employed when he was growing up, often in manufacturing or manual-labor jobs, but jobs nonetheless. The unemployment rate was not as high then as it would become in years ahead. Gang fights, yes, but no drive-bys when he was a kid. Folks seemed to take more pride in their neighborhoods, washing their stoops, keeping their houses up, and so on.

There must have been some drugs around, although he was not conscious of it when growing up. He never actually witnessed anyone using them. Now, they seemed to be everywhere! The more middle-class community members—doctors, teachers, lawyers, insurance salesmen, and so on—had moved out of the inner city, leaving the mostly poor, less-educated people with each other. Now the drug dealer and other criminals were a constant presence! The so-called Black Mafia and others were a known presence. What had happened just when blacks seemed to be on the move? Who had introduced cheap, readily available drugs in the community? Who had started importing and selling guns in the community? Was it African Americans? Sure, there were your big-time drug-dealing kingpins making millions of dollars, like in NYC. Amir had heard of and maybe had met the Jolly Green Giant in a nightclub one night in Philly. He was supposed to be big in pharmaceuticals in Philly and its environs.

But most drug dealers were low-level, poor, poorly educated, inner-city youth, weren't they? Something was afoot. Fortunately, Amir had never been attracted to drugs. He had only taken a few hits from a joint once, at a party. He didn't drink much either. In some ways, he guessed he was a square. Among his close friends and family, he wasn't aware of anyone who was hooked on drugs, except perhaps one beautiful young lady at work. He had to admit, however, that the lure of easy money could be strong. You could make a *lot* of money selling drugs! It didn't justify selling pharmaceuticals, but people had to live. *People want things. We live in a consumer society. Desperate people do desperate things. Madison Avenue often informs our wants and desires. Society often doesn't present a lot of options to poor inner-city black males. Of course, some escape and do quite well, become educated, make good money legitimately, and so on. But most people, black or white, are not exceptional, are not extraordinary. They are average,* he thought, *and fairly easily led. They often fall into traps set for them by the system.*

Other changes in the old neighborhood were also puzzling; as a boy, he had patronized a black-owned-and-run dry cleaners, hardware store, corner grocery store, restaurant, and barber shop, all in the neighborhood. Now, upon visits, it seemed that all the store owners and operators were non–African American! What happened?

That brief period of relative prosperity working-class blacks had seemed to enjoy in Philly during the late 1960s and the early to mid-1970s seemed to be dissipating. Scary times. Sure, among his acquaintances, friends, fellow students, and associates were judges, podiatrists, lawyers, salespeople, corporate types, web designers, and business people. They, obviously highly motivated and educated, would probably be all right. But what about the high school dropouts or even graduates of often low-performing inner-city high schools? Those who couldn't afford to go to college? And those with a record (very easily gotten when he was growing up in North Philly)?

It sort of reminded him of the Black Reconstruction period that occurred in the South and that briefly showed so much promise, only to be ended all too soon. Amir thought that come what may, like the lyrics in the song McArthur Park, "I will have the things that I desire, and let my passions flow like rivers to the sea ..." As long as he lived in "the land of the free and the home of the brave," he would have a fairly comfortable quality of life.

Omar used to famously say, "It's a sorry white man who can't make it in America. They make it, in part, because of the system, when we make it, it's usually in spite of the system!"

Damn, that brother can turn a phrase! thought Amir.

Give Me the Night

Amir always had a love/hate relationship with NYC. Being from Philly, there was some rivalry, of course. Philly folk didn't necessarily look up to NYC and didn't consider themselves inferior in any way.

Years later, he would learn that some New Jersey residents referred to NYC as the city. Philly folk called it New York. They lived in a city also, a city with a lot of history and tradition, of its own, particularly for black Americans. But the vitality, the energy of NYC, could not be denied. People came from everywhere; there were the theater, sports, art and museums, women, schools, restaurants. Few American cities had the variety or number that NYC did.

Periodically, he and the guys or he alone would make the approximately one-hundred-mile journey to NYC either via train, bus, or car. Omar had been traveling to NYC for years, starting as a young teenager, often alone. Amir could understand the attraction of NYC to many. If one was in finance, particularly the stock market, the arts, acting, painting, or modeling, New York was the Mecca. He imagined it could also be a great place to hide or reinvent oneself.

With millions of people there, many recent immigrants, one could get lost in the crowd with some effort. There were many schools, universities, and institutes. Of course, the draw was there as well for criminals. Some of the best were in NYC, he thought, from pickpockets and street hustlers to car thieves and gangsters. There was a large market to sell a variety of products and services to, from the sex trade to pharmaceuticals.

Some of the recent arrivals from Africa, the Senegalese in particular, often could be seen on the streets in Manhattan selling their fake Rolex watches. Many Middle Eastern and Asian/South Asian folk were vendors as well, with their carts. Falafel, gyros, and hummus, among other tasty treasures, often wrapped in pita bread, could be found frequently in Lower and Midtown Manhattan. In later years, folks from the islands were there selling beef patties, rotis, and so on. Other vendors sold gloves, scarves, hats, and designer knockoff pocketbooks, among other items. Souvenirs also abounded. He thought that if one had the right connections, one could buy almost anything, legal and illegal, in the Big Apple. Amir had no desire to move there, however. The excitement, fast pace, electricity, and masses of humanity could be overwhelming at times. One had to queue up for almost everything. The people were so competitive that some were quite rude as they jostled for space and position or to obtain some good or service.

No, Philly was more his speed. It was a big city, then the fourth largest in America, with many of the same attractions as NYC— museums, restaurants, many schools, theater (not as much as NYC, of course), and teaching hospitals, but it was more manageable and less expensive! People were generally friendlier too. No, periodic forays into NYC would be enough for him!

1968—It Was a Very Scary Year

There seemed to be something in the air. When the word got around that Phil had died, of course, Amir and all the guys were shocked. Amir had not seen Phil in a couple of years. His understanding was that he had been teaching in Washington, DC. Phil helping to shape young minds was a frightening thought! He had met one of his sisters briefly years before but no one else in his West Philly–based family. He would remember the rumors of a few years earlier about Phil. One was that he might be gay. The other was that he was an agent. There was some justified paranoia during the height of the black consciousness movement, concerning undercover agents, agent provocateurs, spies, and so on. Lots of folks were suspected of being agents of one kind or another. Of course, there were actual spies, double agents, agent provocateurs, and so on, and there had to be Black operatives in order to infiltrate black organizations. The Philly Police as well as the state and possibly the feds all probably had people infiltrating and watching black and white progressive organizations. Philly had many of those. He and the guys knew Lt. Pencil's Civil Disobedience Squad was taking pictures of people at demonstrations and keeping files. Amir was not particularly concerned because he knew he was not doing anything illegal and would not be prompted by anyone to do something stupid.

His associations, however, were varied and many and did in-clude people in whom law enforcement might be interested—like Mickey from RAM, who was arrested in West Philly with rifles in the trunk of his car as he understood it or Adam, a law school student who was arrested and accused of attempting to poison the Philadelphia Police Force. From the old neighborhood, there was Dathan, a really bright guy, a pharmacist, who had shot two police-men in a gunfight and then driven himself to the hospital! "Hip Bip from the Strip" was allegedly a witness in the Mumia Abu Jamal incident in Center City wherein a Philadelphia Police officer had been shot and killed. One or more hos were also allegedly witnesses to the incident, the newspapers had said.

Lil Johnny had a record and may have been under surveillance by any number of law enforcement agencies. There had been a shooting at the Latin Casino in New Jersey in which Omar's friend Rick's pregnant wife had been wounded.

Of course, both MLK Jr. and RFK were assassinated in 1968. The Chicago police could be seen abusing demonstrators at the DNC in Chicago in the comfort of your own home on television. Urban riots and rebellions, depending on your point of view, followed King's assassination across America. John Carlos and Tommie Smith came under withering criticism and retaliation for raising their arms in black power salutes at the Olympic games.

Many white boxing fans hated Muhammad Ali and were for Joe Frazier because of Ali's antiwar stance and refusal to go to Vietnam and his Muslim conversion. The world was going crazy! Was the black male becoming an endangered species? Was America really Amerika? Another sign of the times was that nightclubs and discos that had not in the past done so were starting to wand and search people seeking entrance.

Meanwhile Back at the House

Mike had the second-floor front bedroom. Mike was a good house-mate, not noisy or loud and always had his share of the rent. Mike rarely entertained at the house. All the guys teased each other all the time, playing the dozens or busting on each other. In Mike's case, it was about his penchant, his obsession with self-gratification, jacking off, beating his meat, choking his chicken, taking matters into his own hands, and so on. They probably overdid it, Amir would conclude years later.

They teased him in many ways. There was the time, for instance, that Omar conducted a two-ring ceremony for Mike, pronouncing him at the end, "man and hand!" and the time they, Amir, Omar, and Phil, waited until late one night and bum rushed his room where he was under the sheets with a girly magazine and a flashlight going to town! Then there was the time they chipped in and bought an inflatable doll with orifices for Mike, carefully placing her in his bed while he was out. Sure, he and Omar unashamedly admitted to masturbation. "Put on some soft music, get some Jergen's lotion, and go for self! Use your left hand, and it seems like someone else." But Mike took it to a new level. How could they resist? The then current popularity of martial arts was even utilized to rag on Mike. He was said to use the famous Kung Fu quivering hand technique when he jacked off and the five fingers of death. Eventually, Mike would live at an ashram in New Jersey, coming to Philly almost daily and making the rounds of Center City bars, such as The Club, a particularly dark, dank, and funky-looking place, where he'd sit at the bar and drink copious amounts of beer. Amir would remember the time he walked into the Yacht Club and encountered Mike sitting at the bar, looking dazed with six to seven beers lined up in front of him. *Shame*, he thought as he pulled up a bar stool next to his.

"What's up, brother?" he asked.

"These bitches are killing me," replied Mike with a smile.

"What happened, brother?" inquired Amir.

"I told the girl to give it up, and she left my apartment!"

Amir felt sorry for Mike and liked Mike. Of course, his personality, his manner, had been shaped in part at least because of that stuff on his face (keloids). The game of love was difficult, but having his particular handicap, he was sure made it more difficult for Mike. How many girls, for instance, wanted to kiss Mike with the facial issues he had. He was truly a nice guy, intelligent, a good conversationalist, and generous. Amir enjoyed Mike's company. They even went fishing together more than a few times, both in Philly and in Maryland, where they caught big channel catfish off a pier.

In later years, Mike would actually pay for sex on occasion, Amir came to believe. *Life ain't fair,* he thought.

SaRon had said he was busy getting his knob polished by a young freak and couldn't meet them for dinner.

SaRon had developed a habit lately of referring to almost all females as freaks. Omar and Amir had discussed this. Would he view Omar's daughter or Amir's niece, both of whom had grown into young womanhood as freaks? They both knew SaRon didn't have, in their shared opinion, a healthy upbringing. His dad, now deceased, had been ancient. He was actually raising his second or third family when SaRon came along. SaRon had two or three sisters; Amir couldn't remember exactly. He did remember they acted butchy in the parlance of the day. SaRon was the only male offspring in the small Manayunk row house.

He and Omar had witnessed one evening while visiting SaRon, one of his sisters gaming a girl SaRon had brought home! Damn, that was cold! Your own sister! She pulled her. The way they addressed SaRon was also denigrating and harsh, causing Amir and Omar to agree as they drove away that night from SaRon's house that they wouldn't allow the sisters to talk to them in that manner! Could this, his oppression, explain his bravado and claims of unbelievable sexual feats, which he was prone to sharing with the guys?

Both Omar and Amir had strong opinions about what they called attack women, black women who deported themselves in a hostile, loud, mean-spirited manner and who were capable of saying harsh and insulting things to a man even in public! These were the women who might tell a guy that he "wasn't no man!" Many would proudly proclaim, "I don't need no man! I can do bad by myself," and other negative declarations. Amir was sure that there must be reasons for this superaggressive, angry manner of being. A missing father or father figure? Sexual abuse? Their own sense of inferiority? Harsh discipline from a present father? A broken heart? Penis envy?

What other ethnic group, however, made such public declarations about the alleged shortcomings of some of their men? *For*

Colored Girls Who Have Considered Suicide When the Rainbow Is Not Enough and *The Color Purple*, which had no caring or normal black males in it, were excellent examples of this negative propaganda about black males. The former even had a black male character dropping his children out of a window to their deaths!

Interestingly, Mom, who was raised in the rural South, saw *Purple* and when asked for her review, famously said, "We didn't act like that!" Many people had real pain in their backgrounds, Amir was learning with time. He had been very lucky to have good, loving, and affectionate parents. He had been spared the trauma that many experience while growing up. The older he became, the more he realized it was so. No matter, he was not a shrink! He was not going to be or at least stay involved with a woman who had a pattern of disrespecting, denigrating, and insulting him or questioning his manhood. On this, he and Omar agreed!

Years later, a female author out of Philadelphia would pen a book titled *The Blackman's Guide to Understanding the Black Woman*. Among arguments made in the controversial book would be that at their core, many black American women do not really respect the black man, in part because of negative media stereotypes that they buy into and in part because of an almost genetic kind of memory of American slavery, when the black man was often not in a position to do the kinds of things men typically did relative to their women (i.e., protection, provision for, and so on) in a normal or more natural and healthy kind of setting, sans chattel slavery. Because of this, her respect was gone. Amir had noticed that the older generations of sisters, his mother, grandmother, and so on seemed to see themselves as partners with their men. Sure, they had their complaints, their gripes, their grievances, and so on but seemed to have more of a notion that their fate was inextricably bound to the fate of their men—sort of a "you and me against the world" attitude. Did today's young black women share that same attitude? He wasn't sure they did.

Of course, there were exceptions, but many seemed to think that because the system often rewarded them better or more than the black man, it was somehow the black man's fault if he did not enjoy those same benefits and goodies. The women who were succeeding were doing so because they were so great, so hardworking, and the brothers who were not succeeding equally must therefore be somehow lacking or lazy or unmotivated.

The notion that the system was not as welcoming to the black man, for a variety of historic reasons, qualified or not, didn't seem to occur to them! That this set of circumstances may very well be by design didn't seem to cross their minds. The brothers, they concluded, in order to validate their own success, must therefore be unqualified, lazy, or lacking in motivation. A classic case, thought Amir, of blaming the victim, *The Pedagogy of the Oppressed*. Those black males who were qualified, worked hard, and were allowed to succeed, particularly in corporate America, often were mated to white women. The sisters, of course, in the main, disapproved of that circumstance. What's a brother to do? Buy into the American dream à la carte? Accept it all except for the white woman part?

SaRon, Amir, Ahmed, and Omar were relaxing in Hank's office at the college that beautiful fall afternoon. Hank had given them carte blanche to hang out in his office when he wasn't using it. As usual, the topics of conversation varied, politics, boxing, race, women, religion, movies, books, music, and so on. "Have you heard the Temptations' *In a Mellow Mood*?" asked SaRon. "They tear up 'The Impossible Dream'!" he explained.

"I'll check it out," replied Amir.

Omar interjected, "I just earned my gray belt in Tongue Fu."

SaRon quipped, "Boy, you crazy. Show me some moves."

"Okay, this is the long lick," he said as he fully extended his tongue and moved it up and down slowly. "This is the flutter," he said as he moved his tongue from one side of his mouth to the other, making waves as he did so. "And this is the curlicue." He curled his tongue in half and moved it in and out of his mouth.

"Thank you, grasshopper," responded Amir with a smile. "With you on the prowl, dude, I better be practicing my forms too."

The next day, Amir went to see *Cleopatra Jones*. This movie starred a tall, sinewy, good-looking unknown named Tamara Dobson. She was a black secret agent for the US government. She wore a lot of leather and pants that looked spray-painted on, and her Afro was huge and immaculately kept. Of course, she would know karate and beat up lots of bad guys. In these so-called black exploitation movies, the bad guys were usually white. There would be at least an interesting soundtrack. The main character would of course win.

The audience, however, was part of the show—at least in theaters, where a high percentage of the audience was black! Call and response was what Amir referred to it as. Loud calls of "Don't be so mean!" "Kick his ass!" "Aww shit!" "Hips, lips, and fingertips," and "dumb bitch" could often be heard. If a man was about to go down on a woman, a response might be elicited as well. "Look out now!" "I told you he was a muff diver!" "Aww sooky sooky now." Growing up in North Central Philadelphia, Amir was accustomed to this call and response. Sometimes, the comments were funny and witty and actually added to the movie-going experience, other times, not. It was a cultural thing.

Love, Peace, and Chicken Grease

The roommates were not at the house on this bitterly cold winter's evening, and Amir was entertaining a young tenderoni. As they sat on the couch necking and petting, he felt good about his choice. They had dated a couple of times, dinner, a movie, a ride. She was cute but not a showstopper. Of average height, she had a good body.

Her reddish-brown hair was cut in a pixie-like style. She had back and nice legs. She wore her heels well, enhancing her sexiness. He and Omar had a penchant for girls wearing heels. "Leave 'um on, gurl" was one of their rallying cries.

Soft music was playing, and incense was oozing all over the room, when Amir whispered in her ear, "James Bond may have a license to kill, but I have a license to thrill!"

She smiled and continued kissing him on his neck and softly blowing in his ear. She took his right hand and placed it on her left breast softly. Her kisses were juicy and good. Soon, they would form the beast with two backs. When they consummated, she threw it back. It was an enjoyable sexual experience. When the evening was over, he put her in a cab and bid her good night. This was not love, or infatuation, just recreational sex between consenting adults with mutual respect. Sometimes this was enough, at least for the time being. Half a loaf is better than no loaf!

Lil Frankie was younger than the guys sharing the house—Amir, Mike, and Phil. He was a high school senior, on the verge of entering college. He didn't live at the house but was from the neighborhood. He was like a little brother to them. He periodically visited the house and sat, listened, and observed for the most part, occasionally asking a question, as they pontificated about women, sex, cars, styles, current events, history, religion, politics, the coming revolution, and various other topics. He seemed like a decent guy. He wore eyeglasses, was of short stature and a little pudgy, and was light-skinned with a reddish hue. He had reddish hair. He clearly looked up to the guys. Their successes with women, their fashion sense, their popularity generally, and all the shit they talked.

The mistake he made was asking to use the house to bring over a girl whom he really liked to romance her and to ask her to go with him. They knew what time he'd bring her over. They lay in wait on the second floor, knowing that they would have to remain absolutely still and quiet. They lay on the floor next to the upstairs portion of the banister or handrail. At the appointed time, Frankie entered the house with the young lady. Of course, they couldn't see her. She sounded nice. Lil Frankie started playing soft, romantic music. He dimmed the lights. They danced, slow dragged, a couple of times. Then they sat on the love seat just below the stairs to the second floor. The silence was deafening. All of a sudden, Frankie, sounding very serious, said to the young lady that he really liked her and then asked, "Mommie, can I stand a chance?"

The young lady then replied quite succinctly, "No."

At this point, they could contain their laughter no longer. They all burst out laughing loudly, of course, embarrassing Frankie and the young lady, who promptly left! When they all walked downstairs, Frankie was standing there in the middle of the living room floor with his mouth open, speechless, but he gave them a look of hurt and surprise. Amir felt bad, but Lil Frankie's rap had been so weak!

Even though the guys generally didn't mess with people unless provoked, they did collectively have this sort of sardonic sense of humor side, which they exercised periodically—the "ode to Fat Frank, lord of fat and funk" and the "double ring, man and hand ceremony" performed for Mike. They hoped Lil Frankie would get over his embarrassing moment eventually.

There is a thin line between humor and ribbing and being mean or cruel. They were young, cocky, and not as sensitive as they should be at times. In their defense, however, no one was exempt—males, females, whites, blacks, Asians, Hispanics, rich, poor, young, old, all were fair game.

The practiced ability to engage in this back and forth, this repartee, this sparring, this banter, would hold Amir in good stead for the rest of his life.

There was the time, for instance, while working for the government when an older white coworker, who was generally liked and affectionately called "Pop," but who did say racially ill-advised things from time to time, casually looked at Amir one lazy afternoon from his desk after taking his usual afternoon nap and randomly stated that if it wasn't for the Thirteenth, Fourteenth, and Fifteenth Amendments, Amir would probably be picking cotton in Georgia. Amir was proud to remember that his response, calmly and cooly made, had been, "Maybe, and if it wasn't for the potato famine, you'd still be back in Ireland!" That comment shut up Pop. Amir assumed that all African Americans had these racial moments. Some claimed they didn't, like one of his middle-aged former supervisors, an African American male, who had served in the US Army and the Philly Police and still claimed he had never experienced overt racism! *Sure, tell me anything*, thought Amir. One way he figured out over time for some blacks to deal with the trauma and pain caused by American racism was to be in denial, to overlook acts that were clearly most likely racial in nature and attribute them to something else or pretend they had not seen, to deny the institutional racism that was part of American society.

He would remember, for instance, even as fair as he was, he had been called the "N-word" out loud at least a few times in his life. He thought of the many job vacancies he had applied for over the years and was obviously qualified for and yet was not hired for. One blatant incident involved the big insurance company in Philly, where he had applied when very young in person many times never to be offered a position but received a post card from once alerting him to a specific vacancy. He followed up, and an appointment was scheduled. Upon arrival at the HR department of the company and of course being seen, all of a sudden, it was a mistake. There had not really been a vacancy after all, he was informed. He remembered the many times he would go to a Center City restaurant, and sitting at the counter, often the only black, in the early days, early 1970s or late 1960s, and he had to ask for a glass of water to be given one, while he observed others, whites, being brought one as a matter of course when seated without asking by the usually white waitresses!

As a very young man, in his early twenties, he had gone to inquire about an apartment in Center City as a result of an ad he had seen in the newspaper only to be told once there that the unit had been rented. He checked the newspaper for the next several days, and the same ad was still running! He went to the city human rights commission and filed a housing discrimination complaint. Eventually, there was a public hearing, and he prevailed. One time, he was walking along a suburban road alone and a car full of white guys passed by. Someone was yelling the "N-word" out at him. And yet upon reflection, he realized these were minor incidents compared to what his forebears had endured!

Amir had had a few jobs by this time in his working life, a few part-time retail sales jobs at department stores, usually in their respective men's departments, selling men's clothes. There was a brief stint at a shoe warehouse, which he hated. There were the adult store job and a city job with the Department of Licenses and Inspections as a housing and fire inspector. He was too immature for that position and blew it by being out and or late too often!

Finally, a civil service position with the government as an investigator that he had applied and taken a written exam for months earlier opened up. He would be interviewed, processed, and hired. Amir would stay in the job for about eleven years, and it would be an invaluable experience. He became grounded for his life's work. He was hired with a group of other young recent graduates—black, white, Hispanic, and Jewish. It was a wild time. One guy, who happened to be white, was actually growing a marijuana plant on the windowsill near his desk. Posters were placed on the walls. These "young Turks" would join a staff of older generation folks, mostly more conservative than they and, as a group, less diverse. One female newbie was a lesbian activist. At least two rode motorcycles. A bonus, there were a couple of foxes working there. Interesting dynamics were in place. Supervision, except for the big boss, who was African American, initially was all white. Several supervisors happened to be Jewish.

When the first director retired, he was replaced by a very attractive, well-dressed, intelligent black woman who spent an inordinate amount of time being nasty and curt to as well as harassing mainly her black staff! It was so bad staff used to joke among themselves, "I see it's your turn this month." She was a political appointee and "served at the pleasure of." But this was a good job, with a pension, benefits, and a decent salary. Over time, it became apparent that the regional director did not like Amir. He was determined that he would not be legitimately terminated from there, however. He would be on time, rarely be absent, do his work, and so on. The director would call folk to her office, and many left visibly shaken, some actually crying. He would not give her the satisfaction when his turn came! He had taken and passed a written exam for this job and had had an interview with bigwigs from Harrisburg, as had the other new hires as part of the hiring process. The southwestern corner of Broad and Spring Garden Streets was where the job was. It was a major intersection in downtown Philly. The offices were in the governmental office building, a tall '60s/'70s-architecture-style office building.

Many governmental agencies were housed there, among them the Boxing Commission and the Civil Service Commission. Certain memories would always stand out—the time two women got into a fight on one of the elevators over a married man who was not married to either of them or how, after evacuations from the building because of bomb scares, some staff would simply disappear and not return to their work stations on nice autumn or summer days. Then there was the time he saw heavyweight contender Pinklon Thomas there to be weighed for an upcoming fight. And, of course, there were the periodic strikes. These were problematic. Not everyone at his job joined the union. You didn't have to. You were still considered part of the collective bargaining unit, so that raises and other benefits the union members had fought for, sometimes including striking, would still be received by nonunion employees without paying their union dues or striking! So in July, when the contract was usually up, one might see some of one's coworkers walking right by and going to work! These scabs caused some hard feelings among those on the picket line. Amir was a union member.

He struck whenever a strike was called and suffered the economic consequences along with his fellow strikers. The Pennsylvania State Police would be stationed around the SOB during the strikes. Amir didn't enjoy being on strike; walking around in the summer heat with a picket sign was not his idea of a good time! He felt, however, as a union member, it was his duty. He had grown up in a union family. Dad was a Teamster, in fact, a shop steward. He occasionally took him to union meetings when he was a little boy. He grew up hearing Dad praise Jimmy Hoffa and dissing Bobby Kennedy!

Of course, he would be clean for his state job. He would wear his Pierre Cardin and Yves St. Laurent sports jackets and suits. Occasionally, he would wear another European designer, like Oleg Casini, for instance. The jacket and coats were usually color coordinated with form-fitting garments. He would receive many compliments from guys and women on how he dressed for the rest of his working life. Of course, there would also be those who envied or disliked him because he was so well dressed or assumed he was a shallow person because he was usually sharp as a tack and ready to stick. Shame. But he would define himself, not be defined by others. Of course, Omar would usually be sharp as well. Whenever they got together, they were sartorially impressive!

Omar had his own business. He was putting deals together for a finder's fee. He was traveling internationally. They were very similar in so many ways—tastes, viewpoints, life experiences. Omar and he could sometimes communicate almost telepathically—a look, a smile, a nod, a wink. They even spoke sometimes in phrases many others couldn't understand. "He's got the bit between his teeth, all right!" It was an old British expression they learned from viewing *Lawrence* numerous times or "the Idaho Resolution," a kind of joke between them, based on the Idaho potato but a reference to women—"If they're big enough, they're old enough" (which they didn't really mean). Of course, there was also "USDA-inspected," another female reference, and the "corn-fed and sugar-cured" references or the "all beef, no filler" reference. "If she wrapped those long legs around you, brother, you'd be in paradise at once!"

Omar had various identities, between the guys, at least. He was at times Count Butchy, Count Buche, Baron Bosch, or Sheik El Bush. All were really sexual references that could be used politely in mixed company. They both enjoyed the fine art of conversation. Being honest, they knew they were elitists on some level but would never admit it. Their elitism, however, was not based on skin color, resources or money, or formal education or the lack of it, family or political connections. No, theirs was based more on certain personal traits—intelligence, being quick-witted and well read, having some style, some class, some sophistication, dressing well, being fiercely proud of who and what you were, and knowing some science but being able to be comfortable in and able to operate in both worlds (black and white), liking the ladies a lot wouldn't hurt either. These traits were what made Phil, Cool Ron, Tarik, Khalil, Roogie, Big Nelson, Jimmy Vinson, and some others so interesting.

Deep in their souls, both Amir and Omar knew they were living in a golden era. They would probably never again be able to interact with so many unique, bold, and interesting black people and others of all races on a regular basis in one place! They would occasionally talk about it. Times were a-changing, and not for the better, they had concluded. "Law and order" was the current theme, but whose law and whose order? Was this just a euphemism for harassing and abusing blacks? After *Brown v. the Board of Education*, many expected great things. Years later, many whites were simply withdrawing their kids from the integrated schools and creating private ones for them to attend. Many whites in Boston and other places had acted downright bestially in response to the busing of blacks into their schools. Was the Nation right? Was separation of the races the ultimate answer? Rev. Jesse Jackson had opined, "It's not the bus; it's us!"

Many African Americans seemed to be losing that energy, that dynamism, that positivity, that rebirth that were a part of the black consciousness movement. Or they thought the revolution had been won after all the killings and assassinations—JFK, Malcolm, MLK Jr., Fred Hampton, other Panthers, Bobby Kennedy, Medgar Evers, Patrice Lumumba, and so on. Gamal Abdel Nasser allegedly had had a heart attack. Nkruma's experiment had failed. Many of the Panthers were executed by the police. There was also Cointelpro. The cumulative effects were devastating! It was a scary time. Then there were the so-called riots, which Amir and his friends called rebellions. Then the timely introduction of cheap and readily available drugs into many of the black communities seemed to complete this combination and deliver the knock-out punch! Clearly, blacks and whites of goodwill who wanted change had powerful enemies who would stop at nothing to preserve the status quo and protect their interests!

On another stage, Phil "chicken man" Testa had been blown up while trying to open the door of his small South Philly row house. Sal Testa, his son, would later be killed also. Crazy Phil Leonetti was on trial. The Philly mob guys were killing each other at an alarming rate. Amir and Omar had to wonder in whose camp or family was Little Johnny? They weren't sure, and asking him was not advisable. Amir thought maybe he should stop hanging around the Hippo so much.

Even in the clubs, when one asked for a dance with a honey on a slow record, the response was often, "I only dance slow with my boyfriend/man!" Folks had to be searched before they could gain entry to discos, clubs, concerts, and so on. Their world was definitely changing! Maybe he should start seriously thinking about getting married? Maybe he should move to Canada or some other country? He had always liked Canada anyway.

Omar had gone to the mattresses and couldn't be located for a while. This happened periodically, either because of a woman he was ducking or a business deal gone south. Amir had grown accustomed to this. He would surface eventually and contact him. In the meantime, honestly not knowing where he was or how to reach him gave Amir some measure of protection. He had plausible deniability. So when he received a phone call from the Essex County Prosecutor's Office from a detective seeking Omar's whereabouts one midmorning day at work in Prudential's HR department, he could honestly say, "I don't know where he is or how to reach him!"

The detective was, of course, cynical but added that "no one wants to give him up!" He explained that Omar had allegedly taken some money from a nice lady. Amir could honestly respond that he didn't know anything about that—plausible deniability.

When Omar eventually surfaced, no explanations were usually offered or asked for. A relationship with a woman could be very complex. Who promised what? Who gave what to whom? What was the basis or nature of their relationship? What understandings did they have? Was this nice lady a woman scorned? Amir didn't know any of that. Omar was his boy.

"I'm Petey Wheatstraw, the devil's son-in-law," Tarik said with a big smile as he shuffled up to the lounge area at the college. Ahmed, Khalil, Omar, and Amir were chilling at the time on the long pleather couch there in the lobby. Amir thought the line was from *Dolemite*, a black exploitation movie that his crowd all agreed was niggerish but entertaining on some level. The group was very critical of the black films that harkened back, in their view, to minstrel buffoonery—greasy lips, eating slave food (like pig's feet, pork rinds, and hog brains), bucking their eyes, and so on.

In some cases, the title alone demanded rejection or censure, like Fred Williamson's "Nigger Charley!" Amir abhorred that word and rarely used it. There was something about Tarik that had always reminded Amir of Charlie Chaplin. Maybe it was his combination of the Chaplin-like moustache, his usual baggy pants, his short stature, and the way he walked. Tarik was a good brother, never a bad word about anyone. His lines for the girls were weak though, usually consisting of "Miss, miss, excuse me" or "Can I go with you?" He probably frightened some of the girls! Of course, he'd always remember the time the guys, after exiting the Harvey House restaurant in Center City around two one Sunday morning after discoing all night, were observing some ladies of the evening on the corner as they walked away, except for Tarik, who lingered and patted one woman on the butt. She immediately spun around and loudly proclaimed, "That'll cost you twenty dollars!" He looked sheepishly at the group. They all turned with smiles and walked away. How could he be so naive or stupid?

"My name's Bennett, and I'm not in it," someone else articulated.

"My name's Wess, and I'm not in that mess!"

"My name's Paul, and that's between y'all!"

They walked away laughing.

It was Saturday evening, and Phil, Amir, and Mike were at this mixed club in Center City, a kind of coffeehouse almost. There was a small stage and a live band; they served food, and there was dancing. A series of round tables constituted the décor. There would be whites, a few blacks, and maybe a few Asians and Hispanics. This was unusual. At this time, most clubs or discos were predominantly black or predominantly white. The guys went to all types of places. After being seated and ordering, Amir noticed a shapely, long-haired white girl. She was cute. She looked foreign to him. He couldn't place her probable origin. Others were on the dance floor, so he asked her to dance. She accepted. Her body felt nice and tight as they slow dragged across the floor. She smelled good also.

He would invite her and her two friends to join them at their table. They accepted. Drinks went around, and conversing began. Her accent was distinctive, causing Amir to ask, "Where are you from?"

"Romania" had been her response. "Transylvania to be more precise."

Was she joking? Dracula's homeland! Amir couldn't help himself. "May I see your teeth?" he asked in a jocular way.

She didn't like the question, judging by her facial expression and body language. He had blown it! Too bad, he thought, but if she didn't have a sense of humor, how much fun would she have been anyway!

Haute Cuisine

While they might not have been gourmets literally, Omar, Amir, SaRon, and some of the rest had developed fairly educated palates. Firstly, they ate out a lot. Single and living on their own, they occasionally actually cooked meals in their respective apartments but dined out frequently, whether takeout, delivery, fast food, a diner, or a real restaurant. Center City, Philly, had come alive, and the choices were legion—Zum Zum, a chain of German-style fast-food offerings, and La Crepe, with those delicious French-style crepes; of course, there were also Book Binders and Old Original Book Binders, Di Nardo's for crabs and seafood, the Middle East with its Lebanese cuisine, Marrakesh with its Moroccan fare, Nyala for Ethiopian food, and others.

Amir only had a couple of dishes that he was semiproud of making himself, his omelets and his pasta. Omar never cooked for Amir and vice versa. Amir had grown up eating some soul food. Mom sometimes prepared mac and cheese, greens, fried chicken, okra, biscuits, deviled eggs, salmon cakes, liver with onions, black-eyed peas, and much to his embarrassment later in life, turkey butts!

As small children, Melinda and Amir often protested when soul food was on the menu, demanding McDonald's instead! Typical spoiled city kids! The irony was that years later, as an adult, Amir often found himself seeking out soul food restaurants, as it became trendier and more mainstream, even developing a penchant for catfish.

But as young men on the town, Italian food, Chinese food, Greek food, German food, Thai food, Ethiopian food, French food, and Lebanese food, among others, were all on the menu. Amir's penchant for Ethiopian food developed as a direct consequence of his relationship with Nadia.

He loved the bread, the injera, and doro watt and tibbs became two of his favorites. This African food and dining in the Ethiopian restaurants in Philly, DC, NYC, or elsewhere were fun. Although usually modest, these restaurants invariably had Ethiopian décor, and, of course, the traditional manner of eating, communal, with one's hands, made the experience even more enjoyable and authentic. Occasionally, a date wouldn't want to mess up her nails by using her hands to eat. Her loss was his reaction. Good pasta, linguine with clam sauce or with chicken livers and mushrooms, if made right, became another favorite, as well as paella, the seafood type. Among other Spanish favorites were rice and beans, codfish, empanadas, tacos, some of the soups or sopas, and flan. Many of Amir's and Omar's dates were dinner dates, and Philly had begun a restaurant boom. In later years, Amir would learn of Newark, New Jersey, and its famous Iron Bound section—Portuguese and Spanish (from Spain) food galore.

Of course, their forays into NYC provided endless choices of cuisine, including Russian, Brazilian, and Afghan food! So they needed to know of good places that were reasonable and preferably with ambiance. The Moshulu, a docked steel-hulled sailing vessel moored at Penn's Landing on what used to be Delaware Avenue was one of Amir's favorites. Talk about atmosphere. On a starry night, one might have drinks on the deck and enjoy the view. Even the Delaware River by moonlight could be scenic and romantic. Another favorite, the Middle East, a large Lebanese-owned-and-operated restaurant in Center City was another of his spots to take the ladies. The fez-wearing waiters, the Middle Eastern décor, and the belly dancers made for an interesting experience and, for some of his dates, a unique one. The late Jim Tayoun, then a city councilman, was the owner, he understood. Philly had a small Lebanese community then, mostly located in South Philly.

After a move to New Jersey, years later, Amir occasionally drove all the way back to Philly to get a real Philly cheesesteak at Pat's, Geno's, or Jim's. Of course, on Amir's trip to London and Paris, he had some good food—bangers and mash, shepherd's pie, a ploughman's lunch, and in Paris, escargot, truffles, soups, and venison. A good meal with an interesting, sexy, sophisticated woman and friends was one of life's pleasures, he would grow to believe.

WHAT'S SO GOOD ABOUT GOODBYE

CHAPTER 11

A mir enjoyed the guys, and gals, warts and all. However, the group was starting to break up. It was inevitable. Time passes. They all had lives and careers to pursue. Never was moving to California. Omar was traveling in Africa on business. Fat Frank had died. SaRon had descended into some kind of sexually freakish almost hermitlike lifestyle and had seemingly and inexplicably lost his game. The formerly seemingly sophisticated, urbane guy had descended into an obsession with girly nude pics and other porno. Tarik was off to who knew which college campus. Flash had also moved to California to work in the computer industry. Mike was living in West Philly like a monk. Nadia was moving to California as well to further her education. Amir's world was changing.

At least he had found and secured a good position with the Commonwealth of Pennsylvania, a civil service job. He had changed his mind a few years ago about becoming an officer and a gentleman. The Vietnam War was the basic reason. It wasn't just fear.

Any sensible person had fears about going to war, he believed.

But after some reading and soul searching, he had decided that the war was wrong. America was fighting the George Washington of Vietnam, Ho Chi Minh! Stopping communism was just a pretext, he decided. A serving officer in the US military would not have the luxury of cherry-picking his wars, he thought. And as Ali had articulated "dem Viet Cong ain't never called me nigger!"

No, his fight was here. Blacks had served in all of America's wars and conflicts, starting with the American Revolution. They had agitated to serve after being refused initially, to prove that they were men and good citizens. Yet when the wars and conflicts were over, they returned to a largely ungrateful and largely unchanged America. Witness the Red Summer of 1919, he thought. Fighting in America's wars was not the key to freedom, justice, and equality obviously, he thought. Philly, to some extent, was still a Quaker town. The antiwar, antislavery Quakers offered free draft counseling. Of course, most inner city blacks were not aware of it. Amir had found out, however, and taken advantage of this free service. He was the only African American he observed in his particular class, composed of essentially middle-class white guys.

The Quakers explained the Selective Service System, how it worked, the main provisions and rules, and how one made a case to become a conscientious objector. They explained what to say to the draft board and how. The fact that Ali was claiming conscientious objector status gave strength to many young men to do the same, particularly black men. He had read somewhere that the Lamb was a CO during World War II. He decided he would become one also. Amir's draft board consisted of older white guys. He was nervous, of course, when he made his argument before them but thought he had done a good job. He got it!

He would learn years later that Thomas Edison High School in North Philly had more young men drafted and killed in Vietnam than any other high school in America! Poor and black, most couldn't claim a student deferment and didn't really know about conscientious objector status or how to get it, couple that with a fear of going to jail, and their fates were sealed. No, from Crispus Attucks, Peter Salem, and Salem Poor, the Civil War to the Buffalo Soldiers, World War I, Montford Point Marines, and Tuskegee Airmen, blacks had proven their bravery and soldiering ability. As far as Amir was concerned, further attempts to prove or demonstrate their worthiness for full citizenship in his family would stop with him!

Amir thought outside the box. He wouldn't serve in Vietnam or go to jail! If the conscientious objector status hadn't worked out, he would do what a large number of mostly middle-class white guys were doing, go to Canada! He had a Maxwell House coffee can he called his Canada money, kept at Mom's, which he frequently contributed to.

Of course, Mom was in agreement and didn't want her only son to go to Vietnam. He liked Canada anyway. If that "Greetings" letter from Uncle Sam ever came "Au revoir." Figured he could settle in Canada comfortably, learn some French, and maybe come back to the States when the climate changed. Years later, these American expats would be pardoned by President Jimmy Carter, and many returned to the United States. He would never forget his mandatory physical at eighteen and a half years of age at 401 North Broad Street. "Mix some alcohol, Listerine, and cough syrup together, and drink it the night before your physical!" Lots of guys drank concoctions beforehand to hopefully raise their blood pressure or heart rate to fail the physical. One guy played crazy while undergoing the physical, proclaiming he was Jesus, wearing a robe, and jumping on top of a table! While undergoing the hearing test with headphones on, Amir refused to raise either hand as instructed by the tester when he heard a sound on the corresponding side of his body.

On paperwork, he checked off nightmares, sleeplessness, dizzy spells, and any other malady he thought he could easily claim or that he thought would be difficult to disprove. He knew they were probably hip to these obvious ways to try to avoid service. He didn't find fault with those who went. He knew most didn't want to go but feared going to jail and knew of no alternative! Amir would hear the stories of returning vets who spoke of sometimes being ambushed by the Viet Cong and spared because they were black. They were asked, "What are you doing here?" or were told, "Our fight is not with you!" The racism experienced in Vietnam from white American GIs was another popular topic, along with stories of the Vietnamese prostitutes. "I give GI very good duck." He would never forget accidentally encountering a guy he had seen at the physical months later on Broad Street in his US Army uniform! Niko, a really nice guy and fellow student at the college, was from West Philly. He wore horn-rimmed glasses, was very energetic, and was part of the extended crew. Nico was in the Army Reserve and had served two tours in 'Nam. Now a part-time student at the college, he had a scar from a bullet wound that ran almost the entire length of his left arm. He explained how it had happened, that he was on point when his squad was ambushed in Nam. Yet, Niko wanted to go back to Nam and do another tour! Amir had met others who didn't really seem to care about the politics of the war. They just enjoyed the combat, the adrenaline rush. Others just wanted to kill somebody legally!

Robert was tall and slim, a few years older than most of the guys, another Nam vet. He explained that he had been in Nam. He had been in Army Intelligence, he recounted. One day, while sitting around in the lounge area of the college with some of the guys, including Amir, Robert told of one of his Nam experiences. Three captured Viet Cong were taken up in a helicopter. They were questioned. The first two refused to talk and were pushed out of the helicopter, while airborne. The third one, frightened to death, who had defecated and urinated on himself, sang like a bird!

Years later, America's less than honorable withdrawal from Vietnam only served to bolster Amir's conclusion that we should've never gone there in the first instance and certainly should've left sooner! Like the popular song says, "War, what is it good for?

Absolutely nothing, y'all!" Only real self-defense justified war, Amir concluded.

Amir both liked and disliked his government job. The security of being a civil service employee was good. The salary was decent for the time, and there were benefits, including a pension. Because they went into the field, this afforded him some measure of freedom from simply sitting at a desk all day, at a desktop, which he would find boring and confining. The work, fighting discrimination, was important, and he was committed to it, although he wondered about a few of his colleagues. Lou, for instance, a friendly coworker who happened to be white, once wondered, because illegal discrimination could hurt the employer's bottom line, why would they discriminate? Lou's sensitivity needed to be heightened, he thought.

He grew to believe over years of doing EEO work that some of the best cases of illegal discrimination were never filed. Minorities and women in our society are so accustomed to being discriminated against in so many ways that many simply soldier on and do not file complaints or lawsuits! The dynamics of the office were quite interesting. The regional director was a black man, initially; most supervisors were white, and several were Jewish. Once Amir's group was hired, the number of black staff increased dramatically. There were at least two generations, possibly three there—the silent generation, the X generation, and the Y generation.

The regional directors served at the pleasure of. They were not civil servants. One had to have certain friends, Amir assumed, to get the position. *Just like a judge is a lawyer who has a politician for a friend*, thought Amir. Joshua or Josh was cool. A middle-aged brother, light-skinned with a full moustache, Josh was old school. He was always sharply dressed, with his hair slicked back. If you didn't bother Josh, Josh didn't bother you! The receptionist, Mabel, was kind of grumpy and taciturn, but she seemed to like him, and he liked her. The next RD was an attractive, brown-skinned, dark-haired, well-dressed, sexy, intelligent, and evil black woman. She seemed to have anger issues. She harassed staff regularly, and curiously, it was the black staff whom she harassed! When they, she and Amir, first met, he knew there'd be trouble. She stated to him, "I've heard a lot about you." What did that mean? She didn't elaborate, and he didn't probe. For however long, she'd be his boss. His gut was correct. One month, for instance, when he was nominated for employee of the month, she put the kibosh on it, telling his then supervisor, "Amir can't get it," according to the supervisor, who added, "She has a hard on for you."

He knew one day a showdown would occur when she would send for him and ask him, in the privacy of her office, to do something unethical or contrary to his true beliefs or his written and signed report as was her practice with staff. When it happened, one beautiful fall afternoon, as he was walking to her office after having been summoned by Lilly, her secretary, an attractive, well-dressed African American woman, he felt this would be it!

"Amir, I want you to change your recommendation in the matter of blank versus blank Cough Drops."

Amir didn't lose it but calmly asked, "May I inquire as to why?"

Her response was "Just change it!"

Life has these moments—aha moments. He needed his job, and she was the boss, but she didn't articulate any reasons, legitimate or otherwise, for him to change his finding in the matter. He would be the one to sign off on and possibly be called to testify in court and defend the report. The RD liked having her way and was becoming visibly upset already. He thought of a good strategy, he thought.

"All right, but I'll need your memo directing me to change the report before I can resubmit it," he said. *If looks could kill*, he was thinking, *rigor mortis would be setting in about now.*

"Good afternoon, Amir," she said curtly as she showed him the door.

Wow, he thought. If she had a legitimate reason for her request, she could write a memo. But if she was doing something unethical, she dared not. Of course, she hated him even more after the incident. He knew he would have to eventually find another position!

When Amir stopped by Dade's Place that late Saturday afternoon, he was feeling good. He had a new job, new girl, a different car—life was good.

"I came up hard," Brother Dade was explaining to him as they sat in a booth in the dimly lit bar. "We were poor and lived in the country. My father was mean. He rarely laughed or smiled. He used to beat my brother and me with a razor strap! I still have a scar on my back from the whippings. If we didn't get our lessons, we went to bed with no dinner! We had to work in the fields, ploughing and picking cotton. We fed the chickens, slopped the hogs, peeled the potatoes, shucked the corn, and did lots of other chores around the farm. Made me drop out of school in the sixth grade so I could help on the farm. When I was seventeen, I ran away from that mother fucker and came to Philly. The rest is history. Got me a business here, a nice house, a nice ride, and a big-legged white woman, but when the revolution come, she'll be the first to go. I'm living the mother-fucking American dream," Dade said with a chuckle.

Amir smiled. "I want to be like you when I grow up!"

"Later, Brother Dade," he said as he walked out of Dade's Place and into the Center City pedestrian traffic.

Amir was standing on the corner of Eleventh and Market Streets, waiting for the light to change, on his way to the college. A young man dressed in a dashiki approached him in an unthreatening manner and started speaking. "Brother, can you dig the complexity of the complication we're in?"

Amir smiled. "You see because the man has poisoned us with pork products (porkitis), we can't think clearly, and because we can't think clearly, we're still mental slaves."

"Throw in natal alienation, and the Confederation of Southern States, the magnification and ramification of which is worldwide, my brother."

"White cognitive dissonance is also a motherfucker!"

"By the way, can you spare a quarter, brother?"

Wow, black folks talk a lot of shit! thought Amir. *Whoever made up the lie that African Americans are inarticulate?*

As he sat on the park bench in Rittenhouse Square that beautiful Saturday afternoon, enjoying the flora and the fauna, a tall caramel-colored sister walked by in skintight jeans. They were so tight she probably had to put them on while lying down. She was rocking them, however. She wore high heels and a leather motorcycle jacket to top off the outfit. Her walk was like poetry in motion. *Every poor boy's dream and every rich man's prayer,* he thought to himself as she passed directly in front of him. Amir was thinking that maybe, in light of all the changes occurring around him, maybe marriage shouldn't be such a distant goal. Surely, for the most part, he enjoyed being single, the freedom to more or less go where he pleased and do as he pleased could be intoxicating at times. He could spend his money on designer clothes, sporty autos, travel, and watches and date whomever he pleased, but there were, of course, also the lonely times, like those rainy Tuesday nights as he often referred to them. So much in our society is geared toward couples and families, from getting seated in a restaurant to taking advantage of coupons and discounts at hotels, restaurants, shows, and so on. Additionally, he did want a child or children and always assumed that one day it would occur, but only in the context of marriage.

Yes, he would have to start taking his love life more seriously! The Lone Ranger had broken his heart and possibly one or two others. Of course, he had broken some hearts also.

Amir heard the car horn beep as he was walking south along Twenty-First Street between Chestnut and Sansom Streets. Initially, he didn't pay attention to it. This was his usual practice. If he heard a car horn beeping, it usually wasn't for him, and in a big city, it could spell trouble, so he just kept walking. But he heard his dad's voice clearly yell, "Sonny!" his nickname. When he turned and looked over his shoulder, it was Dad driving his Lincoln Continental Mark III. It was a powder-blue color with a sunroof. It was a chick magnet, he thought. Dad was single now and had said he'd never marry again. Dad was in his playboy/playa period, wearing western boots, nice slacks, and a nice shirt, trying to dress fashionably. Dad pulled to the curb and Amir went over to the car.

"S-o-n-n-y," he said with a smile.

"Wassup, Dad?" Amir replied.

"Haven't seen you in a while," he stated almost inquisitively.

"Yeah, been busy. These chicks are driving me crazy!" Amir stated.

Dad responded, "Can't live with 'em. Can't live without 'em, huh? Okay, stop by the house when you get a chance."

"I will," responded Amir with a smile.

Dad then smiled and pulled off rather quickly. He only drove at two speeds in those days, fast and faster.

Upon visits to Dad's new place in the West Oak Lane section of Philadelphia, Amir got a two-fer. Biggy had moved in with him, and Biggy was a trip! Sitting comfortably in the living room in her easy chair, while dipping snuff, she began to berate Dad. "Something happened to your father during the war! He had good sense when he left home! I don't know where he's getting these cows from!" Of course, by cows, she meant his current crop of dates or girlfriends. "I wouldn't have Black Lily! She'll move in here over my dead body!" she proclaimed.

In time, that is what happened. Dad and Lily got married. Pop, Biggy's husband, had died years before but just before it became clear that Biggy would have to go into a nursing home. She didn't want that. Dad and she lived alone, and Dad often worked long hours.

Biggy's personality was such that having someone come over to the house and help take care of her while Dad was working was problematic. She was stubborn and could be cranky, temperamental, and not very trusting, except for Amir, whom she seemed to trust without limitation. Regrettably, a nursing home seemed the logical option. Some years later, as Biggy was hospitalized at a certain Memorial Hospital in the Roxborough section of Philly and Amir was there to visit with her, he heard cursing as he walked down the hallway to her room. It was Biggy! She was cussing out the nurses attending to her!

When the nurses left the room, after greeting and kissing her, Amir respectfully said to Biggy, "You really shouldn't talk to them like that. You're in their care!"

Biggy's response was "What's the difference? I'm dying anyway!"

Ha, no good response for that. Biggy was going out as she had lived, taking no prisoners! Shortly thereafter, Biggy died. One of Amir's favorite people, best friends, and supporters in life was now gone. She was only in her sixties. Did her physical maladies alone cause her death, or was it also because she lost her will to live? She really didn't want to go to that nursing home!

Ye Olde Gang

Sharon had peeped Flash's whole card, and they had broken up.

Someone had dropped a dime on Nick, a fellow student, and his alleged planned attack on the Philly Police force, so it looked like he might be on his way to jail. Omar was still traveling on business in Europe and Africa. SaRon had morphed into who knows what. Mike was working for the city and living like a recluse in his West Philly rooms. Who knew where Tarik was? Never was still in Cali.

Amir's current love interest was a tall, lithe, sinewy-looking, attractive, long-legged young woman named Uhura. She had dark hair, big pretty eyes, and golden yellow skin. They had only been dating for a few weeks and were having big fun. She worked for the government also. She really seemed to care for him, stopping by the office to visit him periodically during the workday. At a recent Halloween party they had attended, she looked so sexy in her Cat Woman outfit with her fishnet stockings on. She had recently suggested that they get married. "Stop the presses!" Get married? They didn't even know each other that well, he thought. Sure, he liked her. She was fun, intelligent, sexy, and good-looking, but marriage? She already had one son, who was young. That was not necessarily a problem, he thought, but they really didn't have much time together. Of course, he had to give her a response. No response would be an answer in and of itself! His hesitancy about responding in a definite way meant, he knew, the probable end to the relationship. This woman wanted to be married. As he drove along the Schuylkill Expressway that autumn afternoon, he thought of Uhura and the beautiful and haunting lyrics of Eddie Kendrick's song "Tell Her Love Has Felt the Need." "Diamond rings and wedding plans, children laughing and holding hands, she deserves that kind of man, but my life is like drifting sands. Tell her love has felt the need to leave her, tell her love has felt the need to free her. I could never be what she needs of me!"

A few months after they stopped seeing each other, he heard that she had married someone. A few weeks after that, around midnight one night, as he was sleeping in his apartment, the phone rang. It was Uhura. When he asked her why she was calling him and where her husband was, she responded that he was lying in the bed with her asleep! "He doesn't hold me like you did," she stated. "He doesn't touch me like you did," she added.

Wow, thought Amir, *serious drama*! "I don't know what to say," he responded. "You've made your choice."

The phone went dead on the other end. What is love? Does it change over time? Amir knew the ancient Greeks had several terms designating different types of love. Some people with or without the benefit of marriage were together for years, others not.

The American divorce rate was high, he had always heard. The marriage he believed in was the bond between the people, not the certificate, the piece of paper. Wasn't marriage created basically for the orderly transfer of property and other wealth? He grew to believe that sometimes it was better to be in like than in love, more comfortable, less drama.

Amir thought he knew when he was in love because of not just the wonderful feelings attached, but also the presence of jealousy, some need to control, concern for the safety and well-being of the loved one, and a feeling of ownership of the loved one. There was both healthy and unhealthy love, he figured. The unhealthy relationships, the ones with the wrong person, a lot of drama, an element of danger were often the most fun and exciting, however, truth be told, like the go-go girl he briefly dated or the somebody else's girlfriends he occasionally dated, or the beautiful and sexy fiancée of a guy who would often call her while Amir was visiting.

When young and single, he and his buddies ascribed to the "all in love is fair" axiom—unless of course the roles were reversed! Typical male hypocrites. Romance was, he came to believe, at some level, always competitive. "If you can beat me rocking, then you can have my chair!" Of course, they had a code: hands off your boys' girlfriends, fiancées, or wives. Flash, however, had broken that code, as had Never! To be filed away under useful information.

Awww Sooky Sooky Now

Amir was twenty-five. The teacher was fortyish looking. He had met her at a cabaret. He had hesitantly gone to it with SaRon and his older woman. He didn't particularly care for cabarets but went anyway. He was sorting feeling like a third wheel. SaRon had a date, but he didn't. When he spotted her across the room looking elegant and sexy, dressed in all black, he thought, *Looking that good, she should be with me!* She was about five feet six inches tall and light-skinned with freckles. Her eyes were dark and beautiful; her hair, reddish-brown, was worn in a pixie-like hairstyle. It became her. As he observed the outline of her legs in her pantsuit, he concluded that she had good ones. Her smile was engaging. She said she had no children. Her intelligence and sense of humor showed in her face. She was a sophisticated older woman.

He had been fantasizing about older women. His assumption was that a well-preserved older woman might be easier to get along with than many girls his own age, some of whom had hang-ups, complexes, and insecurities that he couldn't abide, deal with, or understand. Older meant more secure, personally and financially, more self-confidence and maturity, a better grip on who they were, and so on, or so he thought. He asked her to dance. She said yes. It was a slow dance, of course. You can't rap to a woman on a fast record! He could feel that they had chemistry. He confidently asked, "Will our first date be dinner or a movie?"

She responded, "You don't waste any time, do you?"

Amir responded, "Life is short. Don't believe in wasting time."

She then stated, "I'm old enough to be your mother."

He said, "But you're not my mother, and what I'm feeling toward you right now isn't motherly either."

When he picked Pam up from her nice small condo in Nicetown for their first date about a week later, he knew they'd have fun. Pam was bubbly in a mature way with a good sense of humor. *Good*, he thought. They would have big fun! As he seduced her that evening, or she him, or they each other, he thought, *I called this one right*. She said she had been seeing somebody, but he didn't live in Philly. She only saw him occasionally, so it seemed acceptable. She and Amir had an easy, comfortable, fun relationship with no drama, no strings, just great evenings in her or his place.

His phone would ring in his apartment.

"What ya doing?" she would ask.

"Coming over," he would reply.

Candlelight, soft music, incense, and intimacy. It didn't get much better than that, zaats-boogaloo! Many women his age were confused, he felt. Liberated? Old-fashioned? Independent? Abstaining from sex out of fear of AIDS? Sleeping around too much because of their newfound freedom? A combination? It could get complicated. The lyrics to Eddie Kendricks hit "Girl, You Need a Change of Mind" often came to his mind. He always found it interesting in his dating life that so many independent and strong black women still wanted him to pay on dates! "I don't need no man!" unfortunately had become the mantra or battle cry of all too many black women, he felt. Omar referred to them as "attack women."

What other ethnic groups' women said such things about their men? Was this posttraumatic slavery syndrome (PTSS), a term coined by a then popular black author? Sometimes they made more money than he did, or about the same, sometimes less. They were occasionally attorneys or physicians and usually still wanted or expected him to pay! *How self-serving*, he thought. "I'm strong and independent, but you can still pick up the check!" A contradiction? He wasn't interested in debating women on the topic. If a man finds a woman sexy or attractive, if he wants to make love with her, he'll pay—at least for a while and often for the unhealthiest of reasons (e.g., she made him work for it or earn it). Not only will a man finance their dating relationship; he'll do innumerable things to impress her, to seduce her. He'll beg, borrow, and steal in his quest. "Nobody begs like a brother" was one of Amir's favorite sayings. Much of what men do, whether they admit it or not, Amir grew to believe, from the type of car they drove, to the clothes they wore, their choice of cologne, their desire to be in shape, even including their literary or other interests, real or feigned, was done to impress women. Amir felt it had probably always been this way. Weren't the males of many species generally not only bigger than the females but more colorful? Didn't they have more hair or colorful plumage than the females? Wasn't that for the express purpose of attracting the female so that they can mate? Then, we *Homo sapiens* weren't really much different after all, thought Amir.

Amir had been relaxing on his sofa bed in the living room of his small Center City apartment. He was wearing his white thobe, a genuine one from Saudi Arabia. Great for lounging and relaxing, it had been a gift from one of the Saudi friends he had made from his days living at Twentieth and Chestnut a few years ago. He had eaten a frozen Hungry Man TV dinner. His small TV was tuned to the local news. When her picture first flashed across the screen, he didn't recognize her. She was in her police officer uniform with her cap on. It was Patricia all right. She had been involved in a serious car accident. Evidently a panel truck had T-boned her car, and she was hospitalized on life support.

He quickly changed clothes and rushed to the hospital. As he approached the intensive care unit, he saw the policeman guarding Patricia, customary when officers were hospitalized, he thought. He could hear her mother sobbing before he saw her. "I'm not putting my daughter in the ground!" she kept repeating in agony. Patricia's sister was there also, crying, but not very vocally. Amir immediately hugged them both. Words were not adequate in such situations, thought Amir, so he didn't say very much. When he approached her hooked up to all the equipment that apparently was keeping her alive, he almost lost it. But men, he thought, couldn't lose it. He would maintain his composure as best he could. He sat in the small chair beside her bed and held her hand. So many memories. He had never stopped loving her, even though they hadn't been together in years. Sure, she had cheated on him, years ago, but that was then, this was now. His heart was aching.

He had heard she had been twice married and divorced and had a young son. Although usually an optimist, he didn't think she would make it. She didn't. His first love, a genuinely good person, she would forever remain in his consciousness.

IT'S JUST BUSINESS

CHAPTER 12

Several of Amir's friends and associates considered themselves businessmen or women, legal and illegal. Some, like Jimmy Faison, eventually would go into real estate, buying up properties and flipping or renting them out. Others would go into entertainment, producing or managing groups, often singing groups. Others were into retail sales, men's or women's clothing. Omar, he felt, was among the most likely to succeed. Very intelligent, quickwitted, and well read, he had personality plus and was urbane and very sophisticated. Initially, he tried music. His dad had been a jazz musician many years ago. Omar formed his own group and went out on the road. He had an encyclopedic knowledge of music, particularly rock and roll. He could sing as well, having spent some time on a church choir. After a couple of years, however, he gave up on the show side, deciding he'd rather be on the business side. In later years, he was putting together business deals for a fee, a kind of broker. So as they were enjoying lunch that beautiful fall day in Center City, Omar was explaining that he had a business meeting later but was sending his white surrogate or stand-in. It made perfect sense to Amir.

It wasn't that this guy was brighter, more knowledgeable, or more experienced, but he was white, and in 1970s America, all things being equal, that was still a status that could open some doors then still closed to blacks. Omar and Phil were among the first African Americans he had known personally who used racism at times to their monetary advantage. They were agents, not simply victims. Omar was impeccably dressed in his Brooks Brothers pinstriped suit, Cole Haan loafers, silk pocket square, and paisley tie. He was carrying a genuine hippopotamus-hide briefcase. His beard was perfectly trimmed, and he had that gleam and twinkle in his eyes. He and his stand-in would meet after the business meeting and debrief.

Amir couldn't help but think that if Omar, Jimmy, and several other ambitious young black entrepreneurs he knew were white, they probably would've been successful already. A witty, ambitious, energetic, articulate, fast-talking, hardworking young black man was often adjudged a hustler or con man, whereas those same traits in a white guy were often found praiseworthy. He had charisma, and the gift of gab. He was an orator, a raconteur, a real go-getter. *Let's face it*, he thought. *Don't most whites openly or secretly think that they are more intelligent than blacks, somehow more credible, more trustworthy?* Studies seem to confirm this.

Even some black professionals, like lawyers, doctors, dentists, accountants, various consultants, and so on, had to deal with the reality that even some of their own people, their potential clients, would rather patronize a white in their respective professions, believing that whites are somehow almost always more knowledgeable, more skilled, more professional, and so on.

A few, usually very talented and very lucky blacks would somehow beat the odds and successfully run the obstacle course that is American society for nonwhites. But they had to be superstars and fortunate! Some, of course, had sold their souls! Not nearly as talented whites could often still expect an equal measure of success.

Omar used to say, "It's a sorry white man that can't make it in America! Whites succeed because of the system; we succeed in spite of the system!"

America is kind of like your uncle who put you through college but molested you!

Of course, there were *Ebony* and *Jet* magazines, Motown, and Beatrice Enterprises, a few prosperous insurance companies, banks, savings and loans, and individuals who achieved wealth, like Madame C. J. Walker, and much later, there would be Oprah, Bill Cosby, Muhammad Ali, and a few other athletes, who had real wealth. Of course, big-time black gangsters in the pharmaceutical business sometimes were millionaires, maybe billionaires at their respective heights. Prosperous blacks, however, were still somewhat insecure, and should be. Witness the "Black Wall Street" incident in Oklahoma back in the early twentieth century or the Rosewood, Florida, incident.

America never made it easy or rarely even fair for blacks, in spite of false and insincere charges of allegedly so doing. Politicians and others have made false promises, lied, and sold out blacks at significant junctures in American history such as during the "Black Reconstruction" era (Tilden versus Hayes election) and with the half-hearted affirmative action efforts. No, his future would not be easy or assured but a struggle from the womb to the tomb. American blacks, he felt, were born in the struggle, whether they knew it or not.

Hatred or envy of whites or others was not the answer, however, but we do have enemies, forces and people who do not want us to succeed for various reasons. This must be remembered always. A society proudly proclaiming itself to be the heir of ancient Greece and ancient Rome, which at their respective heights, were slave-based societies where most were not citizens but slaves, does not fully really believe in equality. Therefore, don't be poor. Remember, the strong have a tendency to take advantage of the weak, no matter their race or color, ethnicity, or gender. Don't behave like a lamb, or you'll be shorn. Think for yourself. Know yourself. Trust most people, but make strategic alliances when advisable, and be prepared for the unexpected.

Amir had toyed with the notion of becoming a lawyer for years, having observed Cecil B. Moore's mastery of the courtroom, watched Oscar Gaskins and other Philly attorneys ply their trade and *Perry Mason* on TV, and seen certain movies, usually featuring charismatic and sometimes flamboyant criminal lawyers. Philadelphia had a well-deserved reputation in that area. "The Philadelphia lawyer" is a well-known phrase. A. Leon Higgenbotham, Juanita Kid Stout, Cecil B. Moore, Oscar Gaskins, the firm of Deckert, Price, and Rhodes, and many other individuals and firms were staples of the time. After years of spending some time around practicing attorneys, however, seeing how tedious and boring a lot of what they did actually was, and observing several criminal trials, Amir decided against that career choice. LSATs, three years of law school, and huge student debt to—he hoped—land a job with a firm as an associate afterward and hopefully do lots of grunt work to eventually become a partner didn't sound very attractive to him!

It seemed that most major cities had one or two black attorneys who were rock stars. Most, however, seemed to be working for the government or had their own small law firms. No, for that kind of investment of money, time, and effort, he would want more. Throughout his working life, he would be told periodically by others that he would've made a good lawyer.

"You hitting that?" Amir was softly asked by a male acquaintance as he walked on Broadway in Lower Manhattan to an audit meeting with the attractive young Mexican American coworker he was training. It was a beautiful autumn day. His response of "No, brother" was met with a skeptical facial expression. Sure, she was good-looking, with her long jet-black hair, clear and spotless complexion, full and sexy lips, and nice shape, but he wouldn't make a move on her. They were coworkers, after all. It could get complicated. Omar was meeting him for dinner at a nearby Ethiopian restaurant located near the Holland Tunnel, called The Red Sea. He and Omar both enjoyed Ethiopian cuisine with its injera bread.

Doro wat and tibbs were some of Amir's favorites. Those Ethiopian women were very often fine as well. Hummus, falafel, shawarma, gyros, grape leaves, shepherd's pie, bangers and mash, good fish and chips, pasta, moussaka, good Chinese food, couscous, tagines, soul food, Italian cuisine, and Caribbean food were all among their favorites. He and Omar had eclectic tastes in cuisine.

They did in music too: Motown, some blues, Chicago, The Righteous Brothers, The Average White Band, Isaac Hayes, Frank Sinatra, Tom Jones, Bobby Womack, Johnny Mathis, Dionne Warwick, Lulu, Hugh Masekela, Ramsey Lewis, Arthur Prysock, Antonio Carlos Jobim, some Broadway tunes (*Camelot*, *West Side Story*, *Man of la Mancha*, and so on), Lenny Williams and David Ruffin ("Nobody Begs Like a Brother"), and many others. Jimmy Webb's lyrics really resonated with them, as did Smokey Robinson's and Isaac Hayes's.

Commuting to and working in New York City was a major life transition for Amir. He had seen a newspaper ad by NYC's then mayor, Koch, recruiting for jobs with and in NYC. He really liked Philly. Philly was his home. His family, friends, and network were there. So many memories! But he was doing a job search and was sending résumés to Delaware, New York City, New Jersey, and even Connecticut, as well as within Philly. Why not? He was young, single, no children. NYC wasn't that far away! When he got a response from NYC personnel, he was shocked. Would this be the start of another adventure in his young life? His first interview was in lower Manhattan with a NYC agency. He had been a little embarrassed when he asked directions to Houston Street that beautiful fall day. He had pronounced it like the city in Texas, Houston. He learned from the New Yorker that in NYC, although the spelling was the same, it was pronounced "How-ston." He did find the address eventually.

Two women would interview him. He thought the interview was going well. He had arrived early, had extra copies of his résumé, and was dressed in his navy-blue interview suit, not too much cologne or jewelry. He had even gone to the men's room to look in the mirror and check that there was nothing in his teeth. When he was asked, "What do you think of gay people?" he was a bit surprised. It was an antidiscrimination type of job. But where was the balance? He wasn't asked how he felt about employees or applicants over forty, about folks with disabilities, or folks of different religions or national origins. Amir thought his answer was balanced and fair. "I'd advocate for the rights of all the protected class members," he had said. He wasn't offered the position. Flash-forward a couple of months, same agency, different interviewers. Amir was offered a position.

Amir was standing at the counter in the record store in Center City Philly when the young brother walked up to the counter. "I want the soundtrack of *Les Miserables*," but he didn't pronounce it in the French language way. He said, "Less Miserables." The saleslady, who happened to be white, glanced at Amir with a kind of smug expression. Sad, he thought, this young man probably received an inferior public school education at an inferior inner-city school, not his fault. When one doesn't have the foundation, it is difficult to be urbane and sophisticated. He had personally witnessed Africans speaking fluent French, German, Dutch, Arabic, Spanish, Portuguese, and so on. It wasn't a matter of capability but exposure and education.

He was beyond being embarrassed per se by other blacks who said or did things he thought of as being ignorant, criminal, silly, tasteless, bestial, classless, or cruel for the most part. Whites and others didn't seem to be embarrassed by the Son of Sam, Jeffrey Dahmer, Ted Bundy, or John Wayne Gacy! Collectively, American whites had done much worse in terms of their behavior than American blacks had, contrary to the stereotypes. Amir's take on American history led him to believe that it was replete with instances of whites perpetrating terrorism and violence upon blacks. The reverse paled in comparison. Mass murders, riots, serial killers, lynchings, and terrorism—whites seemed to dominate in those areas in the respective death tolls. Omar was fond of saying that African Americans are the "Frankenstein's monster of peoples," meaning that whatever they were, to an extent, was what America had made them!

Here since admittedly and debatably 1619 (some think much earlier) and deprived, for the most part, of their African connections, they were the most American of America's various peoples, most of whom were allowed to retain at least some of their respective heritages if they chose to, like some enslaved by the Spanish who kept the drums and colors and practiced some of their African spiritual beliefs. The late comedian Richard Pryor once famously said in slightly different words that the international slave trade solved the African tribal dilemma—Wolof, Ashanti, Ibo, Hausa, Fulani, and so on were all dumped together, like sardines, and became one tribe, "niggers" or blacks!

Omar also used to say that the great feature of America for Europeans was that they, be they of French, German, Italian, Greek, or whatever ancestry, could come to America and eventually at least become white because of the presence in America of black people and Native Americans! Back in Europe, they historically fought each other and were ethnocentric and xenophobic, constantly jockeying for position around resources, population control, trade, colonies, world domination, and so on. A Frenchman was not an Englishman, and a German was not an Italian in Europe. But in America, they could just be white and enjoy the benefits that flowed therefrom. The presence of blacks in America took the edge off tensions between historic white ethnics to a large degree. Of course, some were not considered white initially, like Southern Europeans, people from the Indian subcontinent, Turks, and some others. There were famous legal cases of those struggling to join the white club. Of course, at the top of the hierarchy were white Anglo-Saxon Protestants. An analysis of American immigration laws reflect who was wanted and who wasn't during various periods of time; the Chinese Exclusion act of 1882, for example, was very telling—no Chinese and no prostitutes or lepers!

Zaats Boogaloo

While he was relaxing in his Center City apartment, Amir's phone rang that Saturday afternoon. It was Omar. There were no cell phones in those days. It was his black telephone, a landline.

"As salaamu alaikum, brother. How are you?"

Amir was truly happy to hear from his brother from another mother.

"Where have you been, akhi?"

"I been traveling, brother, trying to make a living—Rome, London, Cairo."

Amir said, "You're the man."

"Naw, brother, I knew a man once," retorted Omar, continuing with "You taught me everything I know, godfather!"

Amir sensed that he would probably never meet or know any other man in this life with whom he felt he was such a kindred spirit. Others even occasionally commented, "You two sound and talk alike." Their communication was sometimes approaching telepathic, a glance, a look, and a message or thought was conveyed or understood.

Omar was one of the few men on the planet he would totally

trust around his girlfriends and years later his wife and daughter. They had so many shared discussions and experiences and so much joy and sadness.

When visiting Omar in Jersey years later, as he was playing house with his daughter's mother, his daughter, then a young child, had approached Amir and asked, "Are you a scientist?"

He and Omar had smiled broadly. Omar was one of his best supporters and he one of his. They both bolstered each other in good times and bad. They would each be accused of being just alike.

"You can make a way out of no way, brother," he had said to Omar often.

"It is the duty of the civilized man to teach, and you do," Omar often complimented him with.

He sensed that Omar sort of looked at him like an older brother. Who else could he view Lawrence of Arabia with who would truly enjoy it and also know most of the dialogue? Who else knew what nations and states used to be known as the Trucial States?

How many other guys his age from his background would be familiar with phrases such as "He's got the bit between his teeth, all right!" or "wog," or how someone has "queered the pitch" about or for something, or understood "car park," "bonnet," and "boot"? Who else would point out good-looking and sexy women to him unselfishly or share his eclectic taste in cuisine, clothes, cars, music, and women?

They didn't think they were Arabs, but they related to robe wearing, warriorlike, nomadic, and desert-dwelling peoples, Africans and others, often Muslims, not the stereotypical and falsely portrayed loincloth-wearing, spear-carrying, almost nude fake Africans that the American media had been portraying to them since childhood and that were not representative of how most Africans looked, dressed, or behaved but were aberrations or "hillbilly" Africans.

In the same vain, *National Geographic* and similar shows

usually broadcast episodes showing Africans in small villages, bare breasted, often with rings around their necks and dancing. African Hillbillies. They never seemed to show African cities, like Lagos, Dar es Salaam, Accra, Addis Ababa, Harare, and so on. Showing sky scrapers, traffic jams, neatly manicured lawns, and Africans driving around in their BMWs or Mercedes-Benz cars or going to university didn't serve their purposes, he guessed. It was enough to make one angry and paranoid!

Among specific African peoples, he felt an affinity for the Tuareg, the Afar people of Ethiopia, the Zulu, and the Ashanti of Ghana. Both he and Omar had made it a point to read about Africa and Africans. Omar and Yusef had traveled there already. They all knew a few Africans from the motherland. Most were multilingual and educated. One, a professor at the college, was from Morocco and had said he was a Tuareg tribesman from the Atlas Mountains region. He had personality plus and was quite a ladies' man. He taught French. There were also a few Nigerians around. The men tended to be proud and a bit arrogant, he felt. Most of Amir's African acquaintances were middle- or upper-middle-class folk, well-traveled and sophisticated. Of course, colonialism, neocolonialism, white supremacy, and Western propaganda had left scars on some of them. A few didn't relate to African Americans because they were not pure, some because they had been slaves in America, and others because they believed the hype that black Americans were all on drugs or were criminals or uneducated!

"Brother, you were not kidnapped from the motherland but couldn't control it!" Amir had said to more than one native African who expressed such sentiments.

Amir was talking to one such haughty and arrogant African brother on that warm afternoon in Rittenhouse Square as he sat on the bench with Omar and this fellow Chudy. "Look what you let them do to Africa!"

One of the sad phenomena he was becoming aware of was how

some folks of African descent, principally some from the Caribbean and some from Africa, tried to look down on American blacks! He and Omar were having none of it! "What have you read about my people?" he would generally ask. "Do you know of Peter Salem and Salem Poor, Fredrick Douglass, Booker T., Nat Turner, the 'German Coast' rebellion, Harriet Tubman, W. E. B. DuBois, Paul Robeson, MLK Jr., Madame C. J. Walker, the Buffalo Soldiers, the Tuskegee Airmen, the Mumfort Point Marines, Black Wall Street? If not, you're not qualified to have an opinion!" That usually shut them up. These folks were generally ignorant of the many and proud accomplishments of American blacks and were basing their views on ignorance, stereotypes, negative media images, and their own insecurities.

Grown Folk

After twenty-plus years of marriage, his parents were getting divorced—Dad, the fun-loving, strong, friendly, hardworking, social Aquarian, and Mom, the conservative, steady, strong, nurturing Virgo. Amir felt that he had good parents. They were not perfect but loving, consistent folks who led by example. Dad worked, took them on vacations, and provided a good home for them to live in and clothes to wear. Mom was affectionate yet very strong.

While conservative—no drinking, smoking, gambling, or swearing—she also had personality plus. She had a great sense of humor and loved to tease and laugh. They both did actually. Everyone in the family and extended family had stories about Mom! "Remember the time she was waiting in the door on Huntingdon Street with a baseball bat for the cabby who had taken first cousin Marcia, visiting from Georgia, for a ride from the train station and frightened her. Or the time she grabbed a two-by-four on the way to confront a neighbor who had been gossiping about her, or how as a youth she would be the one of her three female siblings to go outside, roll her sleeves up, and fight with boys! Or the time she was shooting at someone across the street early in the morning from the second-floor window in her negligee, because she saw him trying to steal Melinda's car!"

She and Dad were both from small-town Georgia—in fact, the same area.

They were migrants to Philly who sought a better life—better jobs, better pay, less racism and discrimination, more opportunities, a better future for their children, like other immigrants from around the world who came to America. In essence, they were seeking a kind of political asylum from the politics of the South principally and other areas of the country as well. They were seeking jobs, homes, and friendships in all walks of life.

Mom and Dad had been married about six or seven years before Amir, the firstborn, arrived. Another nineteen months and Melinda came along. Both were delivered via Caesarian birth in Philly. He and Melinda never witnessed Mom and Dad physically fighting, but there was a palpable tension between them for a time just prior to their divorcing. This was the era when many men, at least the ones he had been exposed to, had an outside woman, a lover, a gumaa, as some Italians would say, in addition to their legal wives.

He was sure not all married women were accepting or tolerant of this state of affairs, but they could be heard saying, in private, to other women, "At least he comes home," or "He pays the bills," or "I'm his wife that slut/cow/ho is getting leftovers!"

Dad, over the years, had apparently had some of these outside women. "Your father is a good man," Mom could be heard to say on occasion. "He just loves women too much!"

As he grew older, Amir decided that although sad, maybe the real wonder was how they remained married for as long as they did. They were so different in personality and style. Maybe she stayed because of the children, an often-heard reason for staying given by married women. Amir and Melinda were grown-ups, both in their twenties. Maybe it was economic. Mom couldn't hope to earn even half of what Dad did in those times. Maybe it was about appearances in front of neighbors, friends, relatives, fellow churchgoers, and so on. What would they say or think? Does one ever truly understand or know the symmetry of other people's relationships, even one's own parents? Amir loved them both and wished them both well.

No matter what, they would always be his mom and his dad, and he would be eternally grateful for what they both had provided for him and Melinda—a good home to grow up in, a work ethic, love, caring, affection, a sense of dignity, some spiritual guidance, and good genes, including basically good health, good looks, and intelligence.

Fun cousin Michael T. had passed. Amir didn't know what of. He went to his funeral and sat in the back of the funeral home, having arrived late. He couldn't help but notice the several well-dressed younger women who attended the services alone and were not family as far as he knew. That conversation of long ago he had with him as he had been driving him around looking for a timing belt for his Mustang II came to mind.

There had been two funerals for Pop because he died in Philly but had always expressed a desire to be buried in the red clay of Georgia. Amir accompanied Dad to Elberton, Georgia, to attend the second funeral. The body of course had been flown down to Georgia. It was at an old country church. It was on a country road in the woods, as far as Amir was concerned. Dust, smoke, and gravel kicked up as the cars drove along the road. This had been the traditional family church for years, he had been told. It was a small—by Philly standards—church built of wood with a steeple. There was no air-conditioning in the church.

Now, of course, many of his relatives had migrated to different parts of America—New England, California, Philly, and so on. There would always be those handheld fans from local funeral homes located in the pews, and the Baptist minister could usually be counted on to deliver a stirring sermon. "In my father's house, there are many mansions. I would have told you if it were not so." Upon one southern sojourn, a minister at the same church, when it was time to eat the delicious food prepared by the sisters, announced it by saying, "Now it's time to eat something dead!"

Cries of "Amen," "Well," "Preach," and "Take your time" could be heard. It seemed that the Baptist ministers were not happy unless one or more attendees got happy, got the spirit, during their sermons. This would be manifested in a flailing of arms, an odd sort of little dance, and possibly fainting. There would be ushers to attend to people experiencing this. Interestingly, the people who got happy or got the spirit were always women, never a man!

The cemetery was behind the church and very close to it. As they lowered Pop into the ground, Amir knew he would miss him. He would miss what Pop had been and meant to him.

Dad looked sad, but, of course, like most African American men of his generation, he could not cry, at least not in public. It was a generational thing, Amir figured. It had to do with why Dad, who he was sure loved him, never hugged him or kissed him in any way, shape, or form. Older brothers were also reluctant to hold newborns. It took Amir some years to understand that, but finally, he did. Maybe black men of that generation endured so much hell from the larger society, they figured they had to steel themselves to handle it and be seen as men, at least by some. They wanted their children to be tough to be able to withstand the harsh racism, sexism, and classism they were sure to encounter out there in the world, so they could navigate the minefield that was American society for African Americans. Some of them overdid it. Their motives, however, in the main, were good; they were righteous, he felt. Amir had met other young blacks who upon having their first overtly racial experience—that is, being called the *N* word or facing other forms of racism or discrimination in one of its many other forms— were traumatized. He blamed their parents to some extent for not preparing them better, for not having the talk or conversation. Sure, he thought he understood how some parents wanted to spare their children from the ugliness and pain of prejudice, discrimination, and hatred, but the stakes were too high in his estimation to send them out into the world with no preparation. He didn't think parents should teach their black children to hate whites. But surely the history of blacks in America, in relationship to whites—slavery, Jim Crow, segregation, lynchings, white riots, brutality toward blacks collectively—demonstrated that a healthy caution, skepticism, and cynicism were in order.

Amir would find it difficult or frustrating in coming years to try to share with younger blacks and many others how he had grown up in a golden era in America for blacks, relatively speaking. Hope, dreams, pride, and employment were at a zenith. Self-hatred and the internalization of white racist thoughts and assumptions were on the wane. When the terms *brother*, *sister*, and *community* really had some meaning and were not just platitudes, at least for many. "Black is beautiful" became a reality for lots of folks. Blacks had been on the move. He didn't talk about his exploits with Omar, Yusef, SaRon, Luther, Phil, Fat Frank, and the rest too often or with too many. He spoke of them only to a few close confidants.

How many would believe him about staying at the Beverly Wilshire Hotel in Beverly Hills or the Pierre Hotel in New York and hanging out with Italian mobsters and Black gangsters, while also hobnobbing with lawyers, judges, priests, actors, singers, musicians, and ministers? Would they believe him about traveling internationally during a period when not many young blacks did? He would either be met with unbelief and skepticism or resentment and envy by others. It could possibly be seen as bragging.

"Damned if I know," one acquaintance had said as they sat

on a bench just outside the church where Phil's funeral was being conducted.

They were all speculating about what Phil had died from. There had always been some mystery, some unknowns about Phil and his lifestyle. Amir wondered if Phil's death might have been an insurance scam. The coffin had been closed at the funeral. It wasn't clear what the cause of his death was. If he knew anyone capable of such a scam, Phil was certainly at the top of the list! Was he really dead? Could he be on an island somewhere, kicking back and sipping drinks with little umbrellas in them? Or was he on the continent or somewhere else? That could be said about a lot of Amir's friends and associates and maybe about him as well. This air of mystery, this other side, this facility for moving among different strata in society. Amir missed Phil. As eccentric as he was, this Gemini was fun to be around usually. They had spent lot of road time together. Many deep conversations had occurred. They talked about race, sex, geo and local politics, and economics. The subject then changed to Little Johnny. Word on the street was that someone had walked into one of his Center City bars or clubs and shot him to death. This only confirmed what they had believed for years. He was all mobbed up but had always been decent to Omar and him. Amir would never forget the brief conversation they had had after Melinda was killed. Life is not simple, not just black and white, good and evil, right and wrong, with the good guys and the bad guys. There are shades of gray.

"These silly Negroes get on my nerves," Omar was saying. He was responding to the apparent growing popularity of candidate Bill Clinton among African Americans. "He's from Arkansas! He's no JFK! JFK was the original playa! He's corny. Did you see Okrah's [Oprah's] new movie?"

"No, brother," commented Amir. "I'm not big on Okrah."

"She's the national mammy," opined Omar. "She takes you

[white people] to her breast and holds you. But I hope she makes every dollar she can!"

They both had respect, even grudging, for blacks who had found a way to make a lot of money in this society with the exception of drug dealers, pimps, or total sell-outs like Clarence Thomas, whom they considered a traitor based on his anti - affirmative action stand and other conservative court decisions.

Mick, the friend of Omar's who had become an undercover Philly cop had some tragedy in his life. While he was at the old Latin Casino in Cherry Hill, New Jersey, for a show with his pregnant wife, a shooting was allegedly done by some folks in the pharmaceutical business, some kind of dispute. Mick's wife had been injured!

The Latin Casino had been a very popular night spot of the time. Folks would get sharp and go there. Flares, platform shoes—for women and men—polyester, jump suits for men, and shoulder bags for guys were in style at the time. "Put on your high-heeled sneakers and your wig hat on your head." Top musical acts would appear there—Al Green, Jackie Wilson, and others. In fact, it was on the stage at the Latin Casino while performing that Jackie Wilson, a great and seminal entertainer, famously had a stroke and was subsequently hospitalized, comatose, to die years later. Melinda, years before in her attempts to become a reporter, had interviewed Al Green there. When Amir had inquired about her impressions of "Al Grits" (referred to as such because he was allegedly discovered with a man by his then woman who allegedly threw hot grits on him), Melinda had commented that while nice, he seemed a bit light in the loafers.

Throwing hot grits or boiling water on someone, which didn't occur that often in reality, was a black cultural thing. Some of the old heads usually laughingly joked about keeping a pot of hot grits on the stove at all times! Talk of or threats of beating someone up with a two-by-four was also a black thing, Amir had learned.

Although he didn't know of anyone who had done this or had this done to them. "I have a two-by-four I've been soaking in STP!"

As they sat waiting for SaRon to arrive, momentarily Amir's mind fleetingly drifted to thoughts of Melinda. What if she were still alive? Like Amir, she would now be a few years older, her daughter a little older of course as well. Melinda would undoubtedly still be a fox, still have the engaging personality and be sharply dressed. They would probably be closer, he thought, would talk more, visit each other more. He would, of course, be taking her daughter, his niece, out to movies, plays, museums, concerts, the zoo, car rides, and so on since she and Donald had divorced. They would grow old together. But back to reality, they would not grow old together, spend more time together. Melinda was dead, her life cut short by an act of violence. He hoped she was in a better place. He hoped he would see her again one day. He no longer believed in the traditional concepts of heaven and hell, but could there be another dimension? A dual reality? Man does not really understand so much. We flatter ourselves, believing that we know a lot, but in reality, we understand so little. Is there life after death? If so, what kind of life is it? Cherubs playing harps? Gardens with rivers flowing underneath? Beautiful virgins who stay perpetually young? Are we reincarnated? Are the Abrahamic faiths correct? The Buddhists? The Hindus? Or is there simply the cold grave, and we become food for worms? No one has come back and told us of heaven or hell. Matters of belief then. *Most of us, if truly honest, are in no hurry to find out either*, thought Amir.

SaRon had finally arrived at the entry, huffing and puffing from his long trek from his metered parking space. He was too cheap to pay to park at the much closer parking garage.

"Hey, Doctor, what's up?"

"I can't call it, just trying to find me another young freak," replied SaRon.

Omar and Amir slyly glanced at each other. Amir was at the

moment just remembering how last week, he had gone alone to the disco up on City Line Avenue in Bala Cynwood, just out of boredom on a Thursday night. But what a surprise, the legendary Curtis Mayfield was there lip syncing to some of his songs! He only had a three-piece band with him, but still, Curtis Mayfield! His songbook was impressive: "Gypsy Woman," "People Get Ready," "We're a Winner," the *Superfly* soundtrack, "If You Had a Choice of Colors," the anti-drug, "Ain't got No Chain On Me," "(Don't Worry) If There's a Hell Below, We're All Gonna Go," and on and on.

Although he didn't have a chance to meet Curtis on that occasion, Amir reflected on how many celebrities he had met during his as yet young life, often quite accidentally: Muhammad Ali, in a Center City Philly burger joint; comedian and actor Robin Williams at the bar in the Sands Casino disco in Atlantic City; actor Herschel Bernardi at the bar in the Polo Lounge in Beverly Hills; Chaka Khan, Cuba Gooding, Lionel Ritchie, and Betty Davis, all at the Hippo disco; Sidney Poitier in an elevator at a hotel in Philly during the filming of *The Lost Man*; and Gordon Parks Jr. at an oldies dance at the famous Roseland Ballroom in Manhattan. He also met and partied with Melvin Van Peebles at the Roseland Ballroom on another occasion. He met Gary U. S. Bonds at the Uptown Theatre in Philly between shows, Norman Connors while hanging out with Omar in New York City, Isaac Hayes at an afterparty following the Essence Awards when they were held at The Theatre in Madison Square Garden in New York City, Jim Brown standing in a queue at a Center City movie theater with his young Philly elite date, and boxer Joe Frazier walking along Glenwood Avenue fresh from his Olympic boxing victory with his smart-looking US Olympic Team blazer on. His gym on North Broad Street was only a few blocks from Amir's house. He also met Ted Lawson, an actor whom he recognized from *Scream Blacula Scream*, also starring Pam Grier and William Marshall. He briefly chatted with the legendary Ossie Davis and former Atlanta Mayor Maynard Jackson in West Palm

Beach, Florida, at a PGA facility where a Black Enterprise Golf and Tennis Classic was being staged. He couldn't help but respectfully ask Mayor Jackson, "Do you believe little Wayne Williams committed all those Atlanta Child Murders? He had to ask Ossie Davis, "Why don't we see movies about the Moors, Hannibal, as a true African?"

Mr. Davis cited reasons such as the need for funding and backing, the lack of a distribution network, and potential interest.

Floyd McKissick, then the head of CORE (Congress of Racial Equality), actually thought he recognized Amir upon their meeting and behaved that way. He received a hug from Maya Angelou as he was standing in a receiving line at a black-tie event in New York City, which was quite unforgettable. *Not a bad list*, he thought. If you go clubbing enough, travel enough, hang out enough, are daring enough, and have a variety of friends and associates, no telling who you might meet or rub elbows with!

As they slowly strolled from the restaurant along Locust Street heading toward Broad that late afternoon, a very shapely young African American woman in a tight but classy and expensive-looking black dress walked past them. She was pumping. She furtively glanced back at them. When she was out of earshot, Tarik casually said, "Her backfield is definitely in motion!"

Omar replied, "She has a great future behind her!"

SaRon chimed in with "Yeah, her troubles are all behind her too!"

Amir concluded with "Gentlemen, can we all agree that she's sitting on a gold mine?"

They all chuckled as they continued ambulating along.

He and Omar were relaxing at Omar's spot that beautiful fall day. Omar had offered tea, and Amir had accepted. They began to discuss women. Omar's English love was arriving for a visit in a few days.

"That bloody tongue!" he had quoted her as saying to him with a sense of pride.

Amir had not met her yet but had been told she was very sophisticated and urbane. Of course, in the looks department, Omar's reputation spoke for itself. She would be fine. He had met her and her sister while clubbing in New York City one night. He had rented a chauffeured limo to travel from club to club. He did this on occasion. Amir had not been along for this particular venture. *Shame*, Amir thought, because Omar had said the sister was fine also. Omar enjoyed being the center of attention. So squiring this beautiful Brit around New York City was up his alley. He liked arm candy, showing off his women. New York City was the perfect place to do this. There had been walks along Fifth Avenue, visits to Tiffany's, steaks at Peter Luger's, visits to Macy's Harold Square, ice-skating at Lincoln Center, lunch at Tavern on the Green, and the Russian Tea Room. The brother had style! Amir was looking forward to meeting Omar's latest adventure.

"So, professor, will this racism thing ever end here in the good old USA?" Omar had asked.

"I can't call it, brother," Amir had responded. "One step forward and two backward. I've been thinking, akhi, and the thought that scares me is—if we're not who the white man says we are, then he isn't who he says he is either. That's a lot for a man to swallow."

"You're a wise man, godfather," responded Omar with a smile.

"Naw, brother, but I knew a man once!" answered Amir.

It was Thursday evening, and Amir had taken Friday and Monday off from work. A long weekend awaited. His government job had its benefits. Not being out very often, he had accumulated a lot of leave. There was annual, sick, emergency, and bereavement leave, along with personal days and personal business days. Then there were the thirteen to fourteen—he couldn't remember which— paid holidays every year. Yup, he wouldn't become wealthy working for the government, but it had its perks. He had decided he would pack a bag and drive his Datsun 280 ZX Turbo up to Montreal soon. That would keep for about a month. Because right now, Ramadan would be starting at the sighting of the new moon in a day or two. While he didn't practice all the pillars of the faith, he often did the Ramadan fast in those days.

It was difficult for him, especially when it occurred during the summer months when the days were so long! No food or drink from sunrise to sunset! He loved to eat and didn't miss many meals. He did come to realize some of the benefits of fasting, however; over time, he gained more sympathy and empathy for those who were truly hungry and did more reflection and study of Islam, the brotherhood of a community of faith, as they gathered for the evening meal and especially the Id (festival), Id Al Fitr, at the conclusion of Ramadan. Some of the sisters looked so beautiful wearing their Islamic garb, including the hijabs. The first few days of the fast were the hardest for Amir, as his body adjusted to weaning off his normal three squares a day. People all over the world would be observing, of course, which gave him some consolation. There really was a brotherhood among many Muslims.

He would periodically meet some brothers from Saudi, Morocco, or Sudan in a club or elsewhere, and once he greeted them with As Salaamu Alaikum, a bond would usually develop.

"Can I buy you a drink, brother?" was the oft-heard response from them.

Actually viewing Lawrence of Arabia with a group of young Saudis in a small theater on South Street had been quite interesting. They had not heard of T. E. Lawrence. Of course, he would also never forget the time when out in a disco with a bunch of Saudis, a middle-America-sounding couple sitting at the table next to theirs politely asked, "Are you fellas Puerto Ricans?"

Amir smiled and responded, "Si."

Generally, the Arabs he had met over the years had been friendly to him. He would always remember the two Kuwaitis who had approached him on his New York–London flight on his TWA Getaway Tour years earlier and politely asked, "Are you an African American?"

When he responded yes, they had said that they knew of his struggle and were with him.

Ramadan had ended. The Id had been enjoyable. Now on to Montreal! He liked his Z Car, black in color with gold pinstripes; it had T-tops, a tan leather interior, and nice gold-colored mag wheels! He had installed louvers on the rear and side quarter windows. It was fast too! It was also a chick magnet, he was told. His vanity plate read "PA Z Car." The thrill of the turbo spooling up when he stepped on the gas was exhilarating. Other burbles and gurgles the car made were enjoyable also. This was a driver's car. His first Datsun Z Car had been not a turbo but a 2+2, black in color also. It was a nice car, but the turbo edition was boss! He also belonged to the National Z Club.

Amir had the directions in his head—the Pennsylvania Turnpike to the New Jersey Turnpike to the New York State Throughway to the Canadian Northway. It would take about ten hours each way, depending on how often one stopped and for how long. Amir always loved water and drank a lot of it, so he would have to make a few rest stops.

Of course, you also must periodically gas up, stopping to take in the views of Upstate New York, with its many mountains, lakes, and beautiful flora and fauna. Maybe taking some pictures was a clever idea also. No, he wouldn't push or rush. He would enjoy the journey and the destination as well, he hoped. He would go alone. Why take oil to the gas station? Sand to the beach? He had seen and met some good-looking Frenchies up there before. This would be another miniadventure, in a life hopefully full of adventures. He loaded up his Z Car, after putting on a neutral-colored turtleneck, a herringbone sports coat, solid-color pleated slacks, and a pair of burgundy-colored penny loafers. He pulled on his black leather driving gloves and headed out on the highway with his eight-track player beginning to play as he drove. The sun was coming up. The sky was beautiful. "Shaft" by Isaac Hayes was the first selection to start playing. *Life is good!*

CPSIA information can be obtained
at www.ICGtesting.com
Printed in the USA
BVHW090848070819
555303BV00025B/1780/P

9 781480 878709